Everything is Flammable

ALSO BY GABRIELLE BELL:

GET OUT YOUR HANKIES
TRUTH IS FRAGMENTARY
THE VOYEURS
CECIL AND JORDAN IN NEW YORK
LUCKY
LUCKY VOL. 2
WHEN I'M OLD AND OTHER STORIES
GABRIELLEBELL.COM

Color Assist: Clara Lucie Jetsmark & Lilli Richards
Production Assist: Jordan Shiveley
Design: Tom Kaczynski

Uncivilized Books
P. O. Box 6534
Minneapolis, MN 55406
USA
uncivilizedbooks.com

First Edition, April 2017

10 9 8 7 6 5 4 3 2 1

ISBN 978-1-9412501-8-1

DISTRIBUTED TO THE TRADE BY:
Consortium Book Sales & Distribution, LLC.
34 Thirteenth Avenue NE, Suite 101
Minneapolis, MN 55413-1007
cbsd.com
Orders: (800) 283-3572

Printed in China

EVERYTHING IS FLAMMABLE

GABRIELLE BELL

UNCIVILIZED BOOKS

Summer
2014

I'm Doing Fine

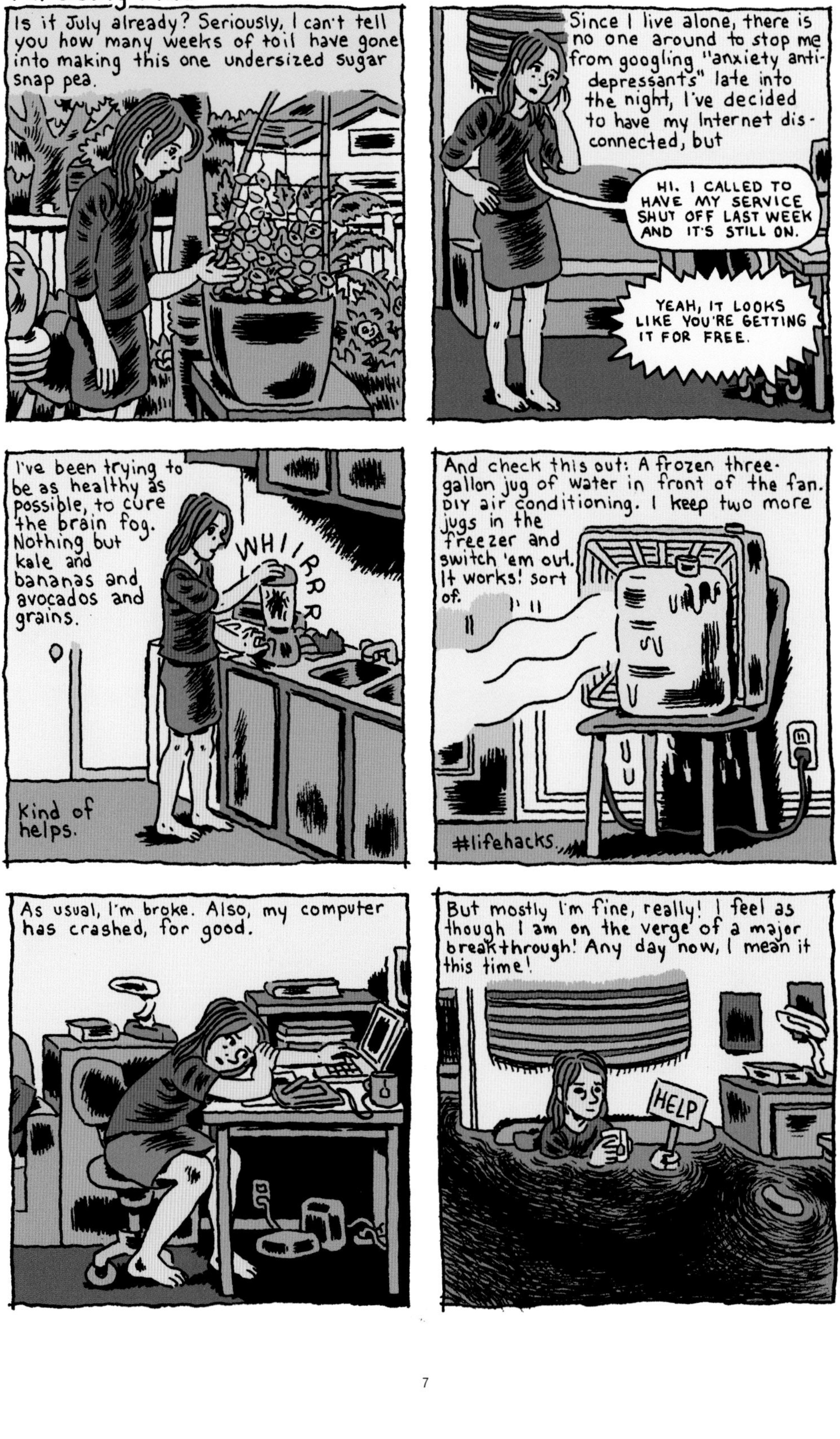

Is it July already? Seriously, I can't tell you how many weeks of toil have gone into making this one undersized sugar snap pea.
Since I live alone, there is no one around to stop me from googling "anxiety anti-depressants" late into the night, I've decided to have my Internet dis-connected, but
HI. I CALLED TO HAVE MY SERVICE SHUT OFF LAST WEEK AND IT'S STILL ON.
YEAH, IT LOOKS LIKE YOU'RE GETTING IT FOR FREE.
I've been trying to be as healthy as possible, to cure the brain fog. Nothing but kale and bananas and avocados and grains.
WHIIRRR
Kind of helps.
And check this out: A frozen three-gallon jug of water in front of the fan. DIY air conditioning. I keep two more jugs in the freezer and switch 'em out. It works! sort of.
#lifehacks.
As usual, I'm broke. Also, my computer has crashed, for good.
But mostly I'm fine, really! I feel as though I am on the verge of a major breakthrough! Any day now, I mean it this time!
HELP

Vigilance

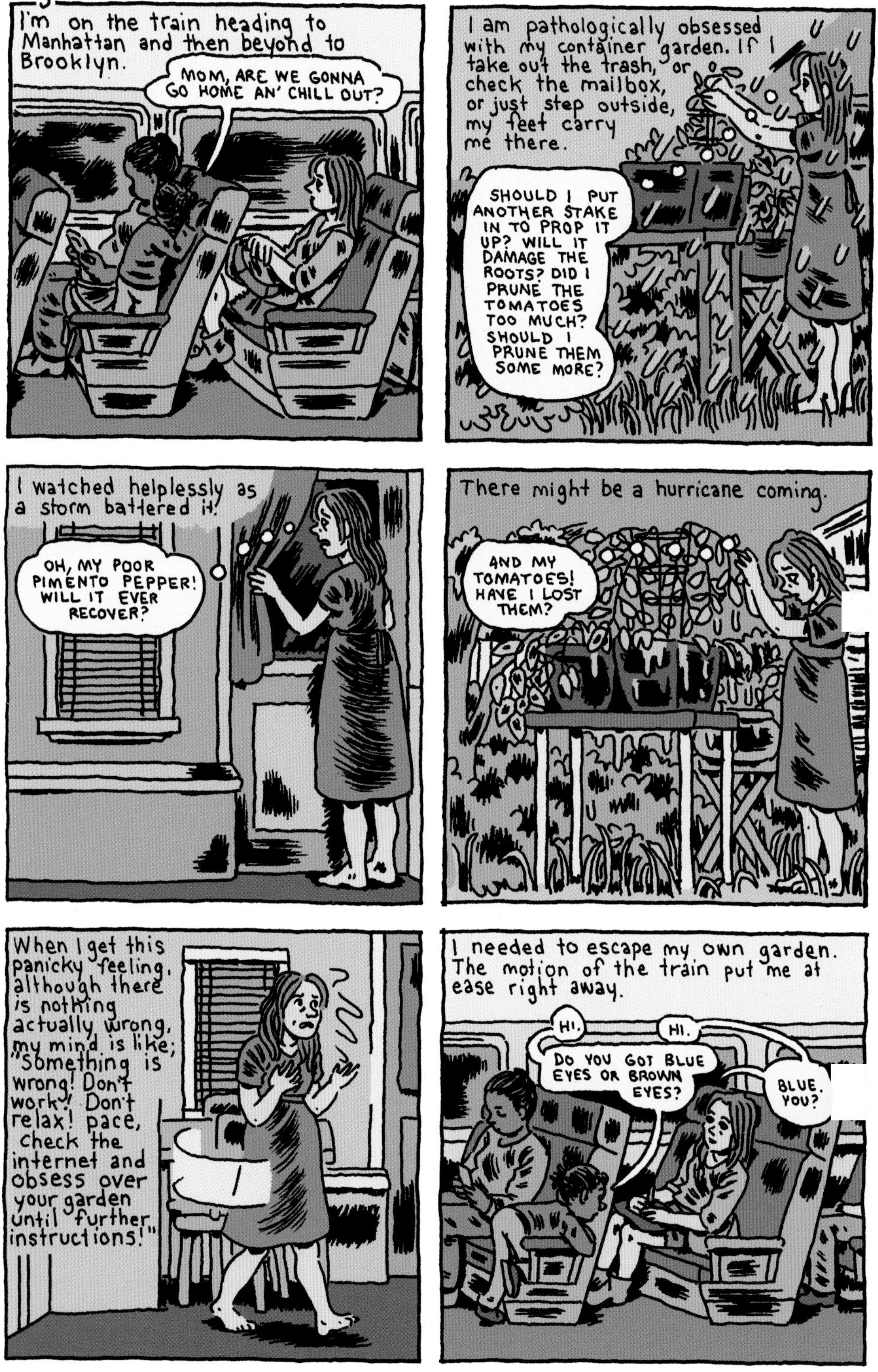
I'm on the train heading to Manhattan and then beyond to Brooklyn.
MOM, ARE WE GONNA GO HOME AN' CHILL OUT?
I am pathologically obsessed with my container garden. If I take out the trash, or check the mailbox, or just step outside, my feet carry me there.
SHOULD I PUT ANOTHER STAKE IN TO PROP IT UP? WILL IT DAMAGE THE ROOTS? DID I PRUNE THE TOMATOES TOO MUCH? SHOULD I PRUNE THEM SOME MORE?
I watched helplessly as a storm battered it!
OH, MY POOR PIMENTO PEPPER! WILL IT EVER RECOVER?
There might be a hurricane coming.
AND MY TOMATOES! HAVE I LOST THEM?
When I get this panicky feeling, although there is nothing actually wrong, my mind is like; "Something is wrong! Don't work! Don't relax! pace, check the internet and obsess over your garden until further instructions!"
I needed to escape my own garden. The motion of the train put me at ease right away.
HI.
HI.
DO YOU GOT BLUE EYES OR BROWN EYES?
BLUE. YOU?

My Friends Help Me

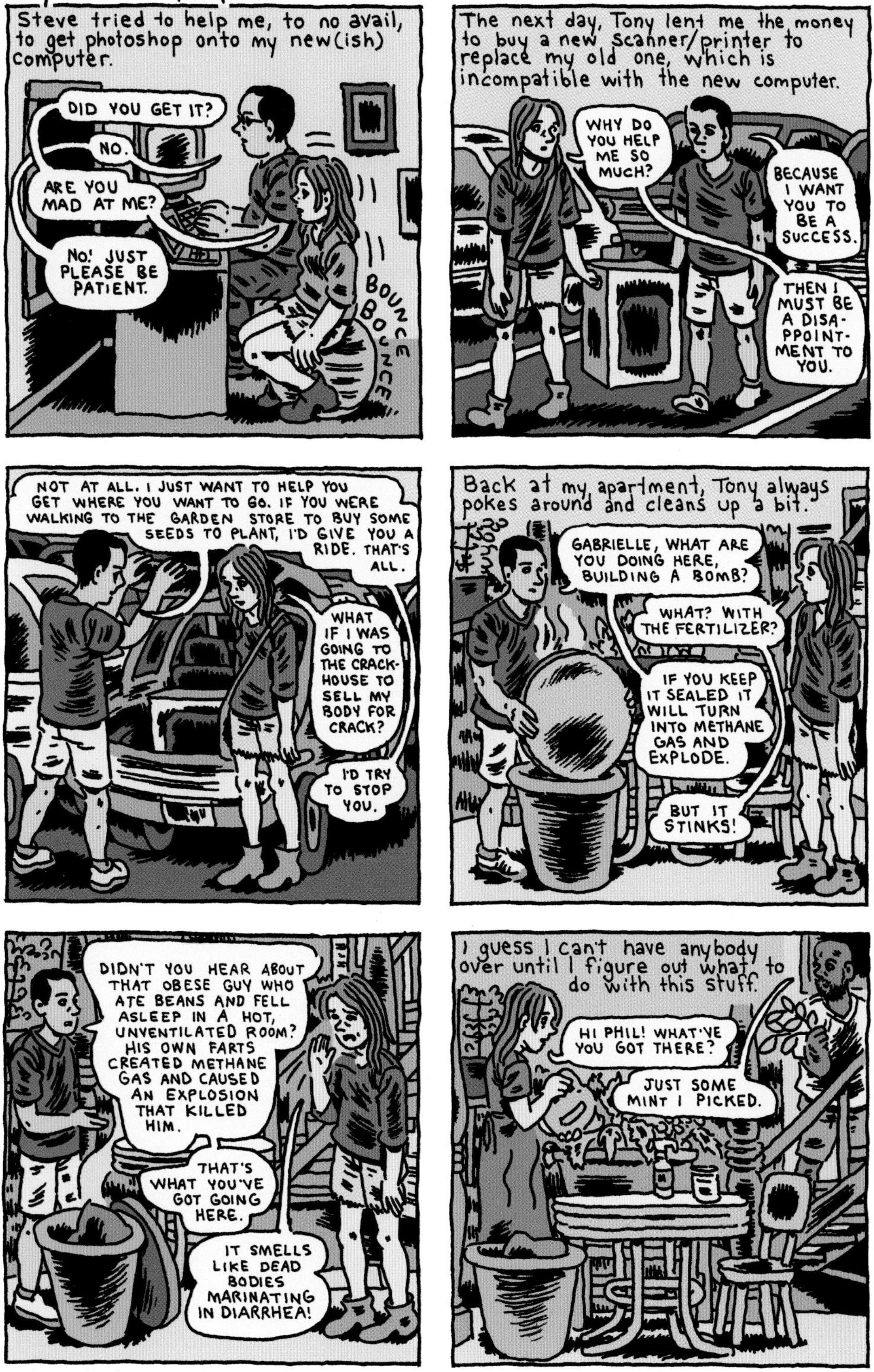
Steve tried to help me, to no avail, to get photoshop onto my new(ish) computer.
DID YOU GET IT?
NO.
ARE YOU MAD AT ME?
NO! JUST PLEASE BE PATIENT.
BOUNCE BOUNCE
The next day, Tony lent me the money to buy a new scanner/printer to replace my old one, which is incompatible with the new computer.
WHY DO YOU HELP ME SO MUCH?
BECAUSE I WANT YOU TO BE A SUCCESS.
THEN I MUST BE A DISA-PPOINT-MENT TO YOU.
NOT AT ALL. I JUST WANT TO HELP YOU GET WHERE YOU WANT TO GO. IF YOU WERE WALKING TO THE GARDEN STORE TO BUY SOME SEEDS TO PLANT, I'D GIVE YOU A RIDE. THAT'S ALL.
WHAT IF I WAS GOING TO THE CRACK-HOUSE TO SELL MY BODY FOR CRACK?
I'D TRY TO STOP YOU.
Back at my apartment, Tony always pokes around and cleans up a bit.
GABRIELLE, WHAT ARE YOU DOING HERE, BUILDING A BOMB?
WHAT? WITH THE FERTILIZER?
IF YOU KEEP IT SEALED IT WILL TURN INTO METHANE GAS AND EXPLODE.
BUT IT STINKS!
DIDN'T YOU HEAR ABOUT THAT OBESE GUY WHO ATE BEANS AND FELL ASLEEP IN A HOT, UNVENTILATED ROOM? HIS OWN FARTS CREATED METHANE GAS AND CAUSED AN EXPLOSION THAT KILLED HIM.
THAT'S WHAT YOU'VE GOT GOING HERE.
IT SMELLS LIKE DEAD BODIES MARINATING IN DIARRHEA!
I guess I can't have anybody over until I figure out what to do with this stuff.
HI PHIL! WHAT'VE YOU GOT THERE?
JUST SOME MINT I PICKED.

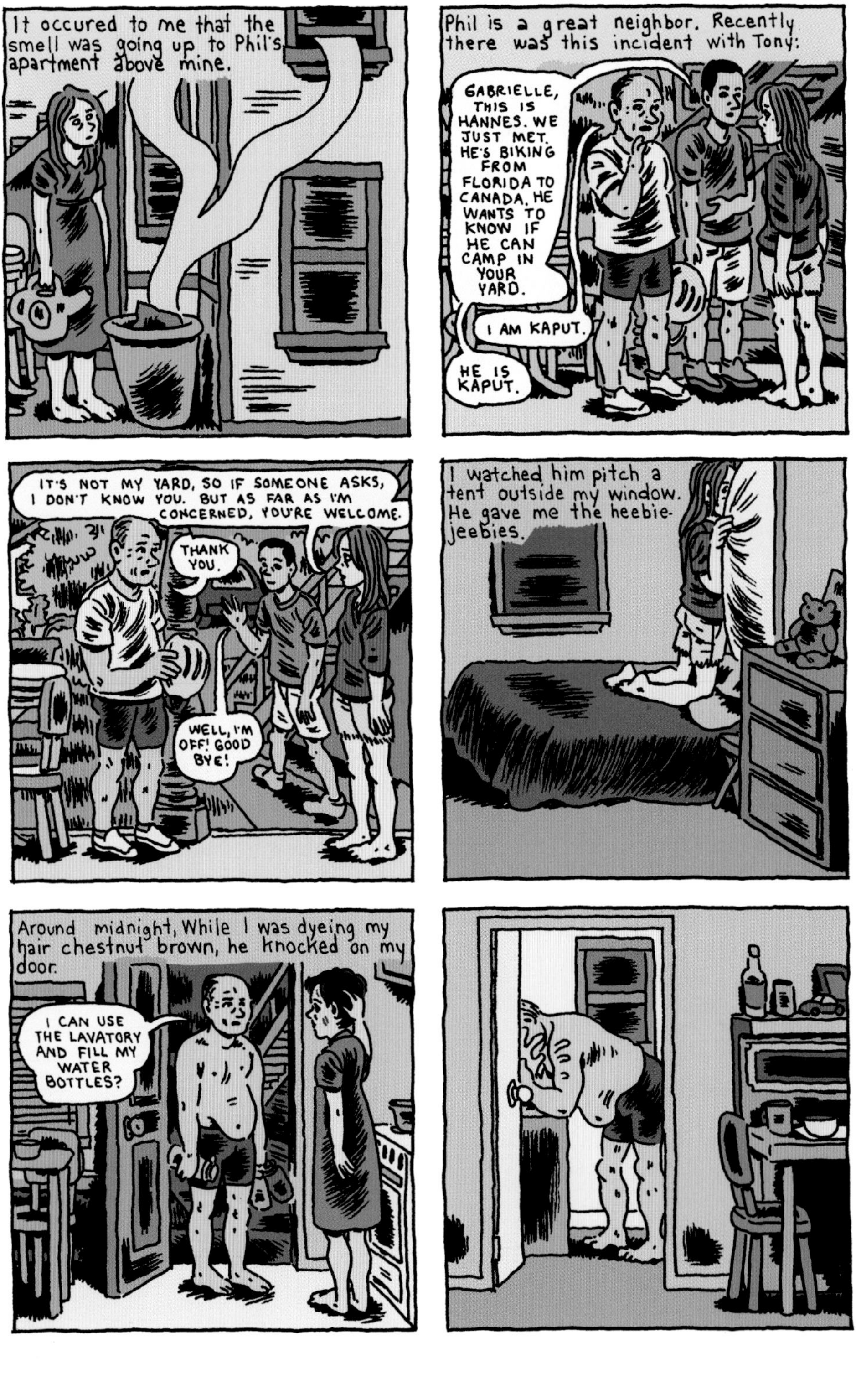
It occured to me that the smell was going up to Phil's apartment above mine.
Phil is a great neighbor. Recently there was this incident with Tony:
GABRIELLE, THIS IS HANNES. WE JUST MET. HE'S BIKING FROM FLORIDA TO CANADA. HE WANTS TO KNOW IF HE CAN CAMP IN YOUR YARD.
I AM KAPUT.
HE IS KAPUT.
IT'S NOT MY YARD, SO IF SOMEONE ASKS, I DON'T KNOW YOU. BUT AS FAR AS I'M CONCERNED, YOU'RE WELCOME.
THANK YOU.
WELL, I'M OFF! GOOD BYE!
I watched him pitch a tent outside my window. He gave me the heebie-jeebies.
Around midnight, While I was dyeing my hair chestnut brown, he knocked on my door.
I CAN USE THE LAVATORY AND FILL MY WATER BOTTLES?

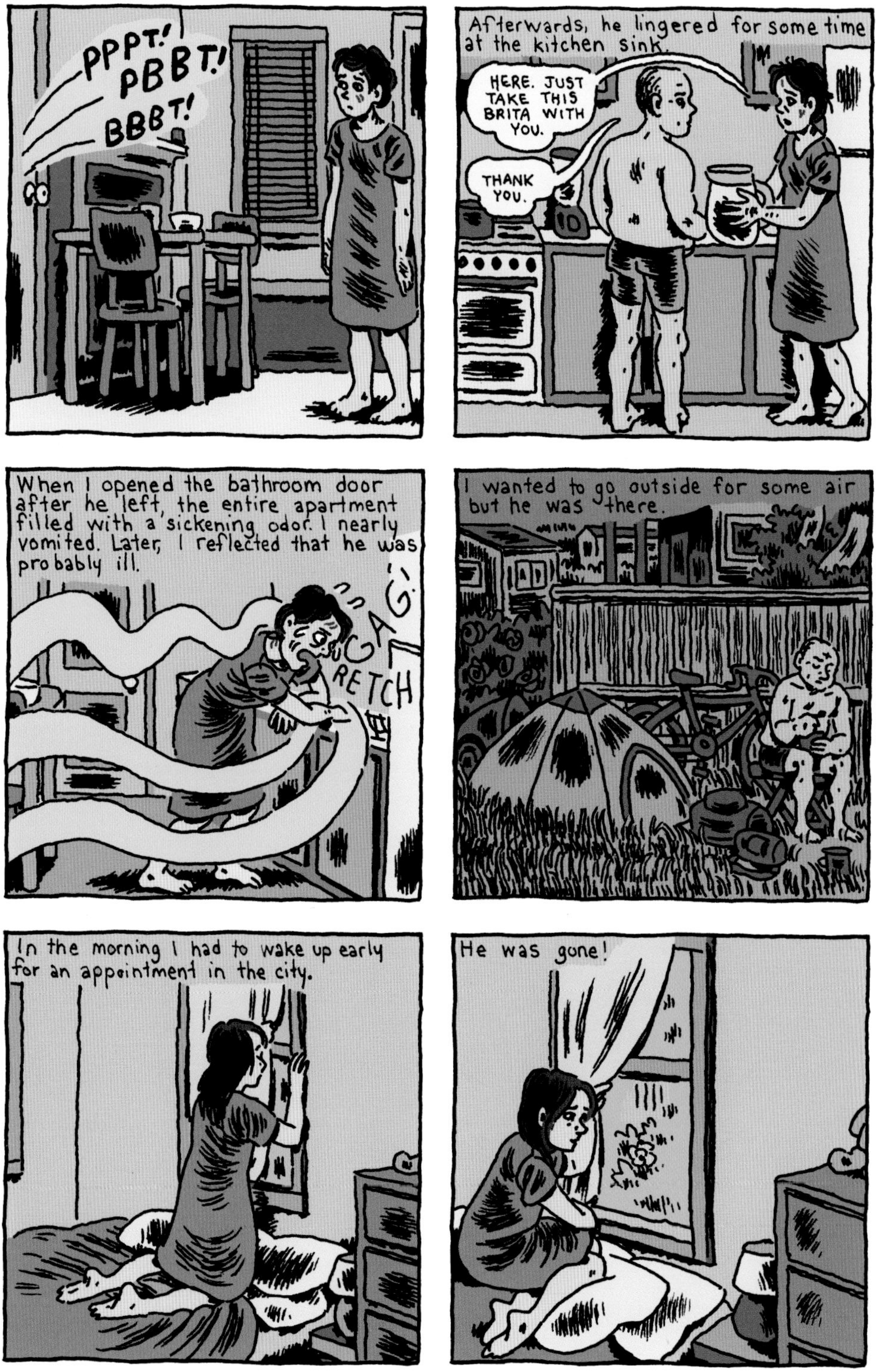
PPPT! PBBT! BBBT!
Afterwards, he lingered for some time at the kitchen sink.
HERE. JUST TAKE THIS BRITA WITH YOU.
THANK YOU.
When I opened the bathroom door after he left, the entire apartment filled with a sickening odor. I nearly vomited. Later, I reflected that he was probably ill.
GAG!
RETCH
I wanted to go outside for some air but he was there.
In the morning I had to wake up early for an appointment in the city.
He was gone!

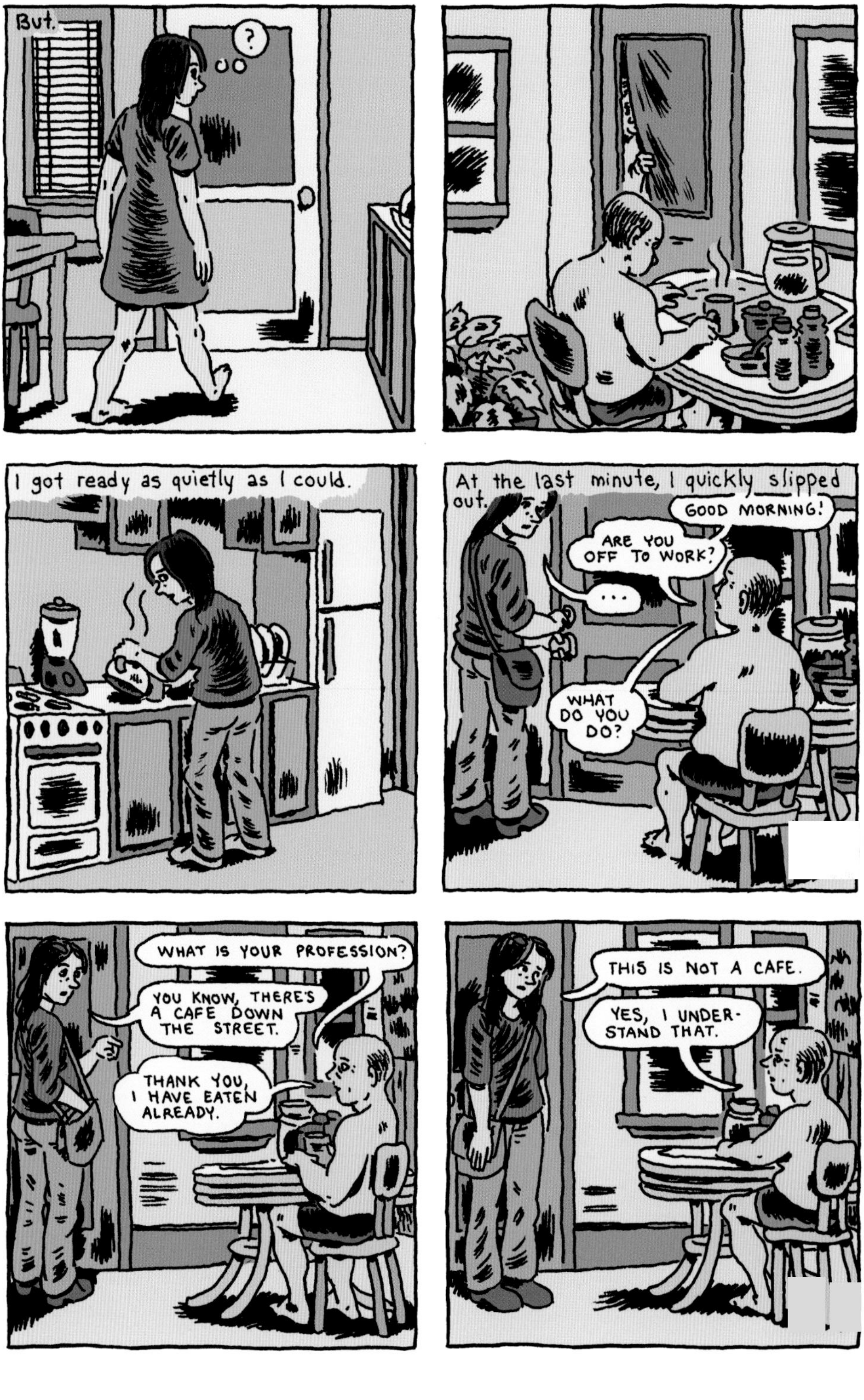
But.
?
I got ready as quietly as I could.
At the last minute, I quickly slipped out.
GOOD MORNING!
ARE YOU OFF TO WORK?
...
WHAT DO YOU DO?
WHAT IS YOUR PROFESSION?
YOU KNOW, THERE'S A CAFE DOWN THE STREET.
THANK YOU, I HAVE EATEN ALREADY.
THIS IS NOT A CAFE.
YES, I UNDERSTAND THAT.

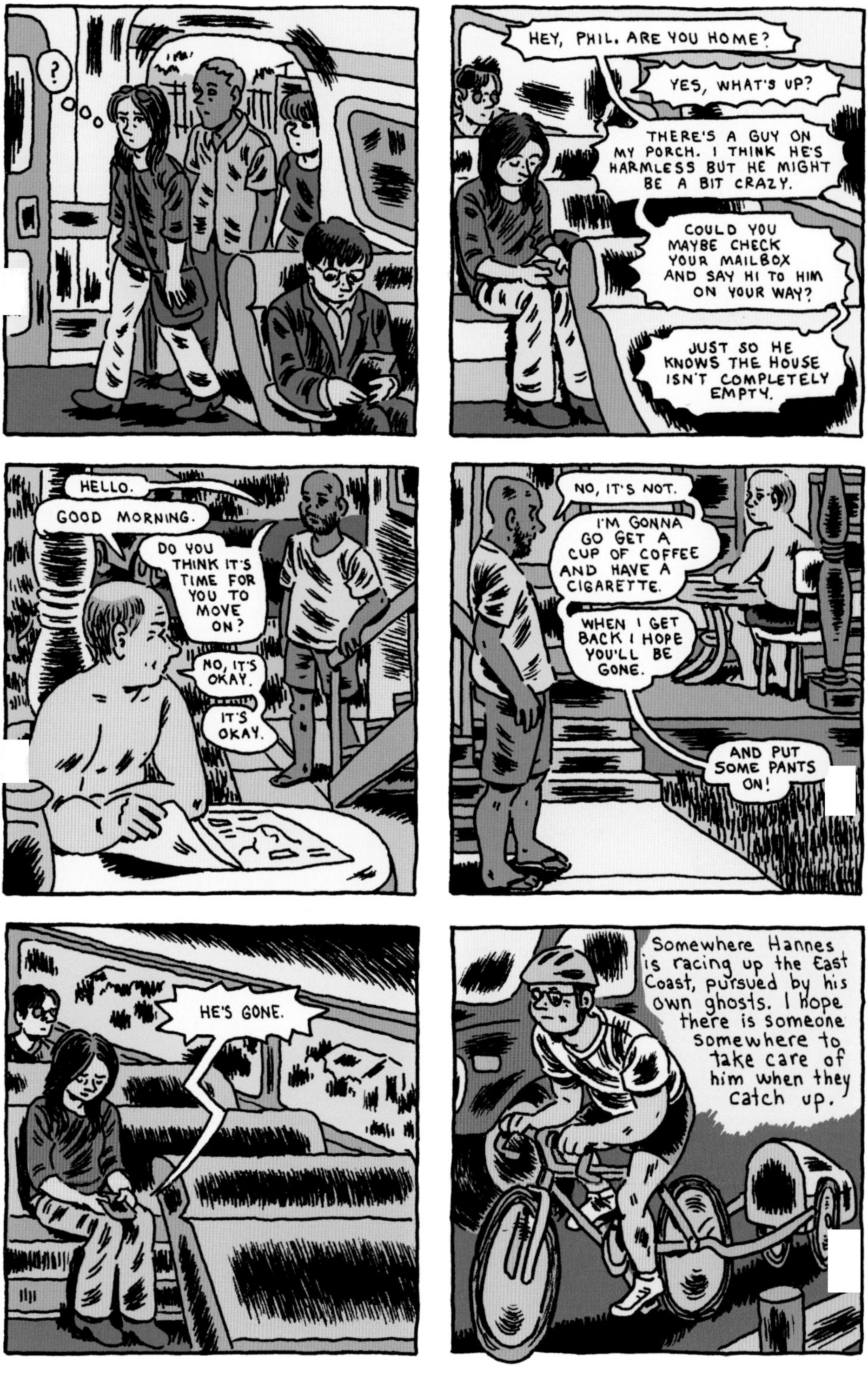
?
HEY, PHIL. ARE YOU HOME?
YES, WHAT'S UP?
THERE'S A GUY ON MY PORCH. I THINK HE'S HARMLESS BUT HE MIGHT BE A BIT CRAZY.
COULD YOU MAYBE CHECK YOUR MAILBOX AND SAY HI TO HIM ON YOUR WAY?
JUST SO HE KNOWS THE HOUSE ISN'T COMPLETELY EMPTY.
HELLO.
GOOD MORNING.
DO YOU THINK IT'S TIME FOR YOU TO MOVE ON?
NO, IT'S OKAY.
IT'S OKAY.
NO, IT'S NOT.
I'M GONNA GO GET A CUP OF COFFEE AND HAVE A CIGARETTE.
WHEN I GET BACK I HOPE YOU'LL BE GONE.
AND PUT SOME PANTS ON!
HE'S GONE.
Somewhere Hannes is racing up the East Coast, pursued by his own ghosts. I hope there is someone somewhere to take care of him when they catch up.

Lucky

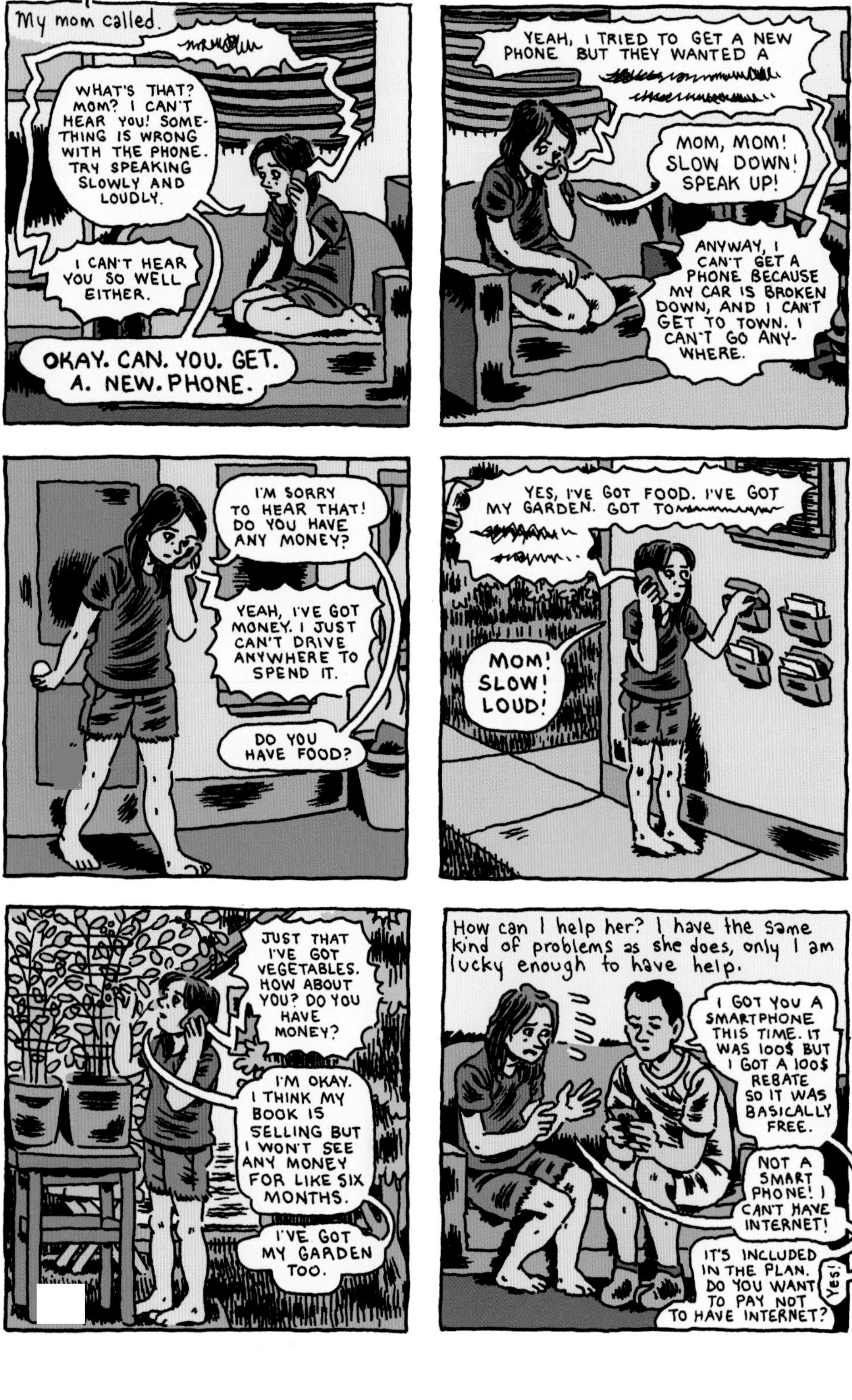
My mom called.
WHAT'S THAT? MOM? I CAN'T HEAR YOU! SOMETHING IS WRONG WITH THE PHONE. TRY SPEAKING SLOWLY AND LOUDLY.
I CAN'T HEAR YOU SO WELL EITHER.
OKAY. CAN. YOU. GET. A. NEW. PHONE.
YEAH, I TRIED TO GET A NEW PHONE BUT THEY WANTED A
MOM, MOM! SLOW DOWN! SPEAK UP!
ANYWAY, I CAN'T GET A PHONE BECAUSE MY CAR IS BROKEN DOWN, AND I CAN'T GET TO TOWN. I CAN'T GO ANYWHERE.
I'M SORRY TO HEAR THAT! DO YOU HAVE ANY MONEY?
YEAH, I'VE GOT MONEY. I JUST CAN'T DRIVE ANYWHERE TO SPEND IT.
DO YOU HAVE FOOD?
YES, I'VE GOT FOOD. I'VE GOT MY GARDEN. GOT TO
MOM! SLOW! LOUD!
JUST THAT I'VE GOT VEGETABLES. HOW ABOUT YOU? DO YOU HAVE MONEY?
I'M OKAY. I THINK MY BOOK IS SELLING BUT I WON'T SEE ANY MONEY FOR LIKE SIX MONTHS.
I'VE GOT MY GARDEN TOO.
How can I help her? I have the same kind of problems as she does, only I am lucky enough to have help.
I GOT YOU A SMARTPHONE THIS TIME. IT WAS 100$ BUT I GOT A 100$ REBATE SO IT WAS BASICALLY FREE.
NOT A SMART PHONE! I CAN'T HAVE INTERNET!
IT'S INCLUDED IN THE PLAN. DO YOU WANT TO PAY NOT TO HAVE INTERNET?
YES!

Impediments

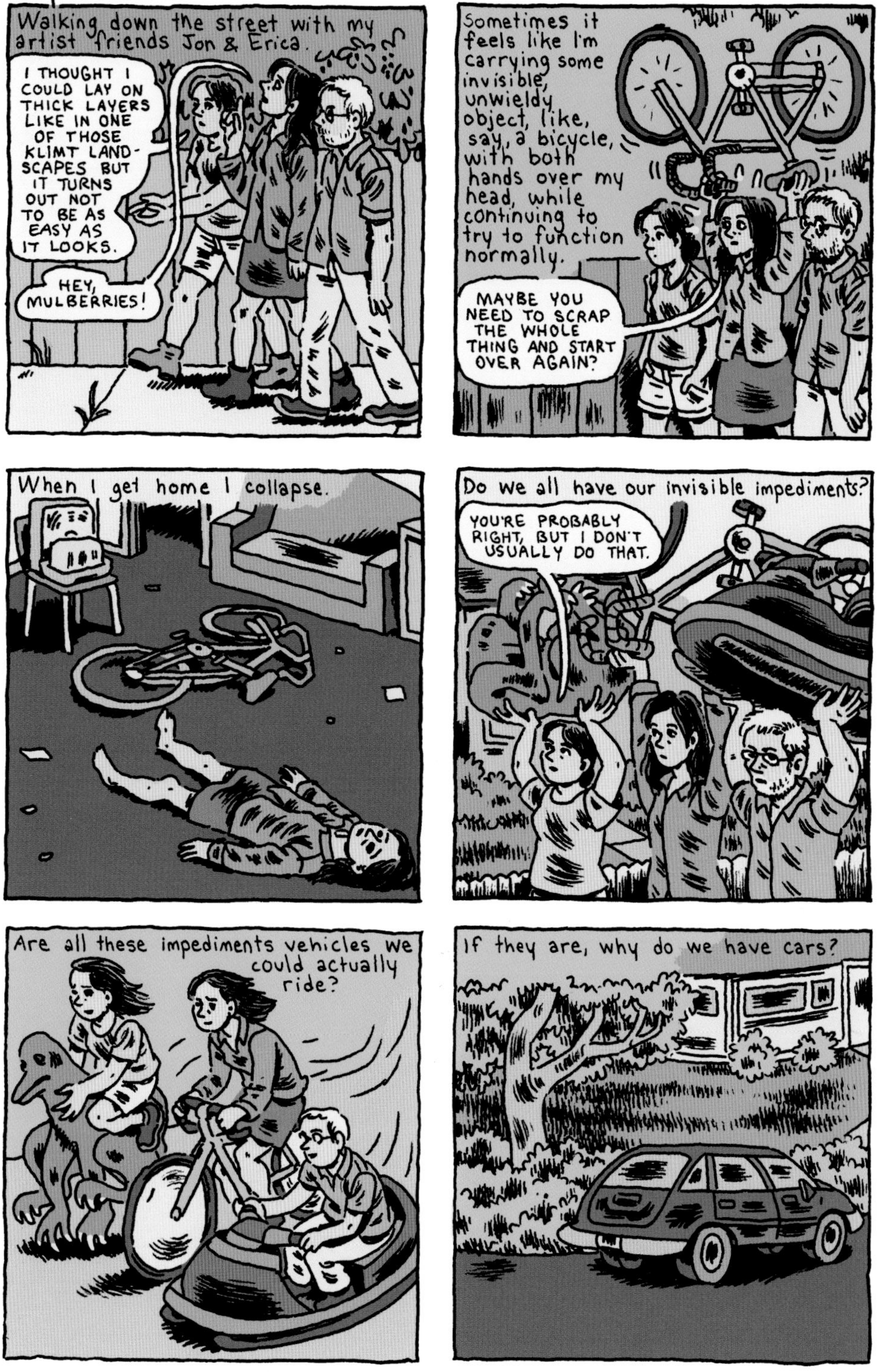

Walking down the street with my artist friends Jon & Erica.
I THOUGHT I COULD LAY ON THICK LAYERS LIKE IN ONE OF THOSE KLIMT LAND-SCAPES BUT IT TURNS OUT NOT TO BE AS EASY AS IT LOOKS.
HEY, MULBERRIES!
Sometimes it feels like I'm carrying some invisible, unwieldy object, like, say, a bicycle, with both hands over my head, while continuing to try to function normally.
MAYBE YOU NEED TO SCRAP THE WHOLE THING AND START OVER AGAIN?
When I get home I collapse.
Do we all have our invisible impediments?
YOU'RE PROBABLY RIGHT, BUT I DON'T USUALLY DO THAT.
Are all these impediments vehicles we could actually ride?
If they are, why do we have cars?

Bad News

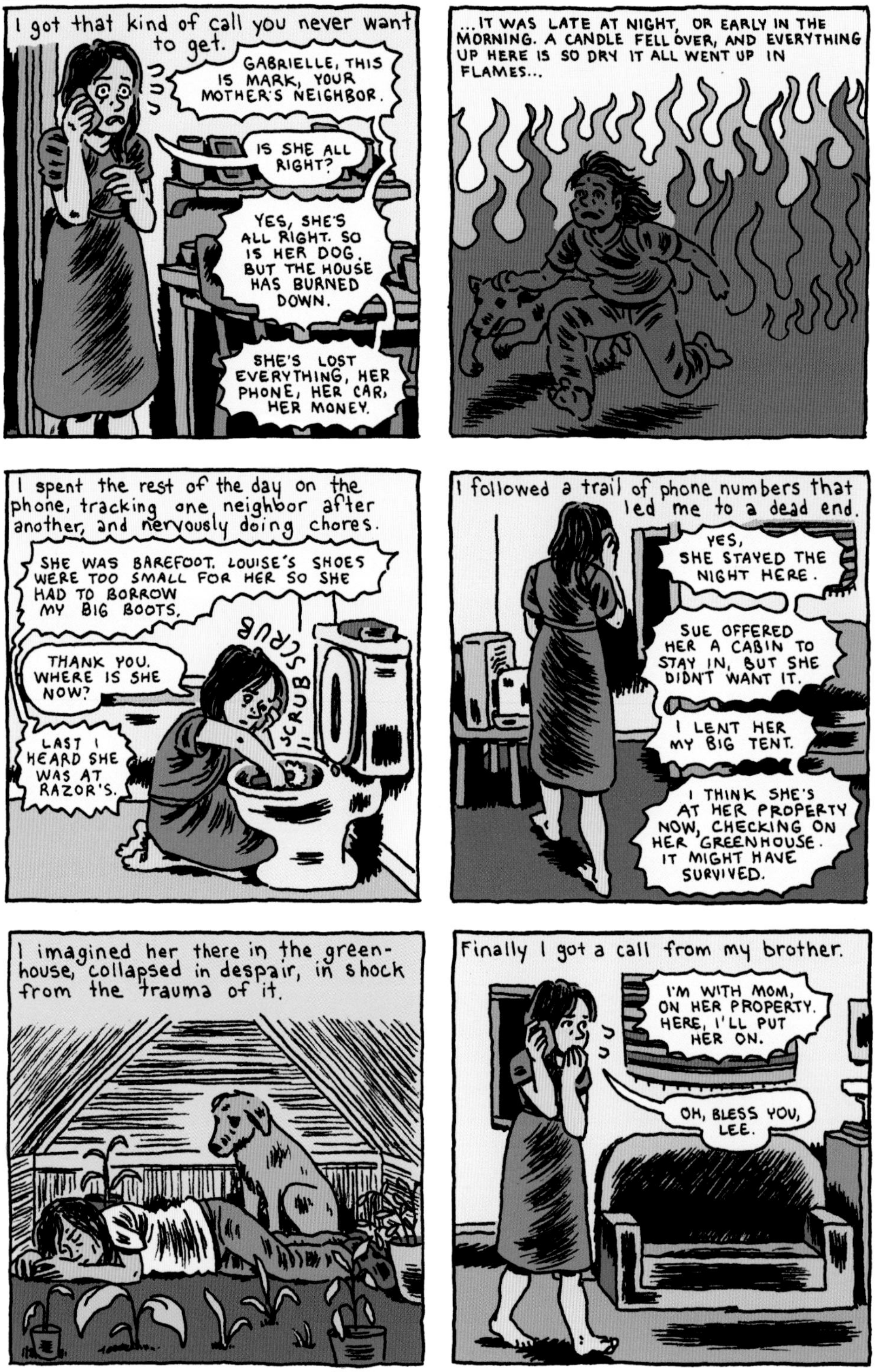

I got that kind of call you never want to get.
GABRIELLE, THIS IS MARK, YOUR MOTHER'S NEIGHBOR.
IS SHE ALL RIGHT?
YES, SHE'S ALL RIGHT. SO IS HER DOG. BUT THE HOUSE HAS BURNED DOWN.
SHE'S LOST EVERYTHING, HER PHONE, HER CAR, HER MONEY.
...IT WAS LATE AT NIGHT, OR EARLY IN THE MORNING. A CANDLE FELL OVER, AND EVERYTHING UP HERE IS SO DRY IT ALL WENT UP IN FLAMES...
I spent the rest of the day on the phone, tracking one neighbor after another, and nervously doing chores.
SHE WAS BAREFOOT. LOUISE'S SHOES WERE TOO SMALL FOR HER SO SHE HAD TO BORROW MY BIG BOOTS.
SCRUB
THANK YOU. WHERE IS SHE NOW?
SCRUB
LAST I HEARD SHE WAS AT RAZOR'S.
I followed a trail of phone numbers that led me to a dead end.
YES, SHE STAYED THE NIGHT HERE.
SUE OFFERED HER A CABIN TO STAY IN, BUT SHE DIDN'T WANT IT.
I LENT HER MY BIG TENT.
I THINK SHE'S AT HER PROPERTY NOW, CHECKING ON HER GREENHOUSE. IT MIGHT HAVE SURVIVED.
I imagined her there in the greenhouse, collapsed in despair, in shock from the trauma of it.
Finally I got a call from my brother.
I'M WITH MOM, ON HER PROPERTY. HERE, I'LL PUT HER ON.
OH, BLESS YOU, LEE.

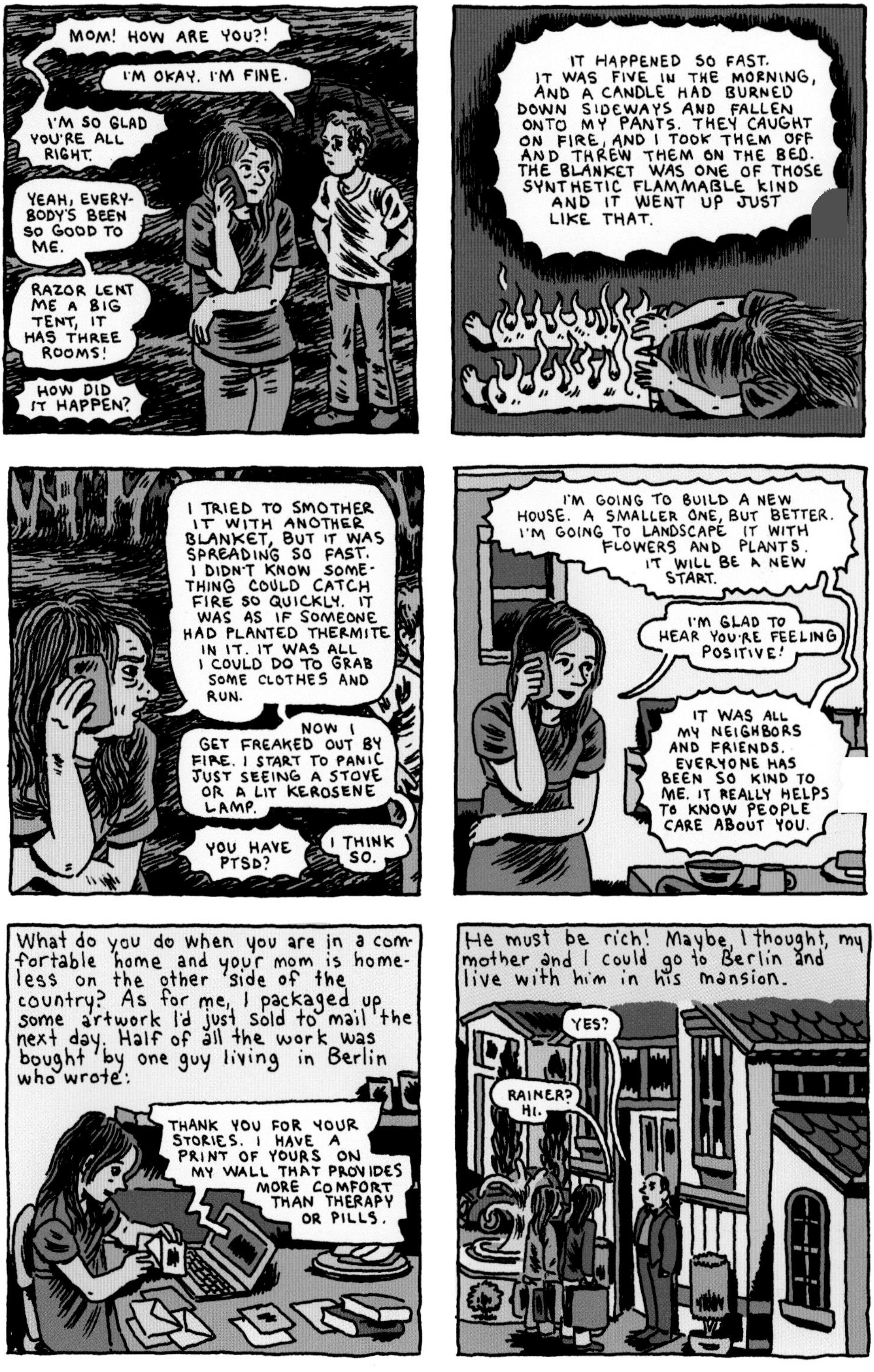
MOM! HOW ARE YOU?!
I'M OKAY. I'M FINE.
I'M SO GLAD YOU'RE ALL RIGHT.
YEAH, EVERYBODY'S BEEN SO GOOD TO ME.
RAZOR LENT ME A BIG TENT, IT HAS THREE ROOMS!
HOW DID IT HAPPEN?
IT HAPPENED SO FAST. IT WAS FIVE IN THE MORNING, AND A CANDLE HAD BURNED DOWN SIDEWAYS AND FALLEN ONTO MY PANTS. THEY CAUGHT ON FIRE, AND I TOOK THEM OFF AND THREW THEM ON THE BED. THE BLANKET WAS ONE OF THOSE SYNTHETIC FLAMMABLE KIND AND IT WENT UP JUST LIKE THAT.
I TRIED TO SMOTHER IT WITH ANOTHER BLANKET, BUT IT WAS SPREADING SO FAST. I DIDN'T KNOW SOMETHING COULD CATCH FIRE SO QUICKLY. IT WAS AS IF SOMEONE HAD PLANTED THERMITE IN IT. IT WAS ALL I COULD DO TO GRAB SOME CLOTHES AND RUN.
NOW I GET FREAKED OUT BY FIRE. I START TO PANIC JUST SEEING A STOVE OR A LIT KEROSENE LAMP.
YOU HAVE PTSD?
I THINK SO.
I'M GOING TO BUILD A NEW HOUSE. A SMALLER ONE, BUT BETTER. I'M GOING TO LANDSCAPE IT WITH FLOWERS AND PLANTS. IT WILL BE A NEW START.
I'M GLAD TO HEAR YOU'RE FEELING POSITIVE!
IT WAS ALL MY NEIGHBORS AND FRIENDS. EVERYONE HAS BEEN SO KIND TO ME. IT REALLY HELPS TO KNOW PEOPLE CARE ABOUT YOU.
What do you do when you are in a comfortable home and your mom is homeless on the other side of the country? As for me, I packaged up some artwork I'd just sold to mail the next day. Half of all the work was bought by one guy living in Berlin who wrote:
THANK YOU FOR YOUR STORIES. I HAVE A PRINT OF YOURS ON MY WALL THAT PROVIDES MORE COMFORT THAN THERAPY OR PILLS.
He must be rich! Maybe, I thought, my mother and I could go to Berlin and live with him in his mansion.
YES?
RAINER? HI.

Burying a Body

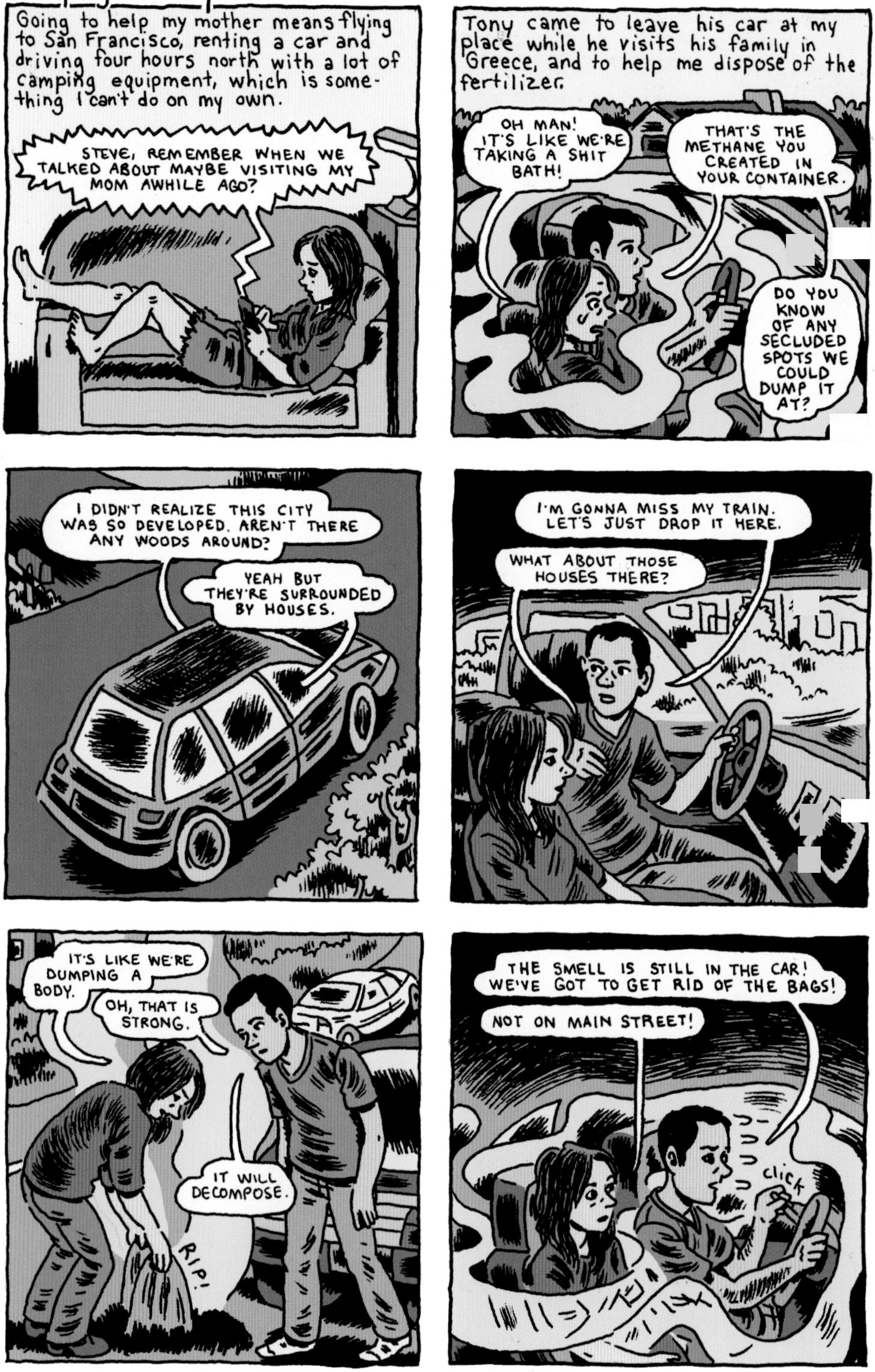
Going to help my mother means flying to San Francisco, renting a car and driving four hours north with a lot of camping equipment, which is something I can't do on my own.
STEVE, REMEMBER WHEN WE TALKED ABOUT MAYBE VISITING MY MOM AWHILE AGO?
Tony came to leave his car at my place while he visits his family in Greece, and to help me dispose of the fertilizer.
OH MAN! IT'S LIKE WE'RE TAKING A SHIT BATH!
THAT'S THE METHANE YOU CREATED IN YOUR CONTAINER.
DO YOU KNOW OF ANY SECLUDED SPOTS WE COULD DUMP IT AT?
I DIDN'T REALIZE THIS CITY WAS SO DEVELOPED. AREN'T THERE ANY WOODS AROUND?
YEAH BUT THEY'RE SURROUNDED BY HOUSES.
I'M GONNA MISS MY TRAIN. LET'S JUST DROP IT HERE.
WHAT ABOUT THOSE HOUSES THERE?
IT'S LIKE WE'RE DUMPING A BODY.
OH, THAT IS STRONG.
IT WILL DECOMPOSE.
RIP!
THE SMELL IS STILL IN THE CAR! WE'VE GOT TO GET RID OF THE BAGS!
NOT ON MAIN STREET!
click

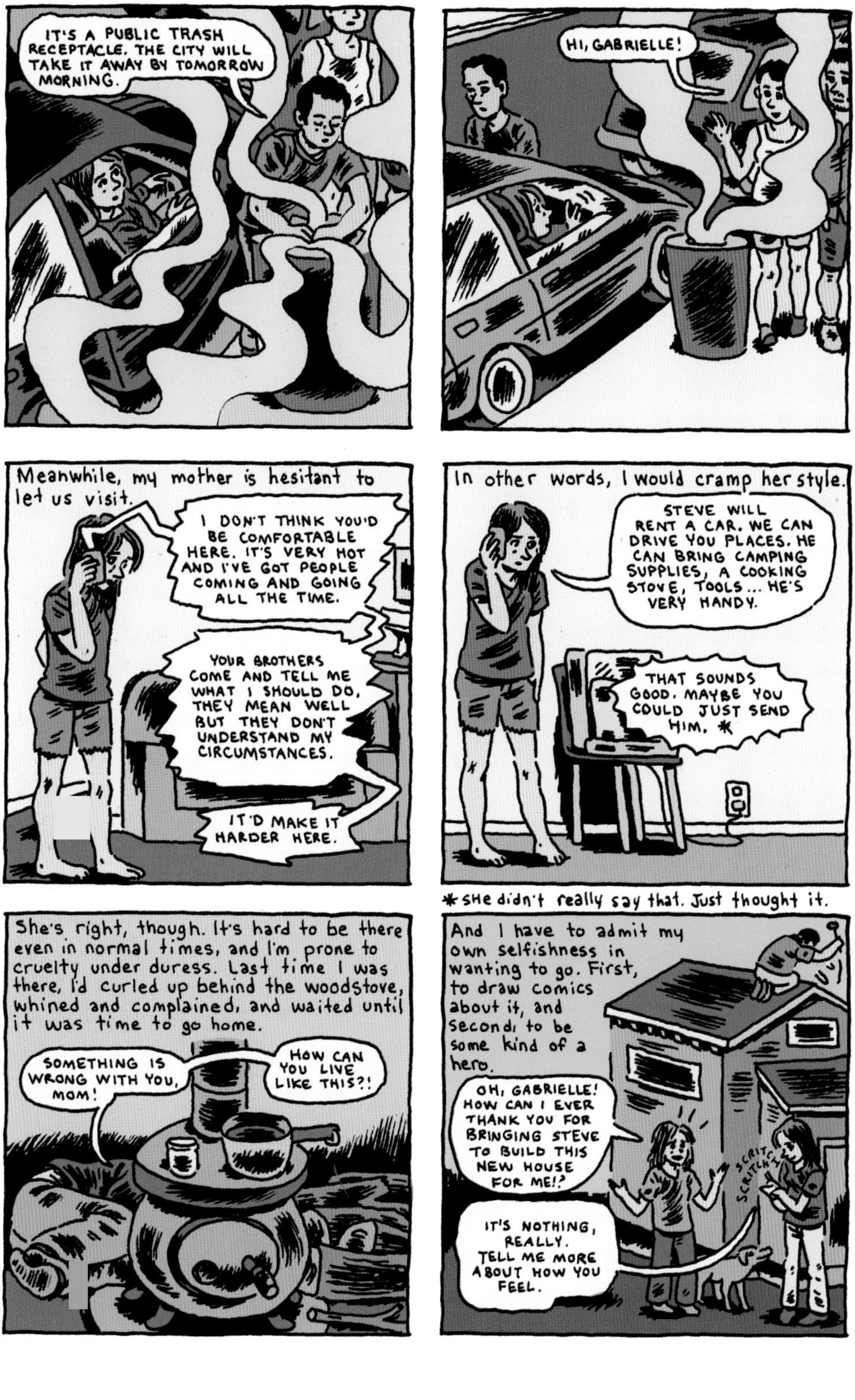

IT'S A PUBLIC TRASH RECEPTACLE. THE CITY WILL TAKE IT AWAY BY TOMORROW MORNING.
HI, GABRIELLE!
Meanwhile, my mother is hesitant to let us visit.
I DON'T THINK YOU'D BE COMFORTABLE HERE. IT'S VERY HOT AND I'VE GOT PEOPLE COMING AND GOING ALL THE TIME.
YOUR BROTHERS COME AND TELL ME WHAT I SHOULD DO. THEY MEAN WELL BUT THEY DON'T UNDERSTAND MY CIRCUMSTANCES.
IT'D MAKE IT HARDER HERE.
In other words, I would cramp her style.
STEVE WILL RENT A CAR. WE CAN DRIVE YOU PLACES. HE CAN BRING CAMPING SUPPLIES, A COOKING STOVE, TOOLS... HE'S VERY HANDY.
THAT SOUNDS GOOD. MAYBE YOU COULD JUST SEND HIM. *
* she didn't really say that. Just thought it.
She's right, though. It's hard to be there even in normal times, and I'm prone to cruelty under duress. Last time I was there, I'd curled up behind the woodstove, whined and complained, and waited until it was time to go home.
SOMETHING IS WRONG WITH YOU, MOM!
HOW CAN YOU LIVE LIKE THIS?!
And I have to admit my own selfishness in wanting to go. First, to draw comics about it, and second, to be some kind of a hero.
OH, GABRIELLE! HOW CAN I EVER THANK YOU FOR BRINGING STEVE TO BUILD THIS NEW HOUSE FOR ME!?
SCRITCH SCRITCH
IT'S NOTHING, REALLY. TELL ME MORE ABOUT HOW YOU FEEL.

Bear Hugs

I went into the city to see my therapist.

SOB

YOU HAVE TO LEARN TO SIT WITH THE HELPLESSNESS.

KNOWING THAT SHE HAS TO GO THROUGH THIS ON HER OWN.

And also a psychiatrist.

MY MOM'S HOUSE BURNED DOWN.

OH, MY.

I WANT TO GO AND TRY TO HELP, BUT I THINK I SCARE HER.

CAN YOU PUT ME ON SOMETHING THAT WILL KEEP ME ON MY BEST BEHAVIOR?

YES, I CAN DO THAT.

On the train heading back, my mother called from her neighbor's phone. She seems determined for us not to come.

DON'T WORRY, I'M FINE. MY TENT LOOKS REALLY CUTE IN THE GARDEN.

PEOPLE HAVE BEEN BRINGING ME TOOLS, BLANKETS, A CAMPING STOVE

LOTS OF CLOTHES. I'VE GOT A WHOLE NEW WARDROBE. I'M BETTER DRESSED THAN I'VE BEEN IN YEARS.

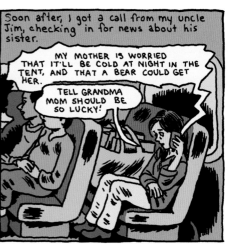

Soon after, I got a call from my uncle Jim, checking in for news about his sister.

MY MOTHER IS WORRIED THAT IT'LL BE COLD AT NIGHT IN THE TENT, AND THAT A BEAR COULD GET HER.

TELL GRANDMA MOM SHOULD BE SO LUCKY!

The Dangerous Web

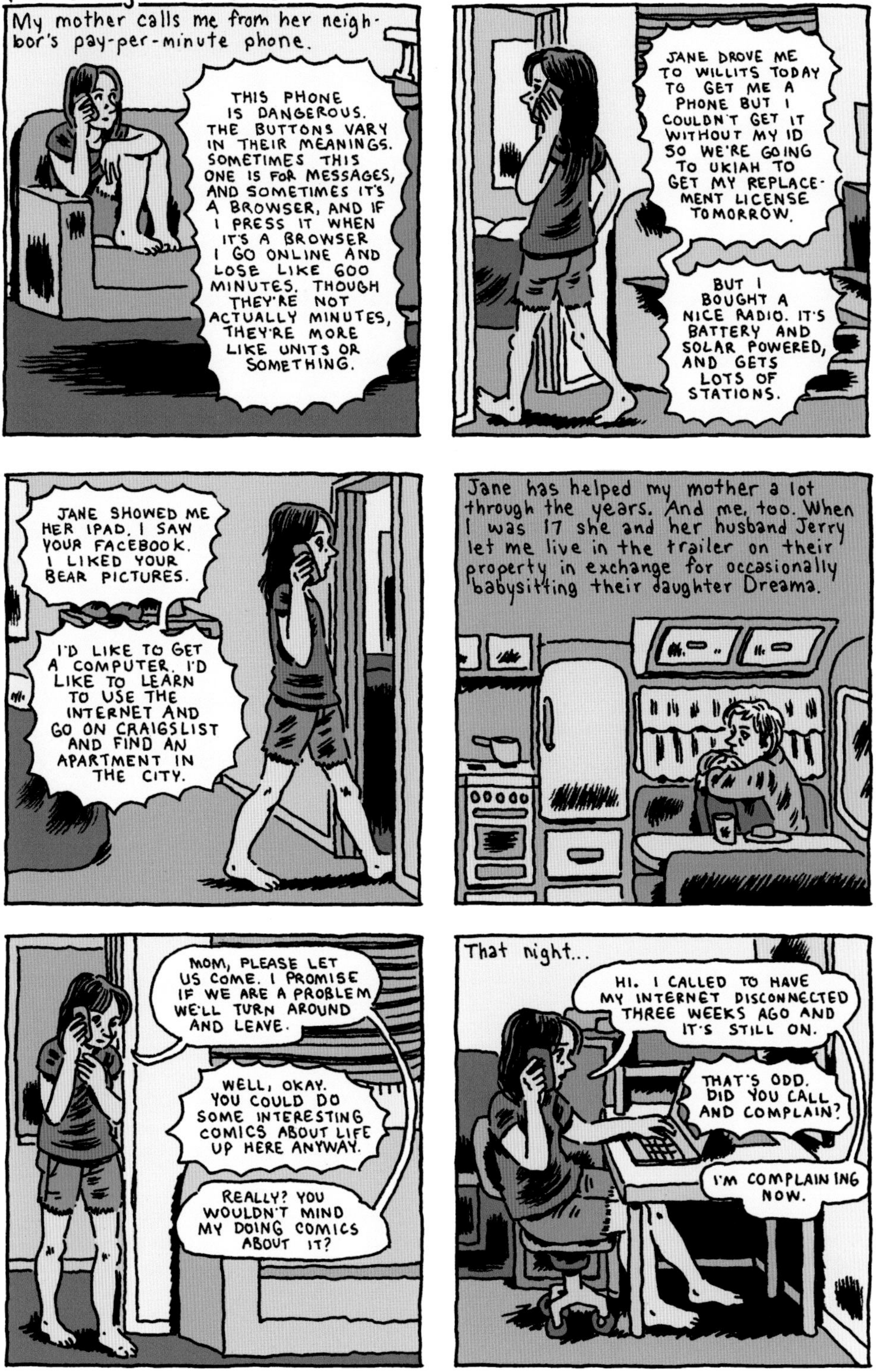
My mother calls me from her neighbor's pay-per-minute phone.
THIS PHONE IS DANGEROUS. THE BUTTONS VARY IN THEIR MEANINGS. SOMETIMES THIS ONE IS FOR MESSAGES, AND SOMETIMES IT'S A BROWSER, AND IF I PRESS IT WHEN IT'S A BROWSER I GO ONLINE AND LOSE LIKE 600 MINUTES. THOUGH THEY'RE NOT ACTUALLY MINUTES, THEY'RE MORE LIKE UNITS OR SOMETHING.
JANE DROVE ME TO WILLITS TODAY TO GET ME A PHONE BUT I COULDN'T GET IT WITHOUT MY ID SO WE'RE GOING TO UKIAH TO GET MY REPLACEMENT LICENSE TOMORROW.
BUT I BOUGHT A NICE RADIO. IT'S BATTERY AND SOLAR POWERED, AND GETS LOTS OF STATIONS.
JANE SHOWED ME HER IPAD. I SAW YOUR FACEBOOK. I LIKED YOUR BEAR PICTURES.
I'D LIKE TO GET A COMPUTER. I'D LIKE TO LEARN TO USE THE INTERNET AND GO ON CRAIGSLIST AND FIND AN APARTMENT IN THE CITY.
Jane has helped my mother a lot through the years. And me, too. When I was 17 she and her husband Jerry let me live in the trailer on their property in exchange for occasionally babysitting their daughter Dreama.
MOM, PLEASE LET US COME. I PROMISE IF WE ARE A PROBLEM WE'LL TURN AROUND AND LEAVE.
WELL, OKAY. YOU COULD DO SOME INTERESTING COMICS ABOUT LIFE UP HERE ANYWAY.
REALLY? YOU WOULDN'T MIND MY DOING COMICS ABOUT IT?
That night...
HI. I CALLED TO HAVE MY INTERNET DISCONNECTED THREE WEEKS AGO AND IT'S STILL ON.
THAT'S ODD. DID YOU CALL AND COMPLAIN?
I'M COMPLAINING NOW.

It's a Process

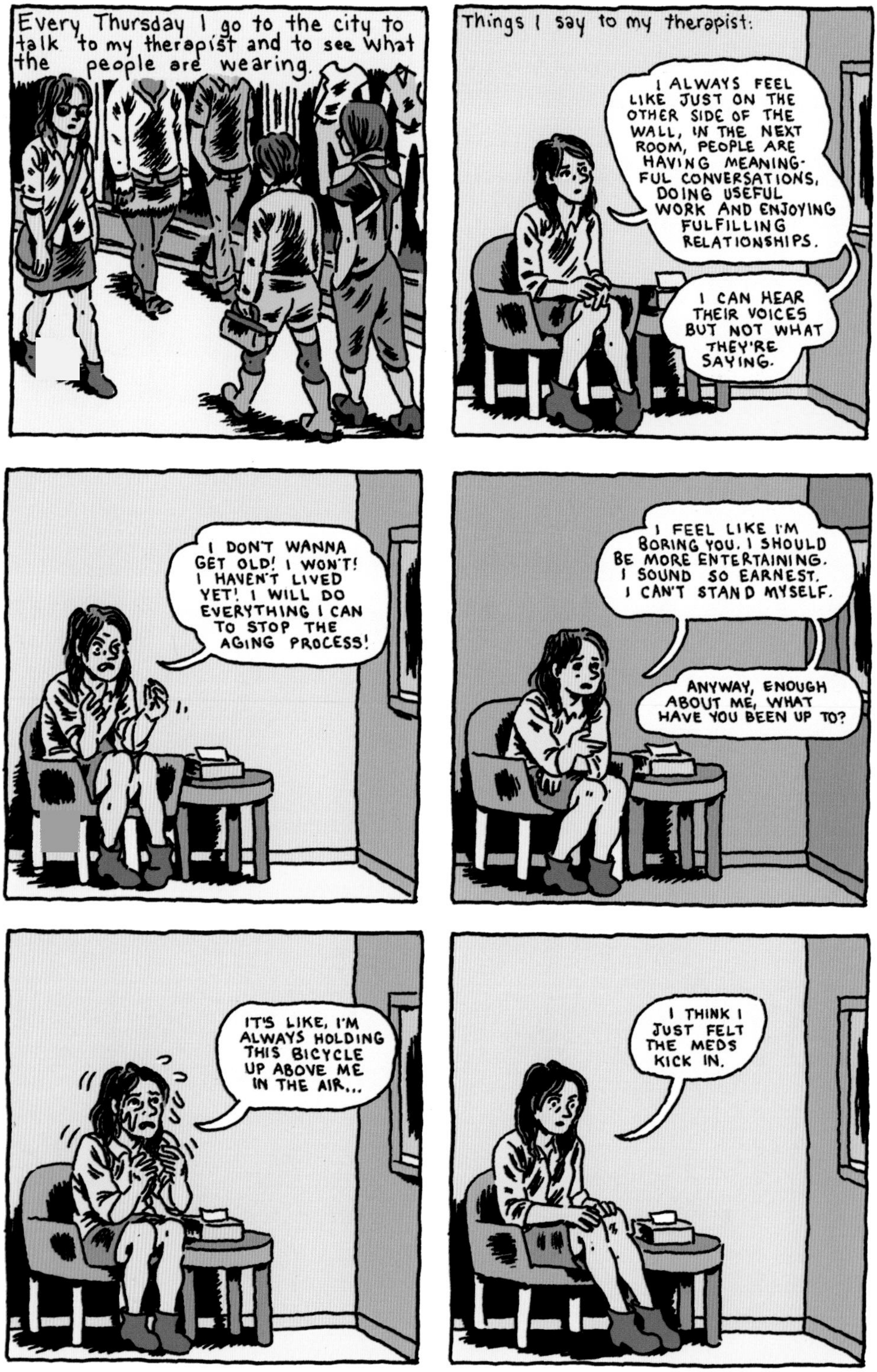
Every Thursday I go to the city to talk to my therapist and to see what the people are wearing.
Things I say to my therapist:
I ALWAYS FEEL LIKE JUST ON THE OTHER SIDE OF THE WALL, IN THE NEXT ROOM, PEOPLE ARE HAVING MEANINGFUL CONVERSATIONS, DOING USEFUL WORK AND ENJOYING FULFILLING RELATIONSHIPS.
I CAN HEAR THEIR VOICES BUT NOT WHAT THEY'RE SAYING.
I DON'T WANNA GET OLD! I WON'T! I HAVEN'T LIVED YET! I WILL DO EVERYTHING I CAN TO STOP THE AGING PROCESS!
I FEEL LIKE I'M BORING YOU. I SHOULD BE MORE ENTERTAINING. I SOUND SO EARNEST. I CAN'T STAND MYSELF.
ANYWAY, ENOUGH ABOUT ME, WHAT HAVE YOU BEEN UP TO?
IT'S LIKE, I'M ALWAYS HOLDING THIS BICYCLE UP ABOVE ME IN THE AIR...
I THINK I JUST FELT THE MEDS KICK IN.

Progress

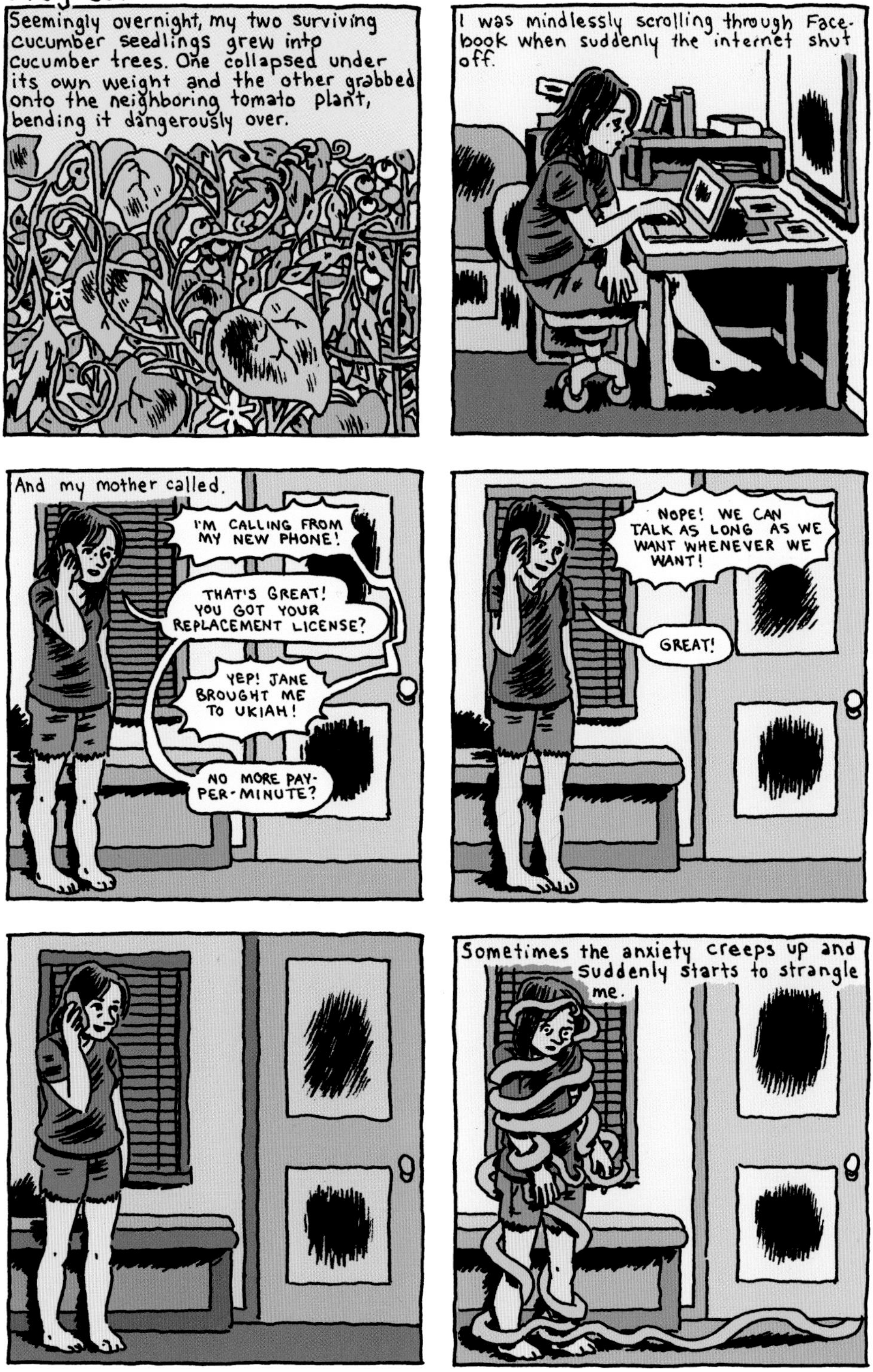
Seemingly overnight, my two surviving cucumber seedlings grew into cucumber trees. One collapsed under its own weight and the other grabbed onto the neighboring tomato plant, bending it dangerously over.
I was mindlessly scrolling through Facebook when suddenly the internet shut off.
And my mother called.
I'M CALLING FROM MY NEW PHONE!
THAT'S GREAT! YOU GOT YOUR REPLACEMENT LICENSE?
YEP! JANE BROUGHT ME TO UKIAH!
NO MORE PAY-PER-MINUTE?
NOPE! WE CAN TALK AS LONG AS WE WANT WHENEVER WE WANT!
GREAT!
Sometimes the anxiety creeps up and suddenly starts to strangle me.

Merciless Nature

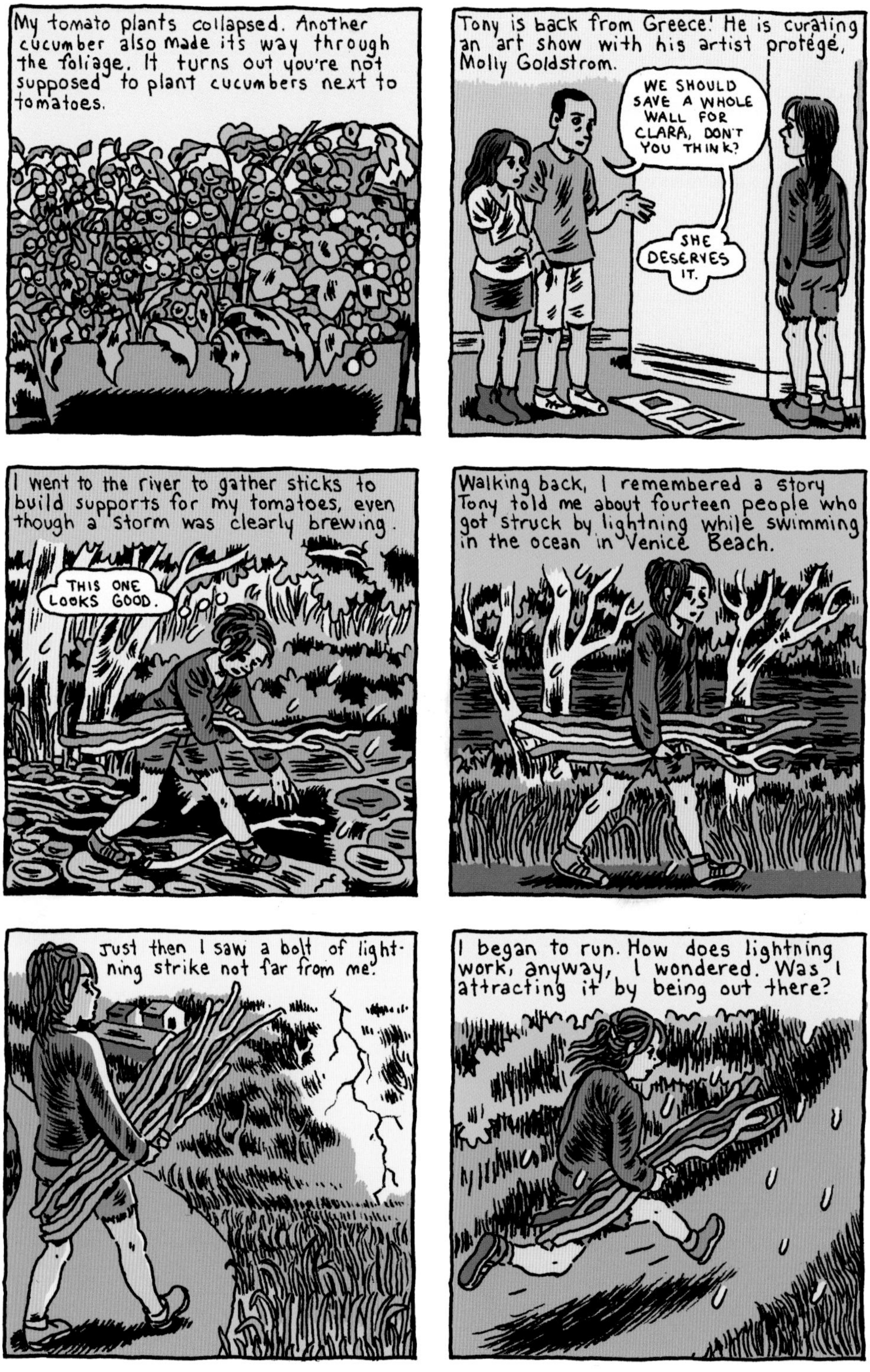
My tomato plants collapsed. Another cucumber also made its way through the foliage. It turns out you're not supposed to plant cucumbers next to tomatoes.
Tony is back from Greece! He is curating an art show with his artist protégé, Molly Goldstrom.
WE SHOULD SAVE A WHOLE WALL FOR CLARA, DON'T YOU THINK?
SHE DESERVES IT.
I went to the river to gather sticks to build supports for my tomatoes, even though a storm was clearly brewing.
THIS ONE LOOKS GOOD.
Walking back, I remembered a story Tony told me about fourteen people who got struck by lightning while swimming in the ocean in Venice Beach.
Just then I saw a bolt of lightning strike not far from me.
I began to run. How does lightning work, anyway, I wondered. Was I attracting it by being out there?

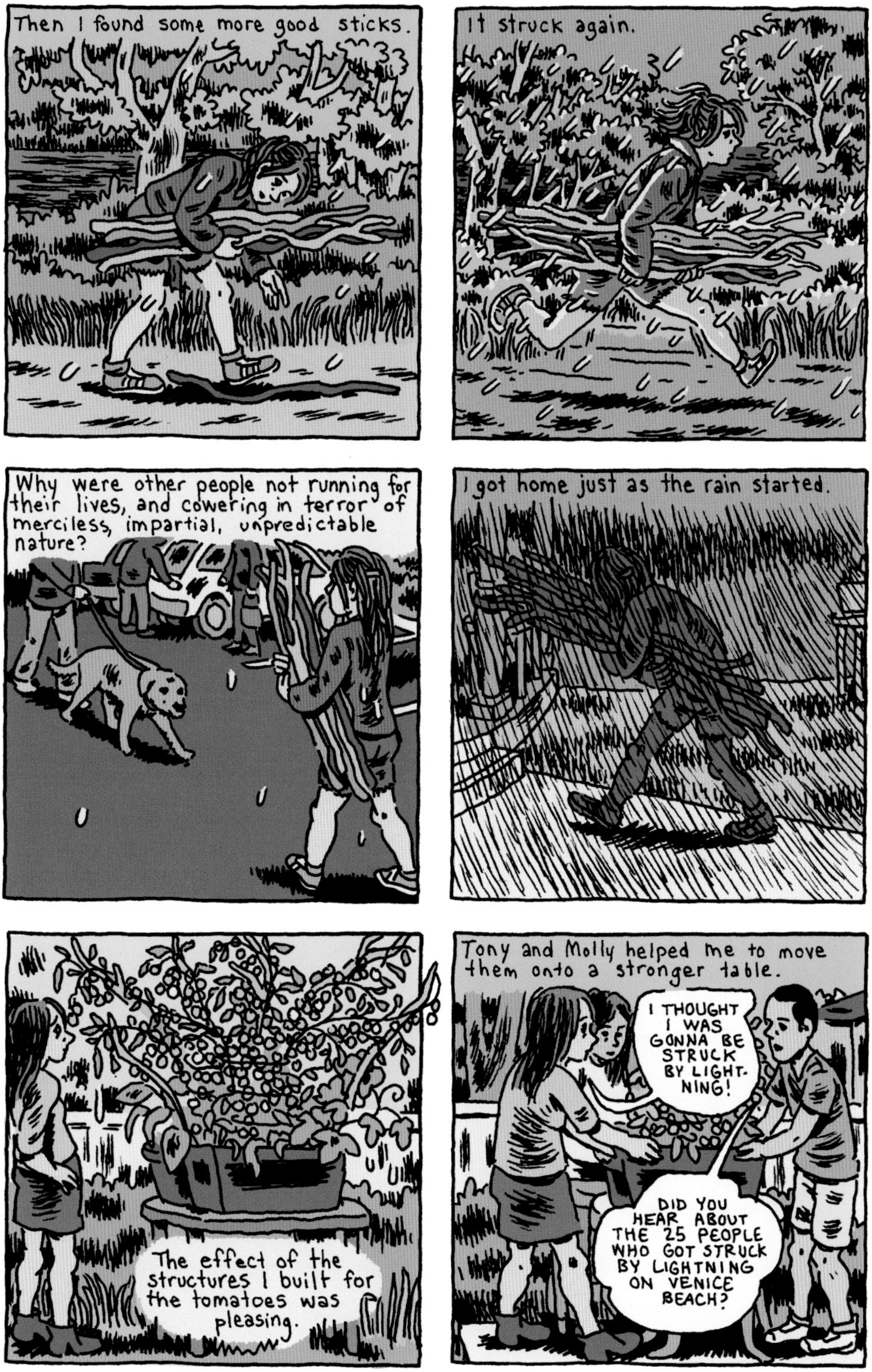
Then I found some more good sticks.
It struck again.
Why were other people not running for their lives, and cowering in terror of merciless, impartial, unpredictable nature?
I got home just as the rain started.
The effect of the structures I built for the tomatoes was pleasing.
Tony and Molly helped me to move them onto a stronger table.
I THOUGHT I WAS GONNA BE STRUCK BY LIGHT-NING!
DID YOU HEAR ABOUT THE 25 PEOPLE WHO GOT STRUCK BY LIGHTNING ON VENICE BEACH?

My Fans Help Me

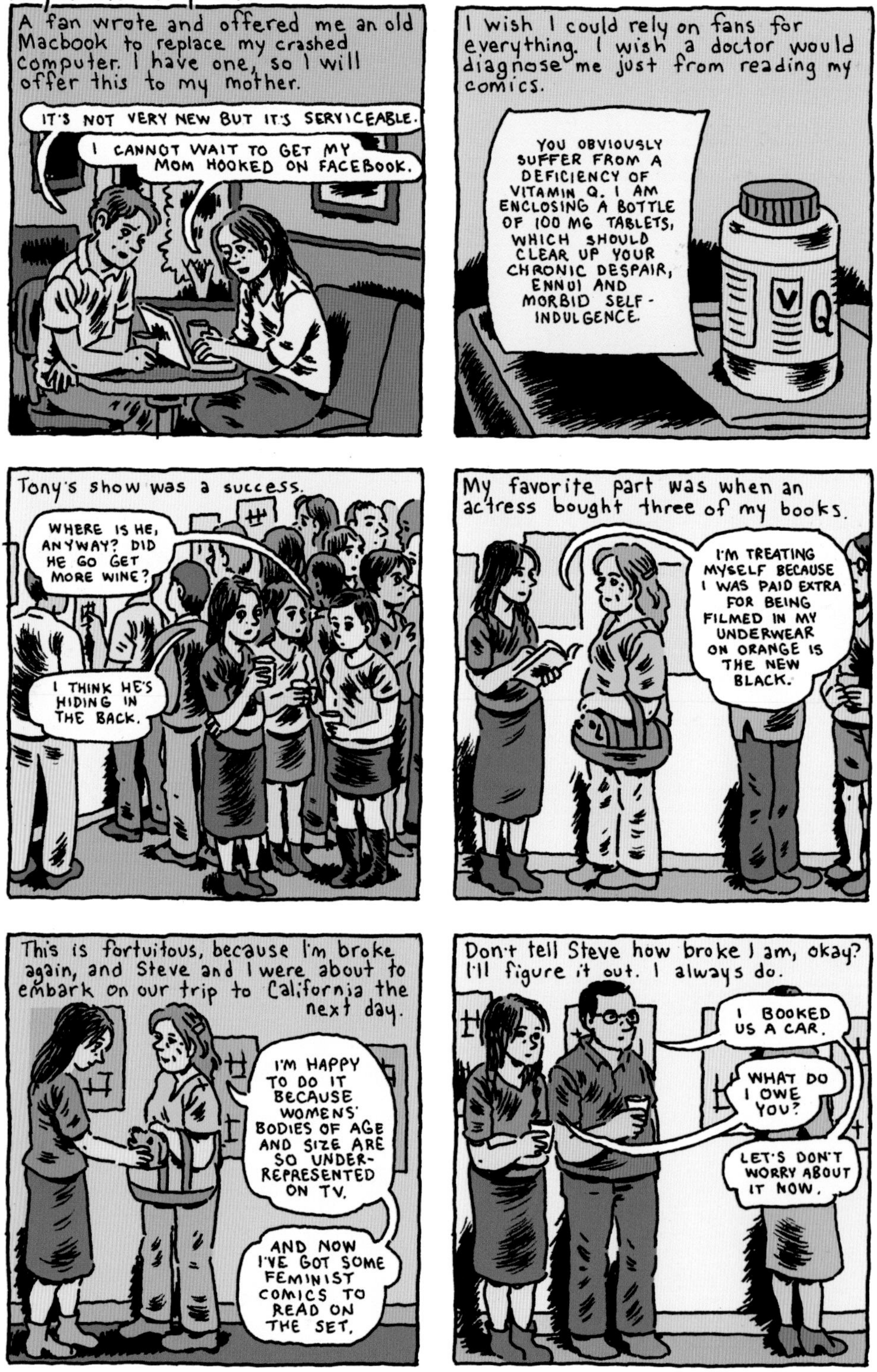
A fan wrote and offered me an old Macbook to replace my crashed computer. I have one, so I will offer this to my mother.
IT'S NOT VERY NEW BUT IT'S SERVICEABLE.
I CANNOT WAIT TO GET MY MOM HOOKED ON FACEBOOK.
I wish I could rely on fans for everything. I wish a doctor would diagnose me just from reading my comics.
YOU OBVIOUSLY SUFFER FROM A DEFICIENCY OF VITAMIN Q. I AM ENCLOSING A BOTTLE OF 100 MG TABLETS, WHICH SHOULD CLEAR UP YOUR CHRONIC DESPAIR, ENNUI AND MORBID SELF-INDULGENCE.
VQ
Tony's show was a success.
WHERE IS HE, ANYWAY? DID HE GO GET MORE WINE?
I THINK HE'S HIDING IN THE BACK.
My favorite part was when an actress bought three of my books.
I'M TREATING MYSELF BECAUSE I WAS PAID EXTRA FOR BEING FILMED IN MY UNDERWEAR ON ORANGE IS THE NEW BLACK.
This is fortuitous, because I'm broke again, and Steve and I were about to embark on our trip to California the next day.
I'M HAPPY TO DO IT BECAUSE WOMENS' BODIES OF AGE AND SIZE ARE SO UNDER-REPRESENTED ON TV.
AND NOW I'VE GOT SOME FEMINIST COMICS TO READ ON THE SET.
Don't tell Steve how broke I am, okay? I'll figure it out. I always do.
I BOOKED US A CAR.
WHAT DO I OWE YOU?
LET'S DON'T WORRY ABOUT IT NOW.

Going to California

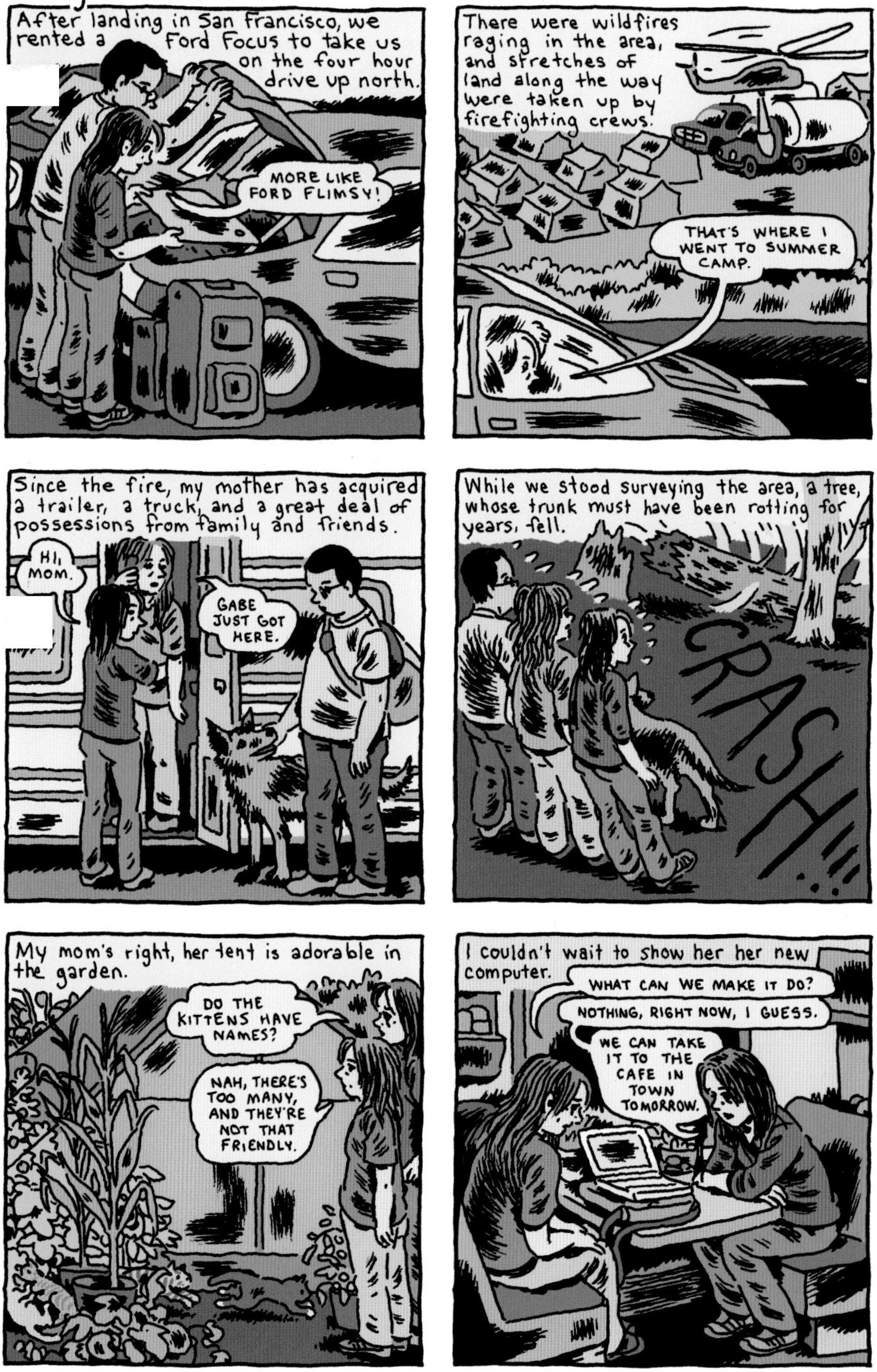

After landing in San francisco, we rented a Ford Focus to take us on the four hour drive up north.
MORE LIKE FORD FLIMSY!
There were wildfires raging in the area, and stretches of land along the way were taken up by firefighting crews.
THAT'S WHERE I WENT TO SUMMER CAMP.
Since the fire, my mother has acquired a trailer, a truck, and a great deal of possessions from family and friends.
HI, MOM.
GABE JUST GOT HERE.
While we stood surveying the area, a tree, whose trunk must have been rotting for years, fell.
CRASH!!!...
My mom's right, her tent is adorable in the garden.
DO THE KITTENS HAVE NAMES?
NAH, THERE'S TOO MANY, AND THEY'RE NOT THAT FRIENDLY.
I couldn't wait to show her her new computer.
WHAT CAN WE MAKE IT DO?
NOTHING, RIGHT NOW, I GUESS.
WE CAN TAKE IT TO THE CAFE IN TOWN TOMORROW.

We Hike up to the Fire Tower

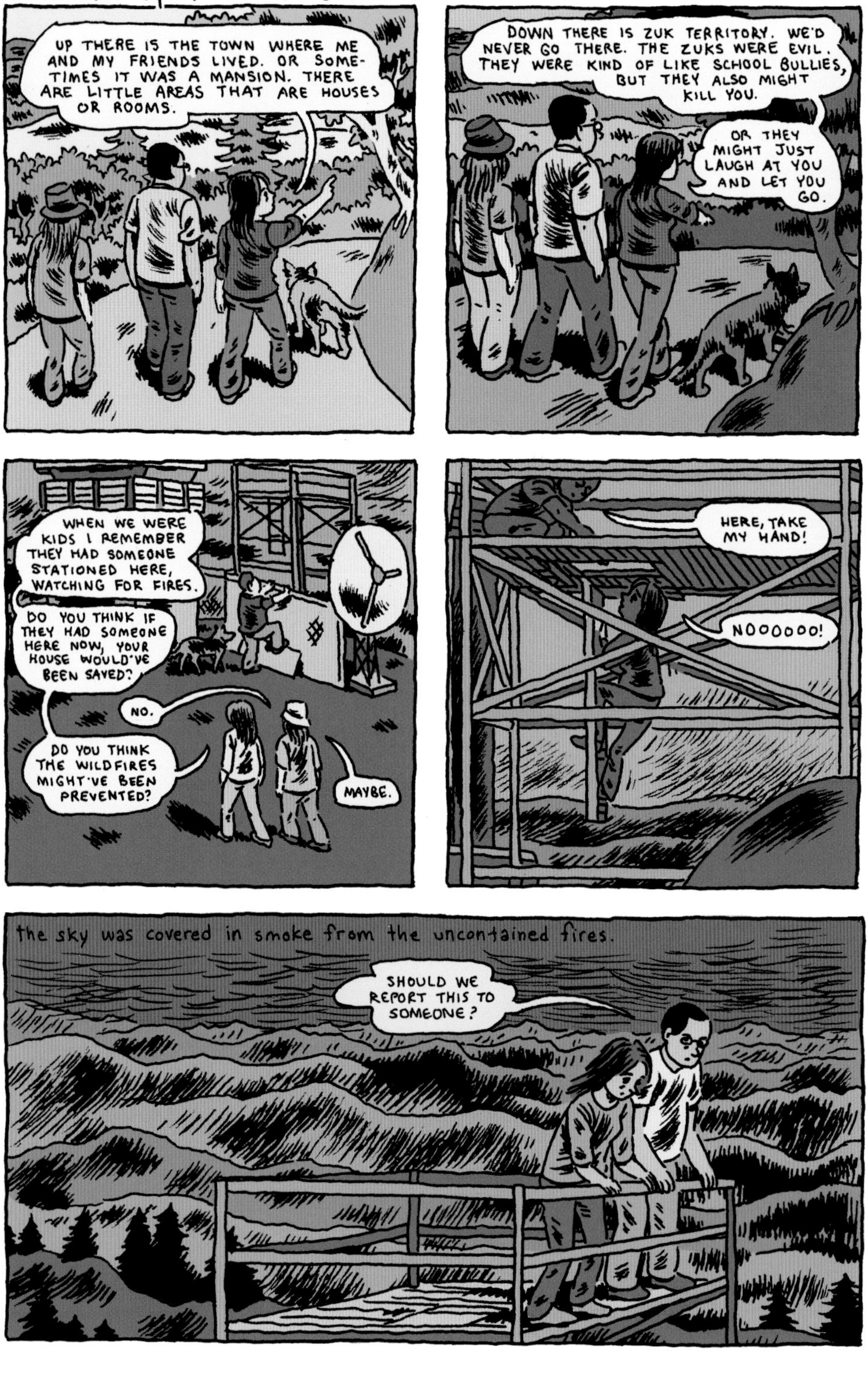
UP THERE IS THE TOWN WHERE ME AND MY FRIENDS LIVED. OR SOMETIMES IT WAS A MANSION. THERE ARE LITTLE AREAS THAT ARE HOUSES OR ROOMS.
DOWN THERE IS ZUK TERRITORY. WE'D NEVER GO THERE. THE ZUKS WERE EVIL. THEY WERE KIND OF LIKE SCHOOL BULLIES, BUT THEY ALSO MIGHT KILL YOU.
OR THEY MIGHT JUST LAUGH AT YOU AND LET YOU GO.
WHEN WE WERE KIDS I REMEMBER THEY HAD SOMEONE STATIONED HERE, WATCHING FOR FIRES.
DO YOU THINK IF THEY HAD SOMEONE HERE NOW, YOUR HOUSE WOULD'VE BEEN SAVED?
NO.
DO YOU THINK THE WILDFIRES MIGHT'VE BEEN PREVENTED?
MAYBE.
HERE, TAKE MY HAND!
NOOOOOO!
the sky was covered in smoke from the uncontained fires.
SHOULD WE REPORT THIS TO SOMEONE?

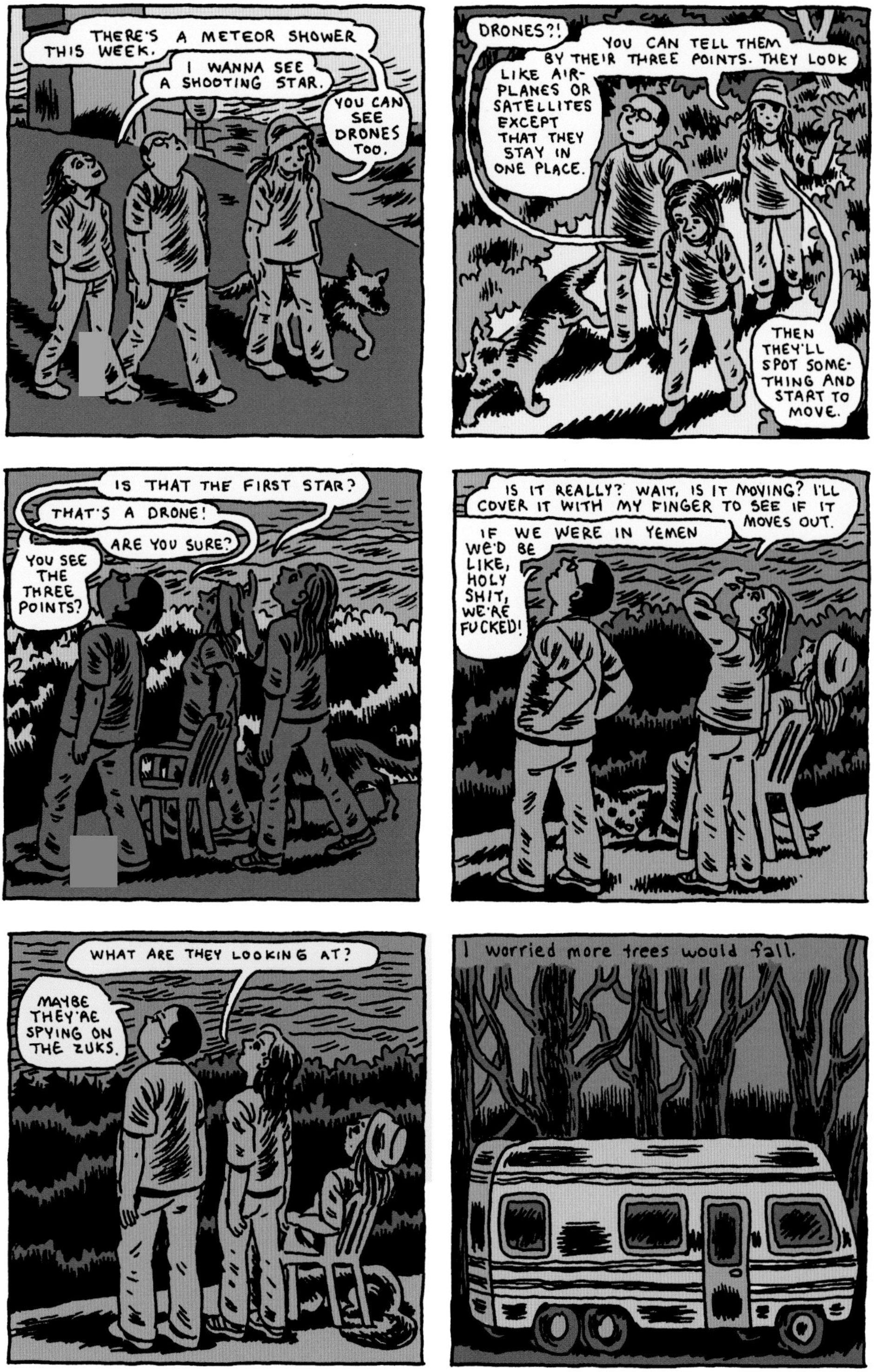
THERE'S A METEOR SHOWER THIS WEEK.
I WANNA SEE A SHOOTING STAR.
YOU CAN SEE DRONES TOO.
DRONES?!
YOU CAN TELL THEM BY THEIR THREE POINTS. THEY LOOK
LIKE AIR-PLANES OR SATELLITES EXCEPT THAT THEY STAY IN ONE PLACE.
THEN THEY'LL SPOT SOME-THING AND START TO MOVE.
IS THAT THE FIRST STAR?
THAT'S A DRONE!
ARE YOU SURE?
YOU SEE THE THREE POINTS?
IS IT REALLY? WAIT, IS IT MOVING? I'LL COVER IT WITH MY FINGER TO SEE IF IT MOVES OUT.
IF WE WERE IN YEMEN WE'D BE LIKE, HOLY SHIT, WE'RE FUCKED!
WHAT ARE THEY LOOKING AT?
MAYBE THEY'RE SPYING ON THE ZUKS.
I worried more trees would fall.

Services

We had to go to Social Services in Ukiah and wait for a long time.

GOT SOME NEW YORKERS.

OH, GOOD.

Luckily, we had a helpful agent.

SO YOU HAVE A TRUCK. IS THERE ANYTHING ELSE YOU OWN?

NO.

THERE'S A TRAILER.

DO YOU HAVE REGISTRATION FOR THE TRAILER?

NO.

I'LL JUST PUT DOWN TRUCK.

We also went to the DMV but the long line depressed us too much and we left.

WHY IS IT THAT THERE'S ONLY POOR PEOPLE HERE? DON'T RICH PEOPLE HAVE TO RENEW THEIR LICENSES TOO?

Then we tried to find a swimming hole i remembered from twenty years ago, to no avail.

I REMEMBER IT WAS PRETTY AND SECLUDED AND THERE WAS A TREE SWING. IT MUST BE AROUND HERE SOMEWHERE.

Later, we went to Starbucks to use their bathroom and wifi.

I DON'T WANT TO HAVE A FACEBOOK. I DON'T WANT TO PUT MY INFORMATION OUT THERE.

OKAY, BUT LET'S SET YOU UP WITH AN EMAIL ACCOUNT.

ALL RIGHT.

LET'S SEE... MAGGIE.BELL AT GMAIL DOT COM? NO, THAT'S TAKEN...

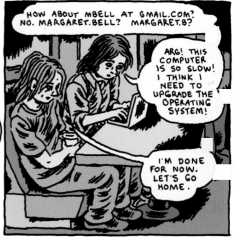

HOW ABOUT MBELL AT GMAIL.COM? NO. MARGARET.BELL? MARGARET.B?

ARG! THIS COMPUTER IS SO SLOW! I THINK I NEED TO UPGRADE THE OPERATING SYSTEM!

I'M DONE FOR NOW. LET'S GO HOME.

Bureaucracy

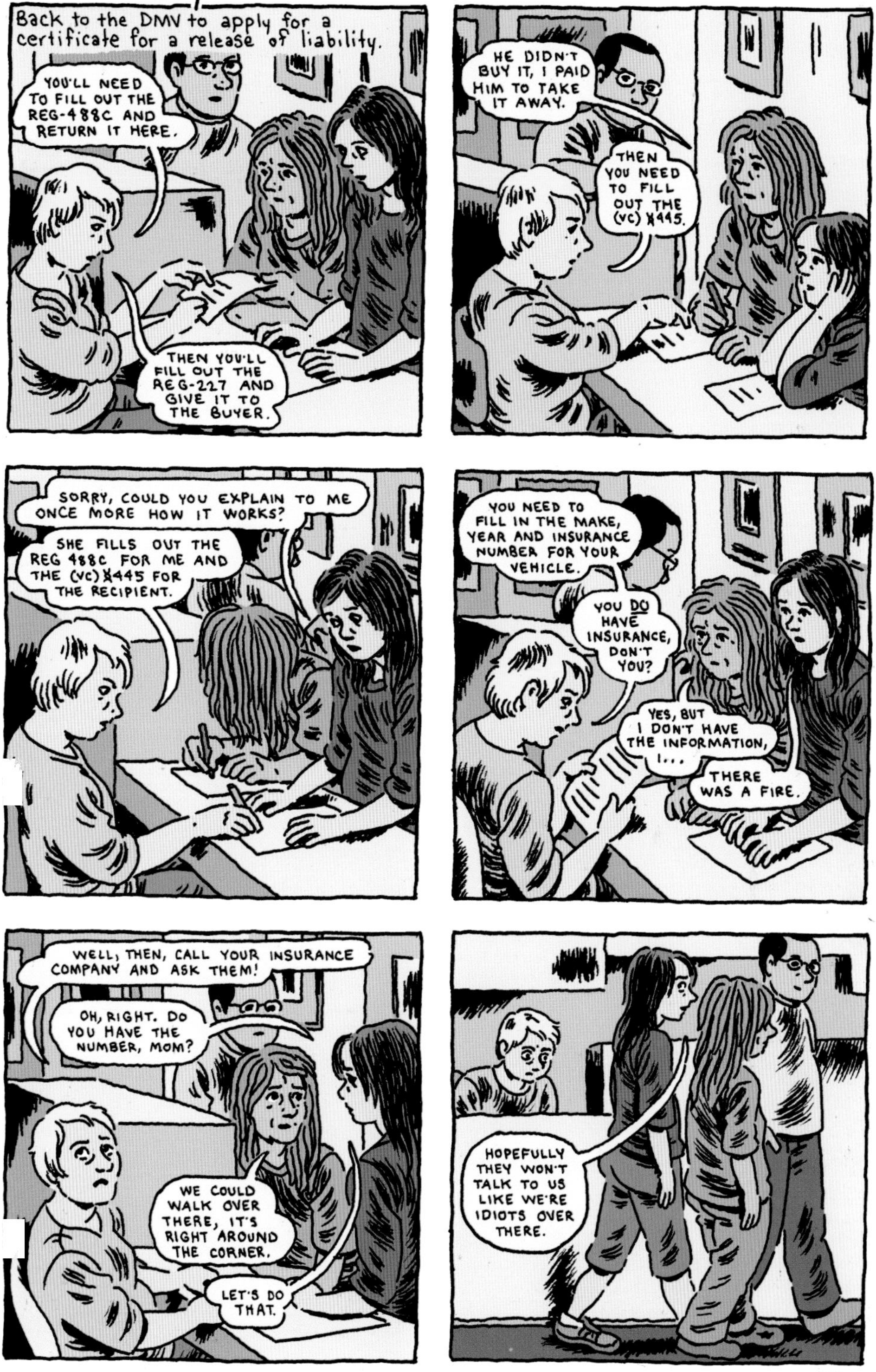
Back to the DMV to apply for a certificate for a release of liability.
YOU'LL NEED TO FILL OUT THE REG-488C AND RETURN IT HERE.
THEN YOU'LL FILL OUT THE REG-227 AND GIVE IT TO THE BUYER.
HE DIDN'T BUY IT, I PAID HIM TO TAKE IT AWAY.
THEN YOU NEED TO FILL OUT THE (VC) §445.
SORRY, COULD YOU EXPLAIN TO ME ONCE MORE HOW IT WORKS?
SHE FILLS OUT THE REG 488C FOR ME AND THE (VC) §445 FOR THE RECIPIENT.
YOU NEED TO FILL IN THE MAKE, YEAR AND INSURANCE NUMBER FOR YOUR VEHICLE.
YOU DO HAVE INSURANCE, DON'T YOU?
YES, BUT I DON'T HAVE THE INFORMATION, I...
THERE WAS A FIRE.
WELL, THEN, CALL YOUR INSURANCE COMPANY AND ASK THEM!
OH, RIGHT. DO YOU HAVE THE NUMBER, MOM?
WE COULD WALK OVER THERE, IT'S RIGHT AROUND THE CORNER.
LET'S DO THAT.
HOPEFULLY THEY WON'T TALK TO US LIKE WE'RE IDIOTS OVER THERE.

Talisman

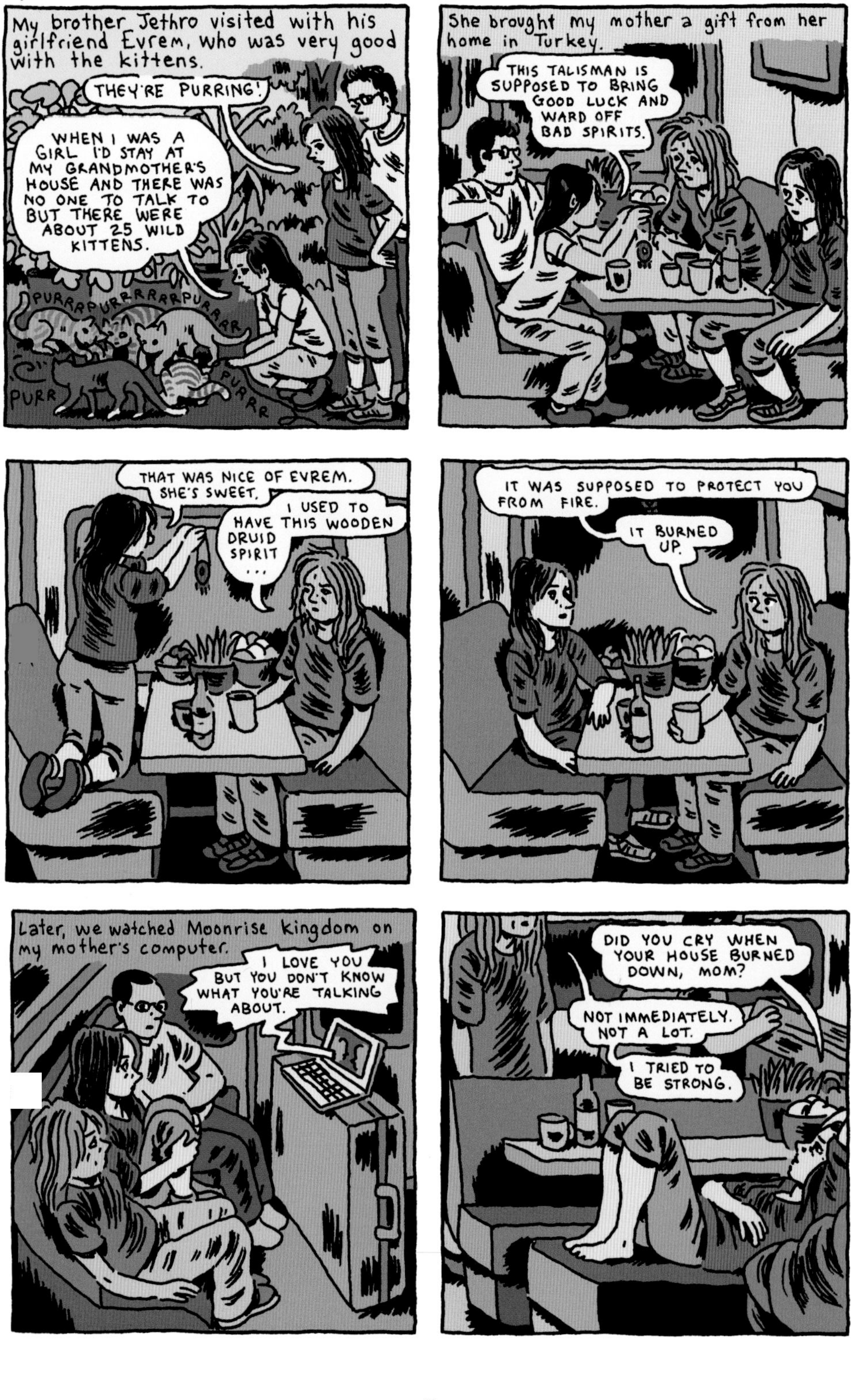

My brother Jethro visited with his girlfriend Evrem, who was very good with the kittens.
THEY'RE PURRING!
WHEN I WAS A GIRL I'D STAY AT MY GRANDMOTHER'S HOUSE AND THERE WAS NO ONE TO TALK TO BUT THERE WERE ABOUT 25 WILD KITTENS.
PURRRPURRRRRRPURRRRR
PURR
PURRR
She brought my mother a gift from her home in Turkey.
THIS TALISMAN IS SUPPOSED TO BRING GOOD LUCK AND WARD OFF BAD SPIRITS.
THAT WAS NICE OF EVREM. SHE'S SWEET.
I USED TO HAVE THIS WOODEN DRUID SPIRIT . . .
IT WAS SUPPOSED TO PROTECT YOU FROM FIRE.
IT BURNED UP.
Later, we watched Moonrise kingdom on my mother's computer.
I LOVE YOU BUT YOU DON'T KNOW WHAT YOU'RE TALKING ABOUT.
DID YOU CRY WHEN YOUR HOUSE BURNED DOWN, MOM?
NOT IMMEDIATELY. NOT A LOT.
I TRIED TO BE STRONG.

The Traumatizer

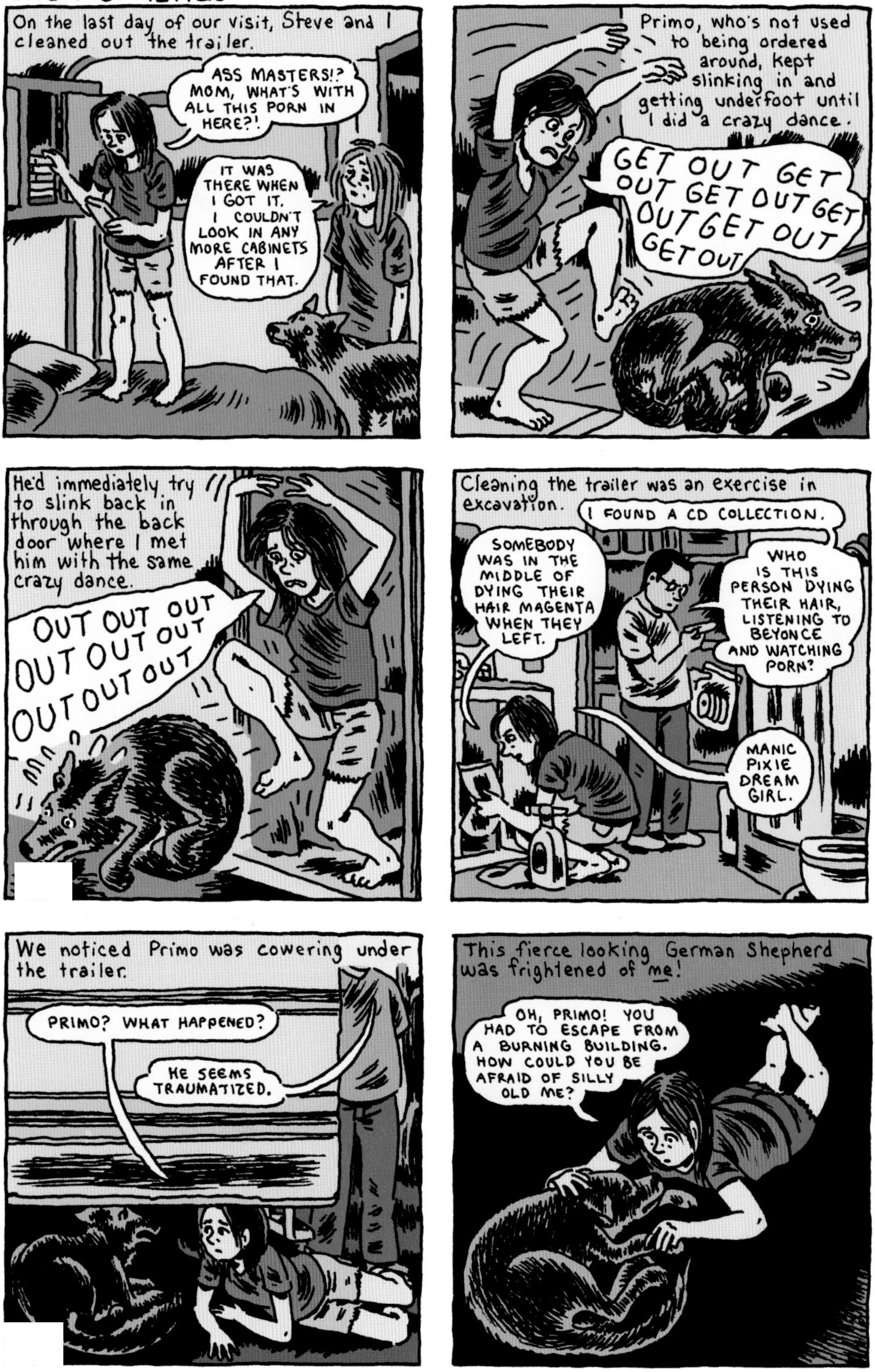

On the last day of our visit, Steve and I cleaned out the trailer.
ASS MASTERS!? MOM, WHAT'S WITH ALL THIS PORN IN HERE?!
IT WAS THERE WHEN I GOT IT. I COULDN'T LOOK IN ANY MORE CABINETS AFTER I FOUND THAT.
Primo, who's not used to being ordered around, kept slinking in and getting underfoot until I did a crazy dance.
GET OUT GET OUT GET OUT GET OUT GET OUT GET OUT
He'd immediately try to slink back in through the back door where I met him with the same crazy dance.
OUT OUT OUT OUT OUT OUT OUT OUT OUT
Cleaning the trailer was an exercise in excavation.
I FOUND A CD COLLECTION.
WHO IS THIS PERSON DYING THEIR HAIR, LISTENING TO BEYONCE AND WATCHING PORN?
SOMEBODY WAS IN THE MIDDLE OF DYING THEIR HAIR MAGENTA WHEN THEY LEFT.
MANIC PIXIE DREAM GIRL.
We noticed Primo was cowering under the trailer.
PRIMO? WHAT HAPPENED?
HE SEEMS TRAUMATIZED.
This fierce looking German Shepherd was frightened of me!
OH, PRIMO! YOU HAD TO ESCAPE FROM A BURNING BUILDING. HOW COULD YOU BE AFRAID OF SILLY OLD ME?

Animals

Our flight from San Francisco was for six the next morning, so we decided to stay until midnight then drive all night.

WE CAN'T LEAVE TIL WE SEE A SHOOTING STAR OR A DRONE.

THERE'S A SHOOTING DRONE!

THAT'S A SATELLITE!

How did my mother live here, I wondered, with nothing between all this darkness and her. Still, we didn't want to leave.

As I was putting some things away in a storage container outside, one of the kittens ran up onto me, suddenly very friendly.

I guessed that she probably thought I was my mom, in the dark with the flashlight, and when she realized I wasn't, she didn't mind, I would do.

PURRRRRRRRRR PURAAAAAAR

My mom has a way with animals.

HEY!

The Traumatizer, part two

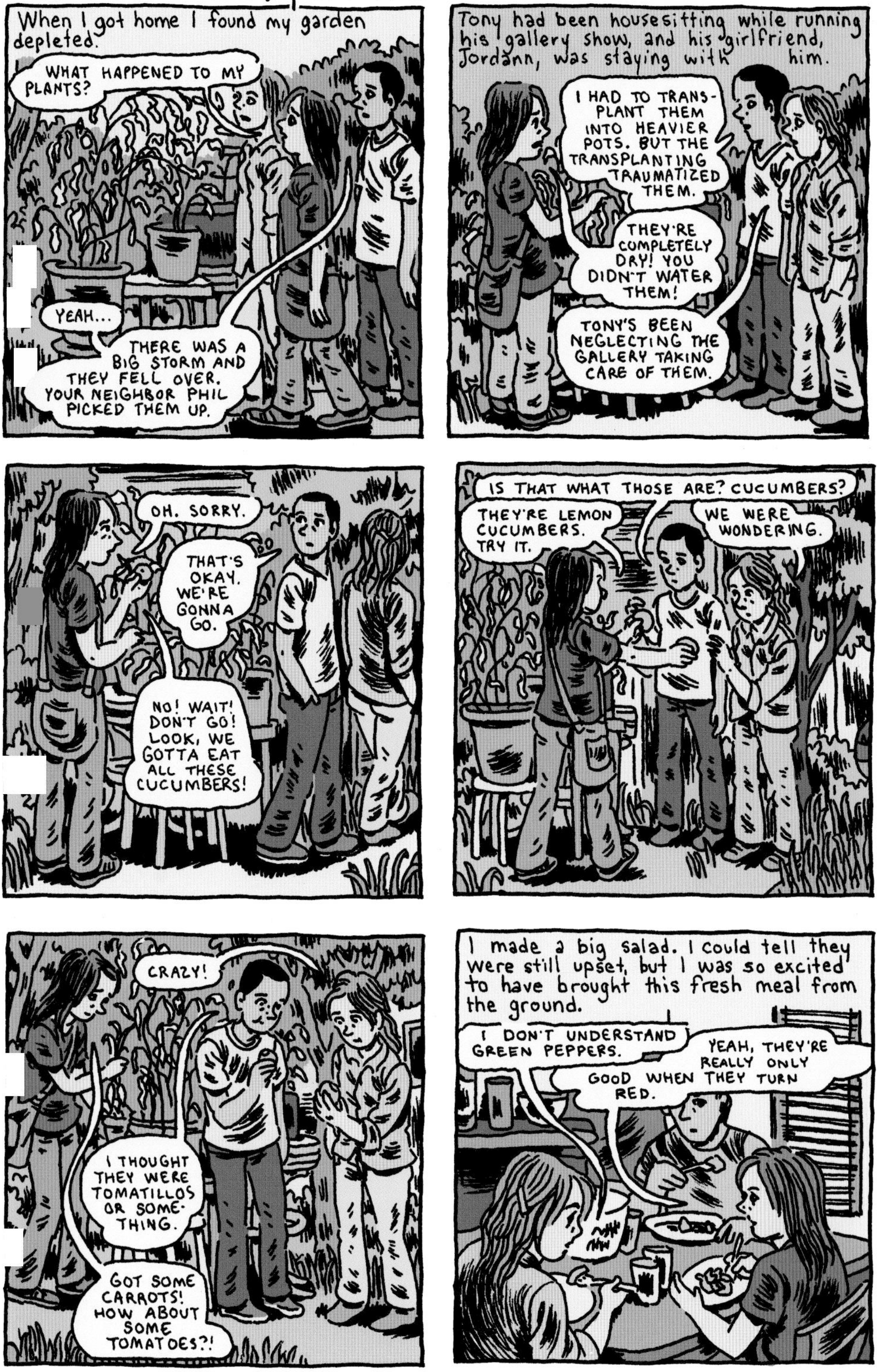

When I got home I found my garden depleted.
WHAT HAPPENED TO MY PLANTS?
YEAH...
THERE WAS A BIG STORM AND THEY FELL OVER. YOUR NEIGHBOR PHIL PICKED THEM UP.
Tony had been housesitting while running his gallery show, and his girlfriend, Jordann, was staying with him.
I HAD TO TRANSPLANT THEM INTO HEAVIER POTS. BUT THE TRANSPLANTING TRAUMATIZED THEM.
THEY'RE COMPLETELY DRY! YOU DIDN'T WATER THEM!
TONY'S BEEN NEGLECTING THE GALLERY TAKING CARE OF THEM.
OH. SORRY.
THAT'S OKAY. WE'RE GONNA GO.
NO! WAIT! DON'T GO! LOOK, WE GOTTA EAT ALL THESE CUCUMBERS!
IS THAT WHAT THOSE ARE? CUCUMBERS?
THEY'RE LEMON CUCUMBERS. TRY IT.
WE WERE WONDERING.
CRAZY!
I THOUGHT THEY WERE TOMATILLOS OR SOMETHING.
GOT SOME CARROTS! HOW ABOUT SOME TOMATOES?!
I made a big salad. I could tell they were still upset, but I was so excited to have brought this fresh meal from the ground.
I DON'T UNDERSTAND GREEN PEPPERS.
YEAH, THEY'RE REALLY ONLY GOOD WHEN THEY TURN RED.

The Dishrack

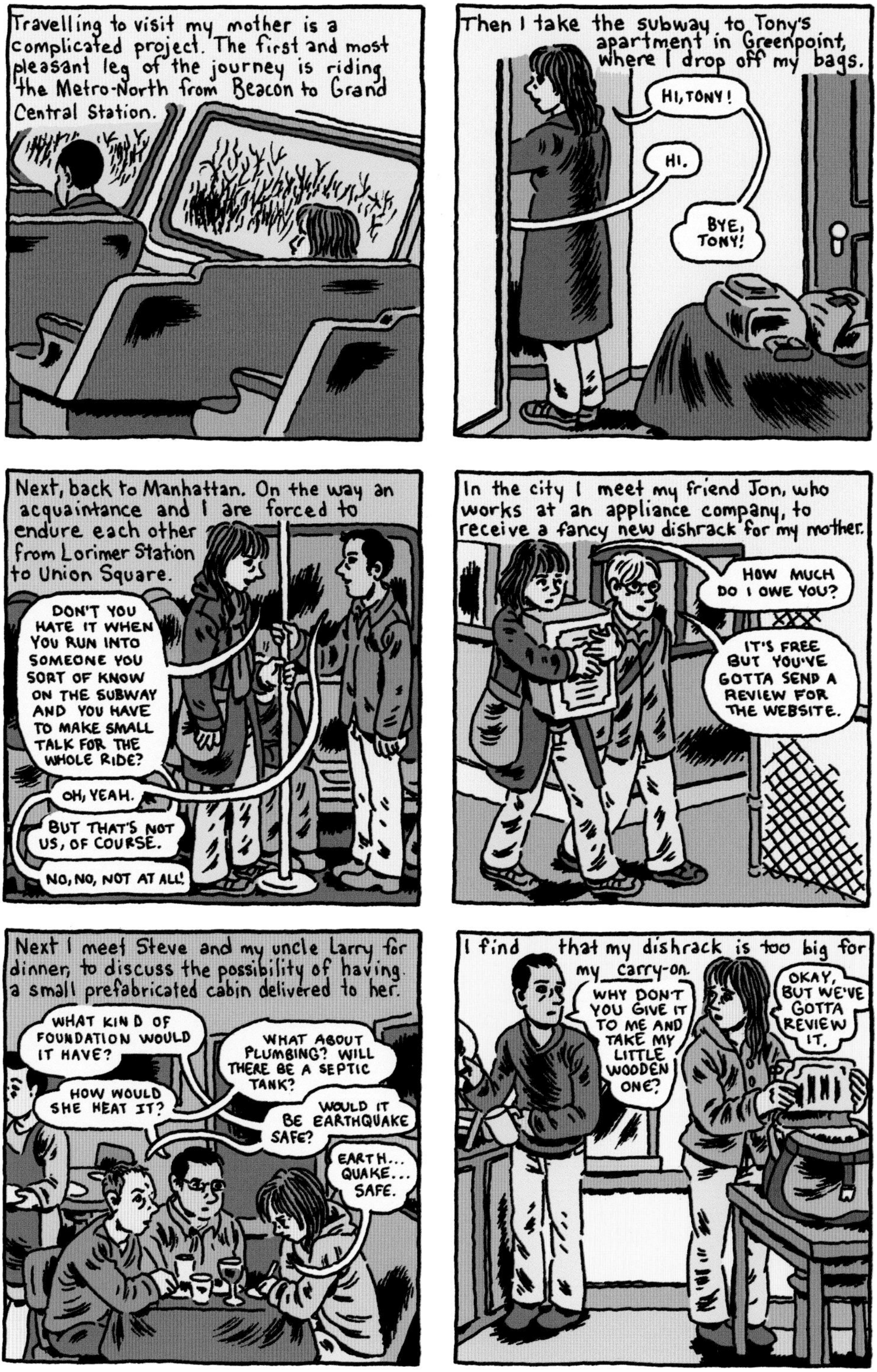
Travelling to visit my mother is a complicated project. The first and most pleasant leg of the journey is riding the Metro-North from Beacon to Grand Central Station.
Then I take the subway to Tony's apartment in Greenpoint, where I drop off my bags.
HI, TONY!
HI.
BYE, TONY!
Next, back to Manhattan. On the way an acquaintance and I are forced to endure each other from Lorimer Station to Union Square.
DON'T YOU HATE IT WHEN YOU RUN INTO SOMEONE YOU SORT OF KNOW ON THE SUBWAY AND YOU HAVE TO MAKE SMALL TALK FOR THE WHOLE RIDE?
OH, YEAH.
BUT THAT'S NOT US, OF COURSE.
NO, NO, NOT AT ALL!
In the city I meet my friend Jon, who works at an appliance company, to receive a fancy new dishrack for my mother.
HOW MUCH DO I OWE YOU?
IT'S FREE BUT YOU'VE GOTTA SEND A REVIEW FOR THE WEBSITE.
Next I meet Steve and my uncle Larry for dinner, to discuss the possibility of having a small prefabricated cabin delivered to her.
WHAT KIND OF FOUNDATION WOULD IT HAVE?
HOW WOULD SHE HEAT IT?
WHAT ABOUT PLUMBING? WILL THERE BE A SEPTIC TANK?
WOULD IT BE EARTHQUAKE SAFE?
EARTH... QUAKE... SAFE.
I find that my dishrack is too big for my carry-on.
WHY DON'T YOU GIVE IT TO ME AND TAKE MY LITTLE WOODEN ONE?
OKAY, BUT WE'VE GOTTA REVIEW IT.

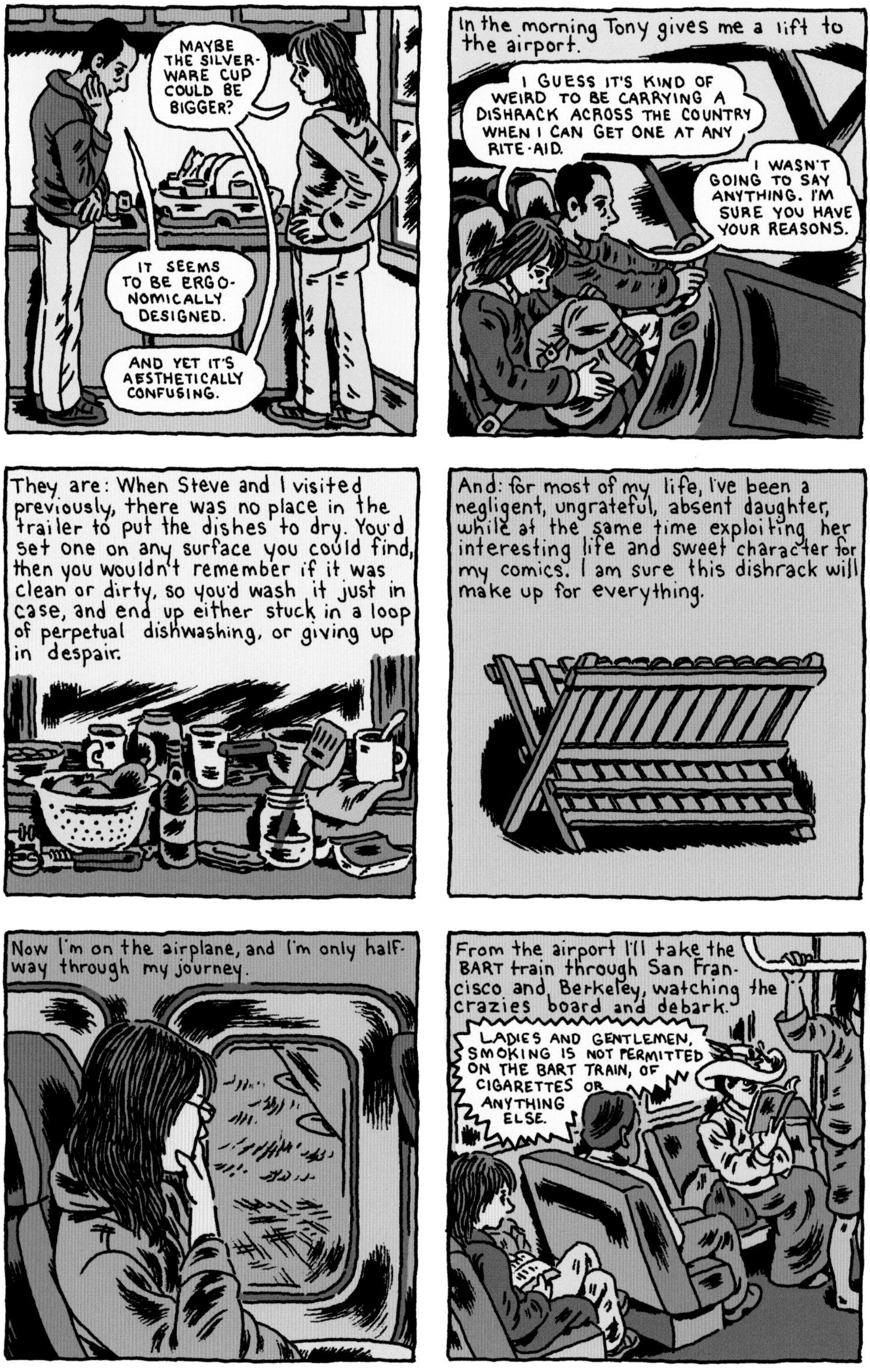
MAYBE THE SILVER-WARE CUP COULD BE BIGGER?
IT SEEMS TO BE ERGO-NOMICALLY DESIGNED.
AND YET IT'S AESTHETICALLY CONFUSING.
In the morning Tony gives me a lift to the airport.
I GUESS IT'S KIND OF WEIRD TO BE CARRYING A DISHRACK ACROSS THE COUNTRY WHEN I CAN GET ONE AT ANY RITE-AID.
I WASN'T GOING TO SAY ANYTHING. I'M SURE YOU HAVE YOUR REASONS.
They are: When Steve and I visited previously, there was no place in the trailer to put the dishes to dry. You'd set one on any surface you could find, then you wouldn't remember if it was clean or dirty, so you'd wash it just in case, and end up either stuck in a loop of perpetual dishwashing, or giving up in despair.
And: for most of my life, I've been a negligent, ungrateful, absent daughter, while at the same time exploiting her interesting life and sweet character for my comics. I am sure this dishrack will make up for everything.
Now I'm on the airplane, and I'm only half-way through my journey.
From the airport I'll take the BART train through San Francisco and Berkeley, watching the crazies board and debark.
LADIES AND GENTLEMEN, SMOKING IS NOT PERMITTED ON THE BART TRAIN, OF CIGARETTES OR ANYTHING ELSE.

I'll get off in El Cerrito, dragging the wobbly, too-short suitcase that I bought at an estate sale along the sidewalk like an unruly pet.

I'll stay with my 96-year-old grandmother, who will stand at attention whenever I enter the room.

WHAT CAN I GET YOU, GABE? MORE COFFEE?

GRANDMA, PLEASE, RELAX, I'M JUST GOING FOR A WALK.

I'll wake up before it gets light and go out to see somebody's large dog walking by itself.

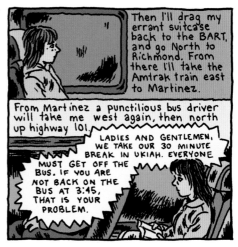

Then I'll drag my errant suitcase back to the BART, and go North to Richmond. From there I'll take the Amtrak train east to Martinez.

From Martinez a punctilious bus driver will take me west again, then north up highway 101.

LADIES AND GENTLEMEN, WE TAKE OUR 30 MINUTE BREAK IN UKIAH. EVERYONE MUST GET OFF THE BUS. IF YOU ARE NOT BACK ON THE BUS AT 3:45, THAT IS YOUR PROBLEM.

He'll drop me off in Laytonville, where my mother will have come to pick me up as if I were just getting out of school. I know what you're thinking: why don't I rent a car and drive myself?

COOL HAT! YOU LIKE IT?

I'm pretty sure that by the time I'd have learned to drive, passed the driver's test, gotten a license, obtained a credit card and saved enough money to rent a car, automobiles will have become obsolete, and our main mode of transportation will be rafts built from the salvaged detritus of our sunken civilization.

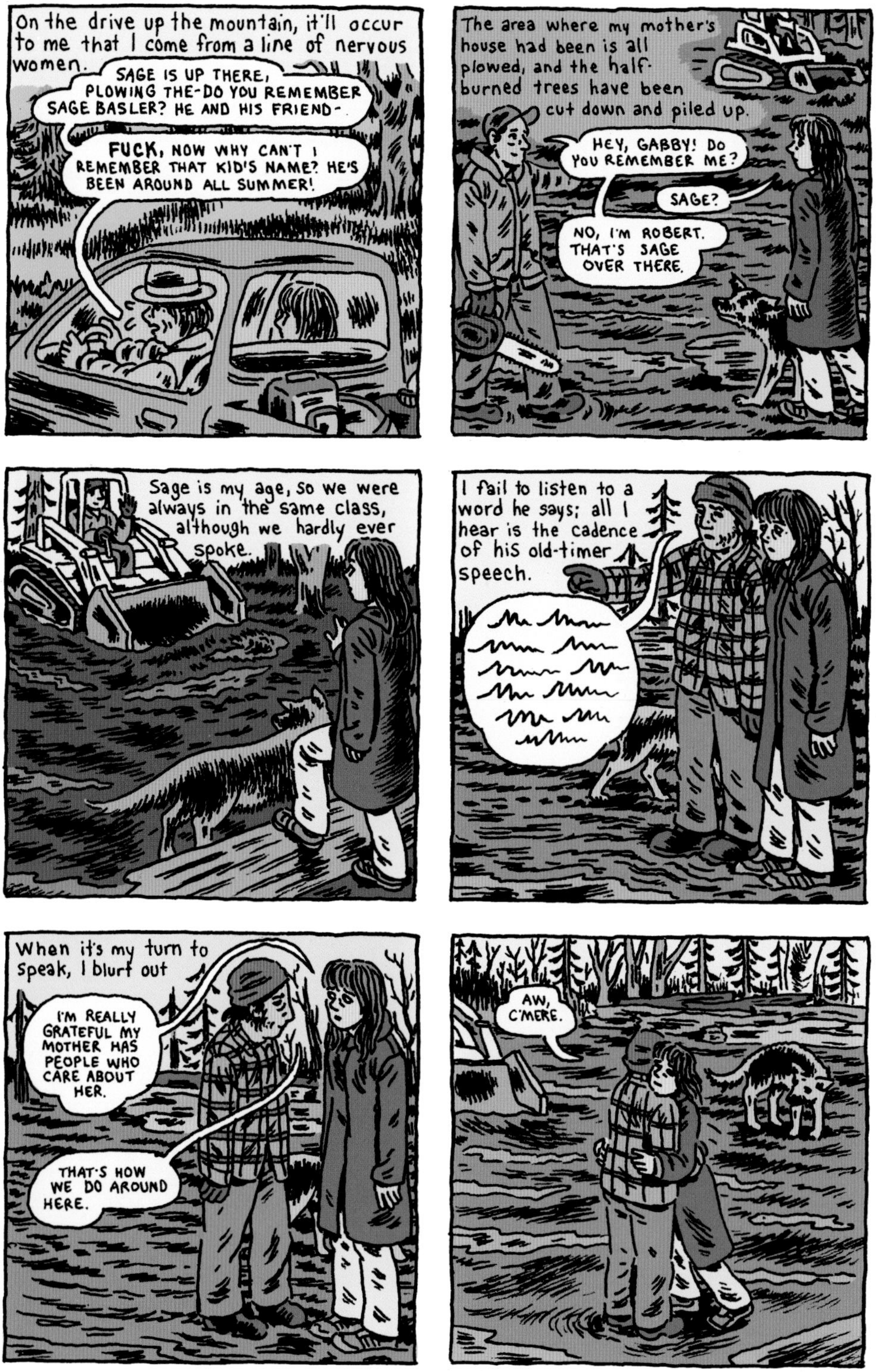
On the drive up the mountain, it'll occur to me that I come from a line of nervous women.
SAGE IS UP THERE, PLOWING THE-DO YOU REMEMBER SAGE BASLER? HE AND HIS FRIEND-.
FUCK, NOW WHY CAN'T I REMEMBER THAT KID'S NAME? HE'S BEEN AROUND ALL SUMMER!
The area where my mother's house had been is all plowed, and the half-burned trees have been cut down and piled up.
HEY, GABBY! DO YOU REMEMBER ME?
SAGE?
NO, I'M ROBERT. THAT'S SAGE OVER THERE.
Sage is my age, so we were always in the same class, although we hardly ever spoke.
I fail to listen to a word he says; all I hear is the cadence of his old-timer speech.
When it's my turn to speak, I blurt out
I'M REALLY GRATEFUL MY MOTHER HAS PEOPLE WHO CARE ABOUT HER.
THAT'S HOW WE DO AROUND HERE.
AW, C'MERE.

Ghost Cats

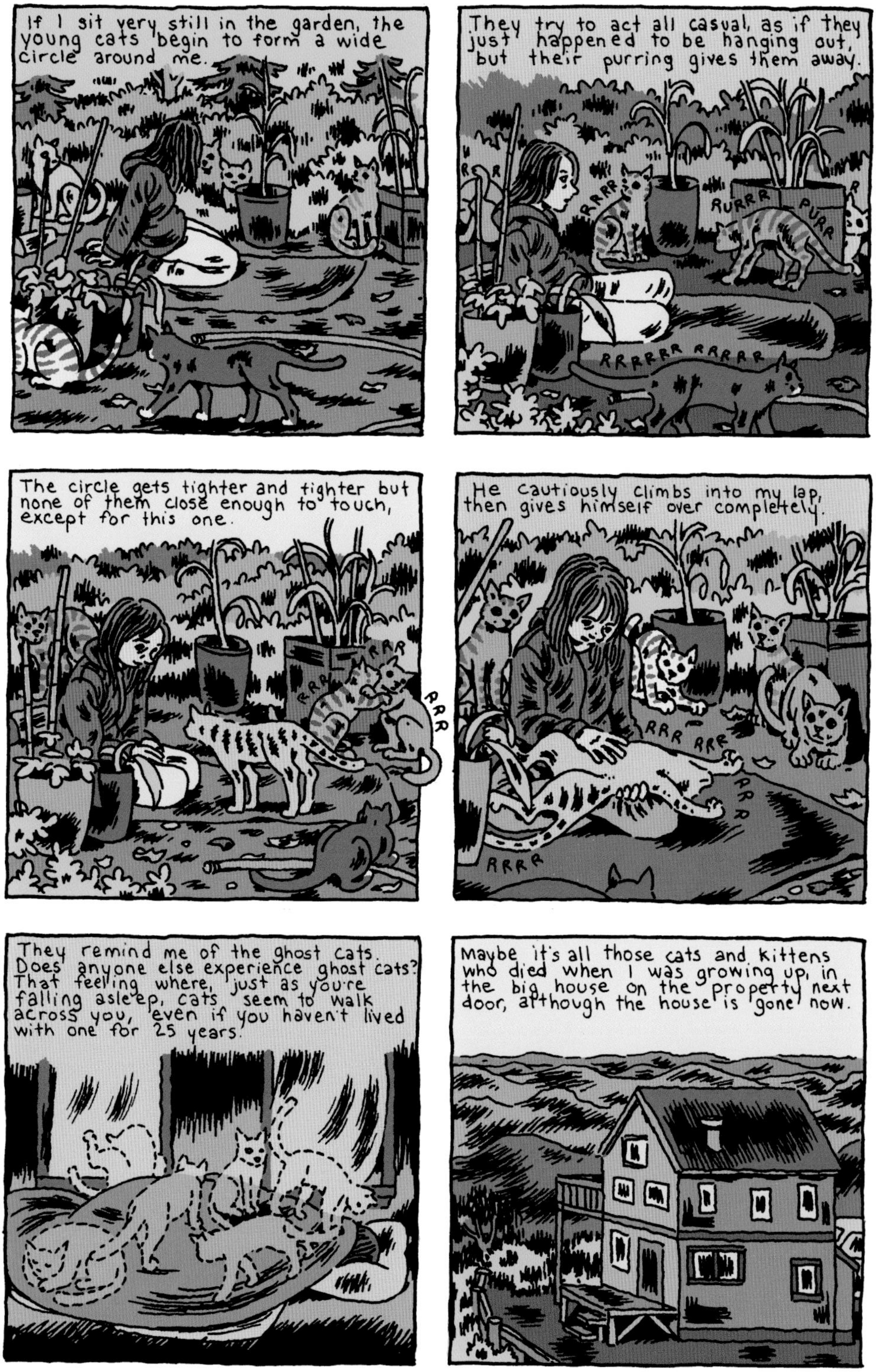
If I sit very still in the garden, the young cats begin to form a wide circle around me.
They try to act all casual, as if they just happened to be hanging out, but their purring gives them away.
RRRR
RURRR
PURR
RRRRRR RRRRR
The circle gets tighter and tighter but none of them close enough to touch, except for this one.
RRR
RRR
RRR
He cautiously climbs into my lap, then gives himself over completely.
RRR RRR
RRR
RRRR
They remind me of the ghost cats. Does anyone else experience ghost cats? That feeling where, just as you're falling asleep, cats seem to walk across you, even if you haven't lived with one for 25 years.
Maybe it's all those cats and kittens who died when I was growing up, in the big house on the property next door, although the house is gone now.

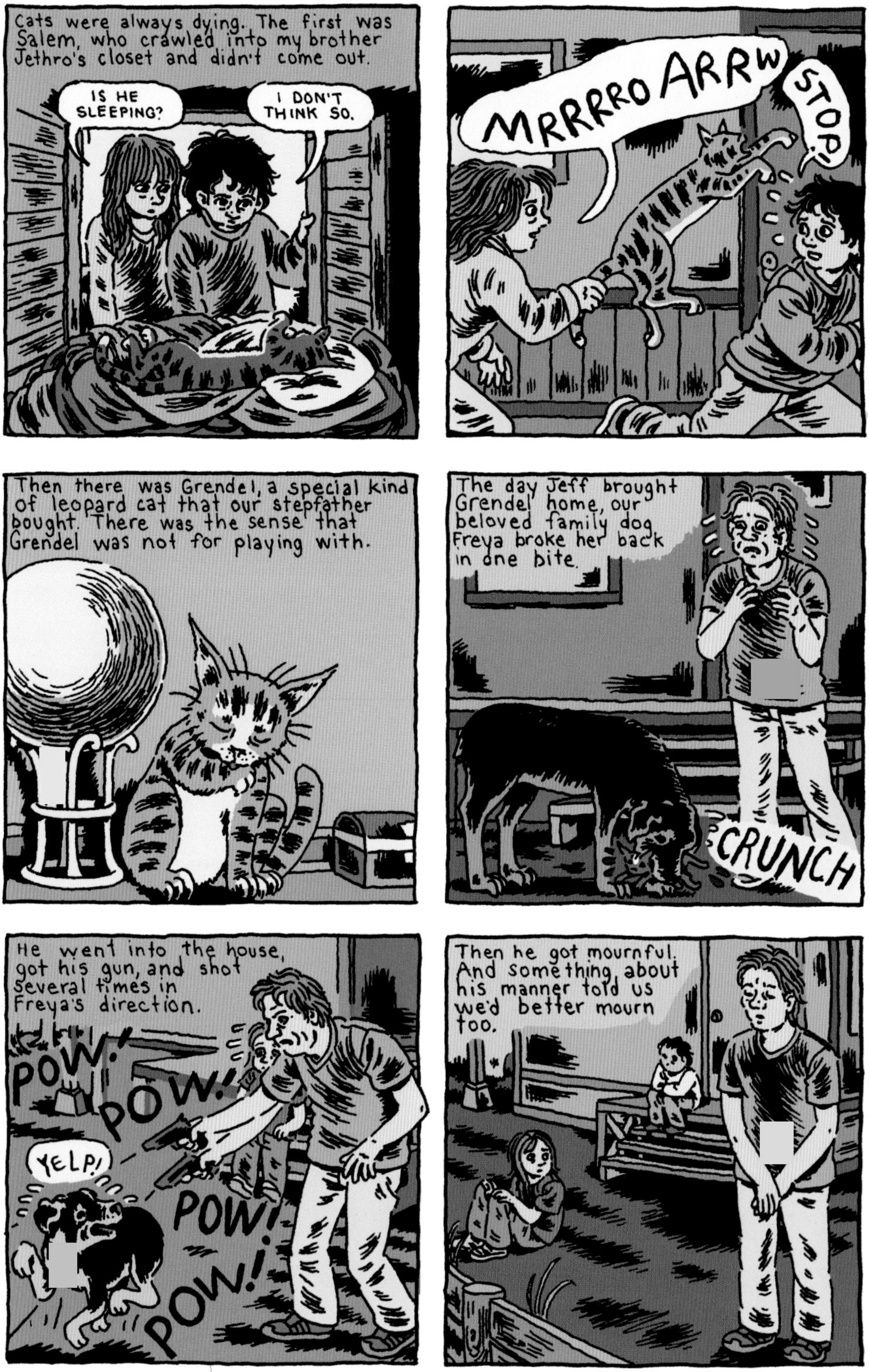
Cats were always dying. The first was Salem, who crawled into my brother Jethro's closet and didn't come out.
IS HE SLEEPING?
I DON'T THINK SO.
MRRRRO ARRW
STOP!
Then there was Grendel, a special kind of leopard cat that our stepfather bought. There was the sense that Grendel was not for playing with.
The day Jeff brought Grendel home, our beloved family dog Freya broke her back in one bite.
CRUNCH
He went into the house, got his gun, and shot several times in Freya's direction.
POW!
POW!
YELP!
POW!
POW!
Then he got mournful. And something about his manner told us we'd better mourn too.

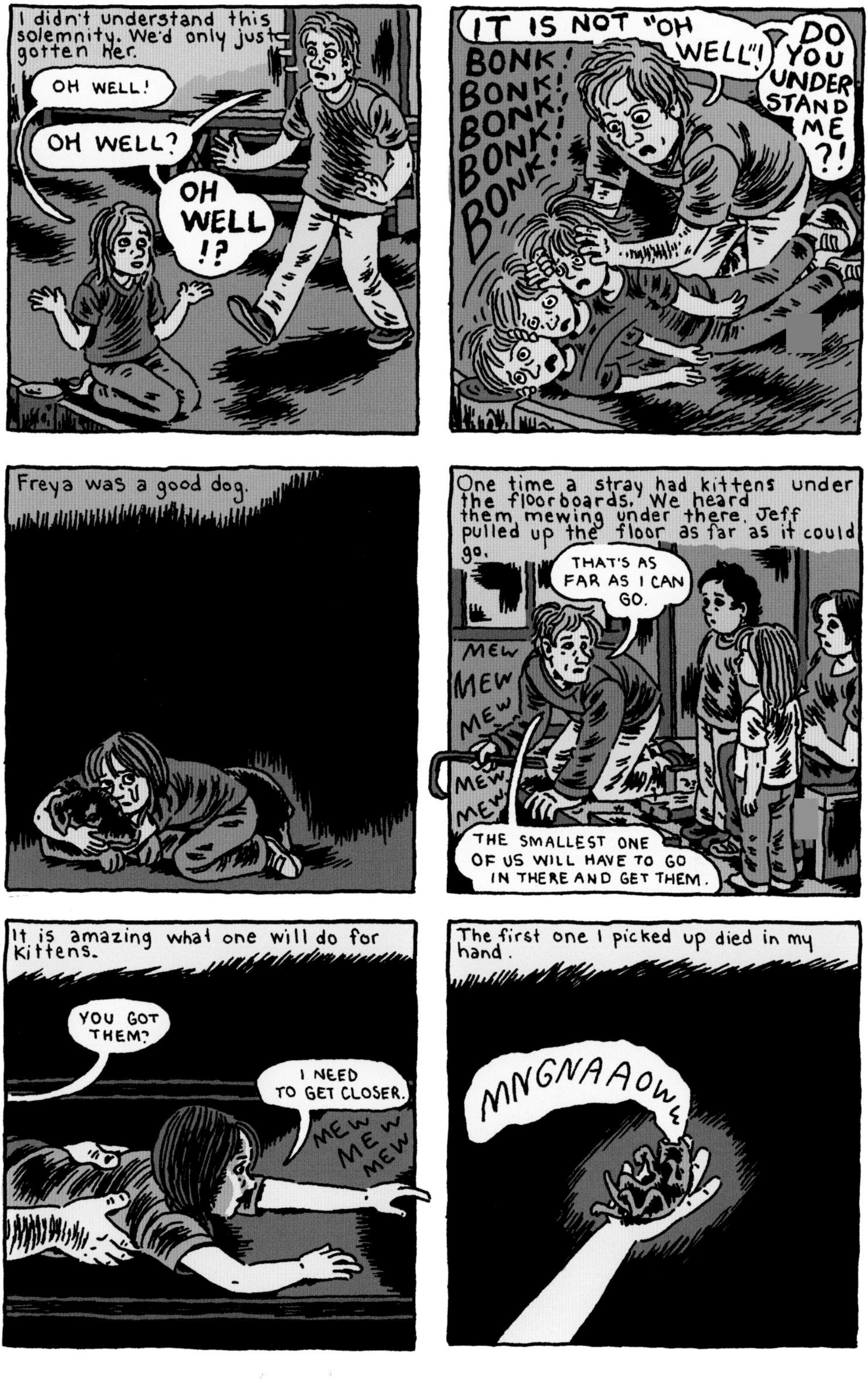
I didn't understand this solemnity. We'd only just gotten her.
OH WELL!
OH WELL?
OH WELL !?
IT IS NOT "OH WELL"!
DO YOU UNDERSTAND ME ?!
BONK! BONK! BONK! BONK! BONK
Freya was a good dog.
One time a stray had kittens under the floorboards. We heard them mewing under there. Jeff pulled up the floor as far as it could go.
THAT'S AS FAR AS I CAN GO.
MEW MEW MEW MEW MEW
THE SMALLEST ONE OF US WILL HAVE TO GO IN THERE AND GET THEM.
It is amazing what one will do for kittens.
YOU GOT THEM?
I NEED TO GET CLOSER.
MEW MEW MEW
The first one I picked up died in my hand.
MNGNAAOW

All but two died.

They were too little to be played with, but nonetheless I brought them to sleep with me in my bed.

In the morning one of them was dead, killed by me.

The other one, Cleo, lived to be a full grown cat, and was found (by me) dead in the road, hit by a car.

Then there was Red, a drooly old Tom who showed up at our house one day. I loved Red, as I loved anything that would let me love it.

RRRR RRRRRRR RRRR RRRR

For some reason, Freya, and two Dobermans who we'd late'r get rid of, had it in for Red.

ARF ARF ARFARFARF ARFARF ARFARF ARF ARF ARF ARFARF

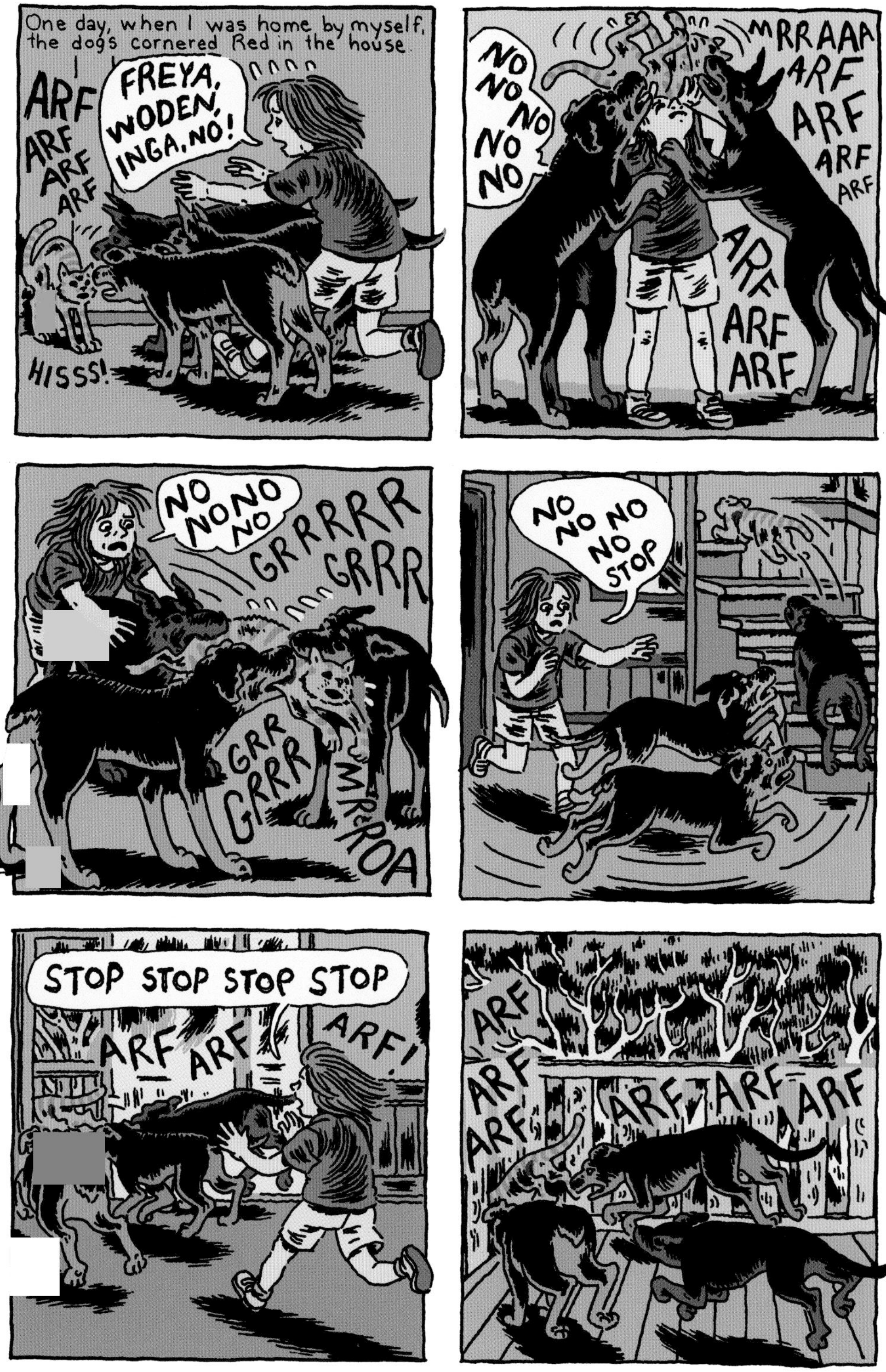
One day, when I was home by myself, the dogs cornered Red in the house.
ARF ARF ARF ARF
FREYA, WODEN, INGA, NO!
HISSS!
NO NO NO NO NO
MRRAAA
ARF ARF ARF ARF
ARF ARF ARF
NO NONO NO
GRRRRR GRRR
GRR GRRR
MRROA
NO NO NO NO STOP
STOP STOP STOP STOP
ARF ARF ARF!
ARF ARF ARF ARF ARF ARF

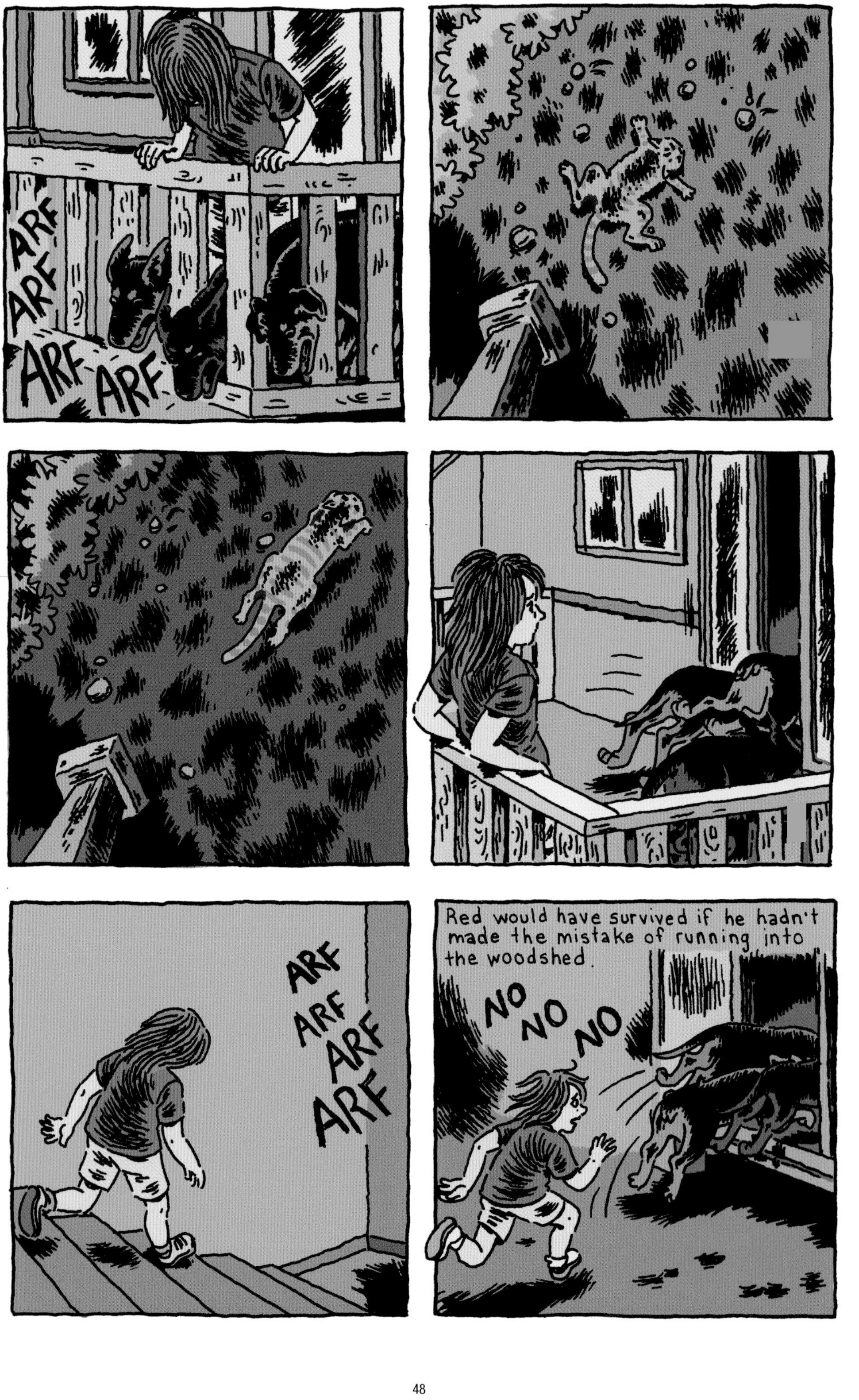
ARF
ARF
ARF
ARF
ARF
ARF
ARF
ARF
Red would have survived if he hadn't made the mistake of running into the woodshed.
NO
NO
NO

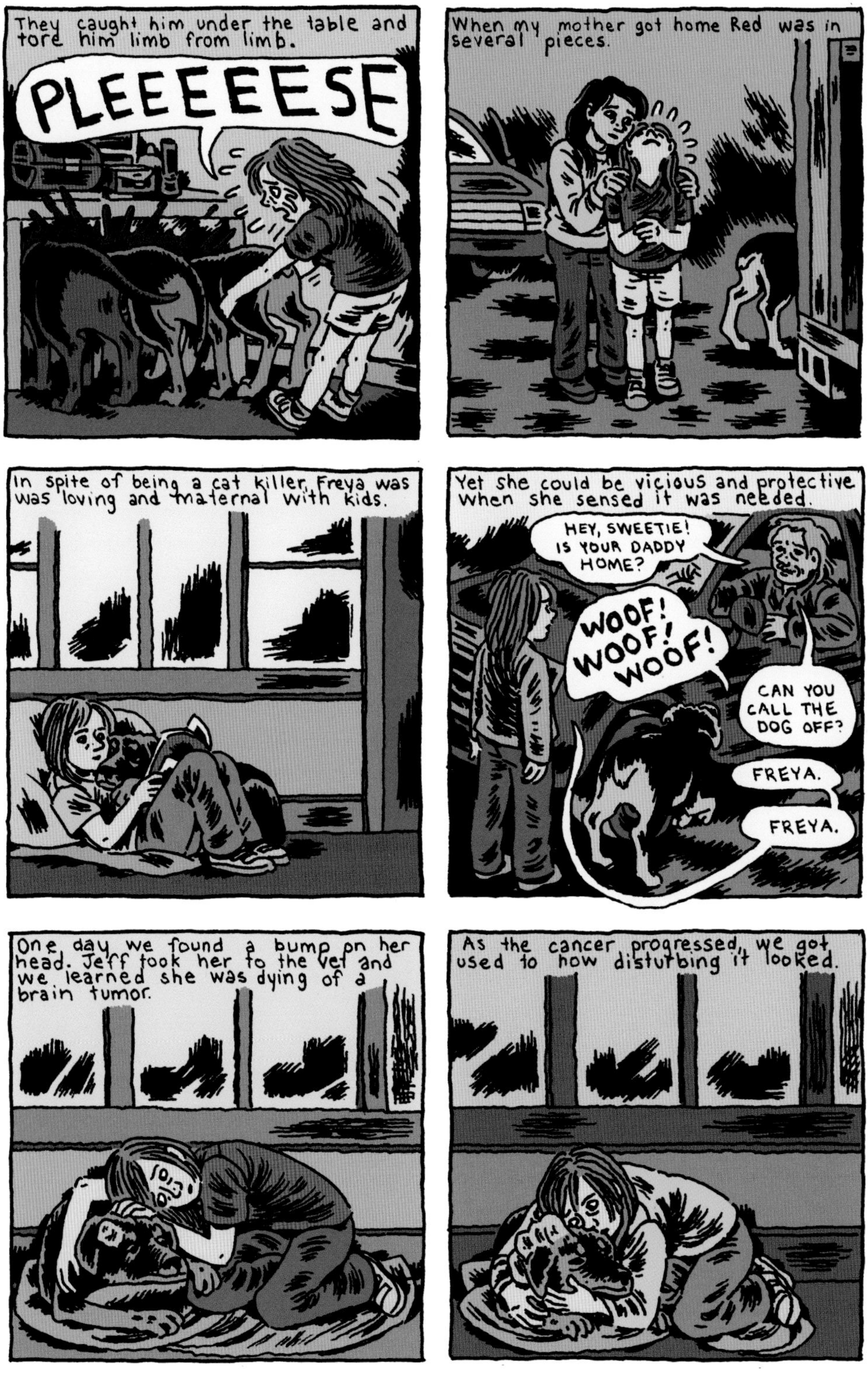
They caught him under the table and tore him limb from limb.
PLEEEEEESE
When my mother got home Red was in several pieces.
In spite of being a cat killer Freya was was loving and maternal with kids.
Yet she could be vicious and protective when she sensed it was needed.
HEY, SWEETIE! IS YOUR DADDY HOME?
WOOF! WOOF! WOOF!
CAN YOU CALL THE DOG OFF?
FREYA.
FREYA.
One day we found a bump on her head. Jeff took her to the vet and we learned she was dying of a brain tumor.
As the cancer progressed, we got used to how disturbing it looked.

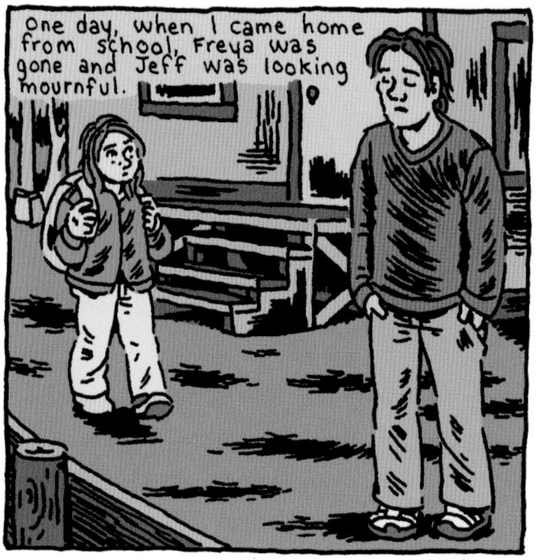
One day, when I came home from school, Freya was gone and Jeff was looking mournful.

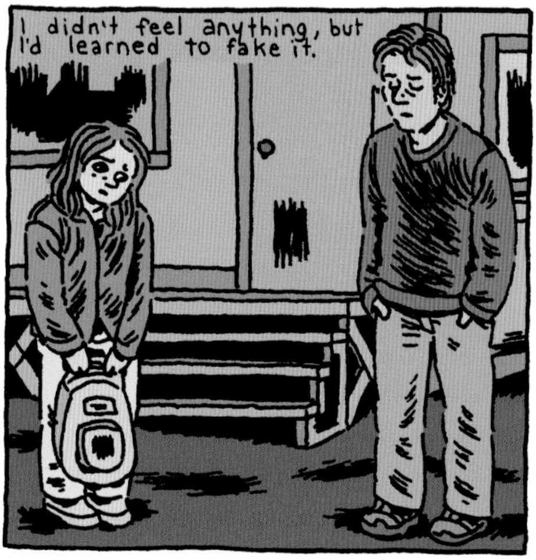
I didn't feel anything, but I'd learned to fake it.

A Mermaid
in a Ship's Cabin

My mom made me a cozy bed out of the trailer's couch. I'm concerned about this leaky window. The rain is warping the wall around it.

MOM, PRIMO'S VERY MUDDY. SHOULD I PUT HIM OUT OR IS IT TOO RAINY?

OH, LET HIM STAY. HE DOESN'T EVEN LIKE TO BE INSIDE MUCH. HE JUST LIKES TO FEEL INCLUDED.

YOU DON'T LIKE REJECTION, PRIMO? I CAN UNDER-STAND THAT.

The dishrack fits perfectly, but at the moment we have no running water.

WE HAD TO DISCONNECT IT WHEN WE MOVED THE TRAILER SO SAGE COULD PLOW.

ALSO I THINK THERE'S A LEAK SOMEWHERE. I'VE GOT TO GO FOLLOW THE LINE AND SEE.

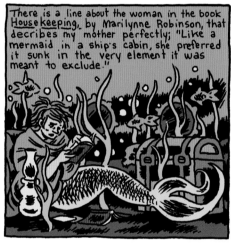

There is a line about the woman in the book Housekeeping, by Marilynne Robinson, that describes my mother perfectly; "Like a mermaid in a ship's cabin, she preferred it sunk in the very element it was meant to exclude."

And this is Gus, who lives in another trailer on the property with his three dogs.

MAIZIE! JUNIOR! PATCH! CUT IT OUT!

WOOF! WOOF!

AW, JUNIOR, DON'T YOU RECOGNIZE ME?

THEY WON'T HURT YOU.

WOOF WOOF WOOF WOOF

POW! POW! POW!

WHAT'S THAT?

STUPID PUNK KID JUST MOVED IN NEXT DOOR FIRING OFF HIS AK-47.

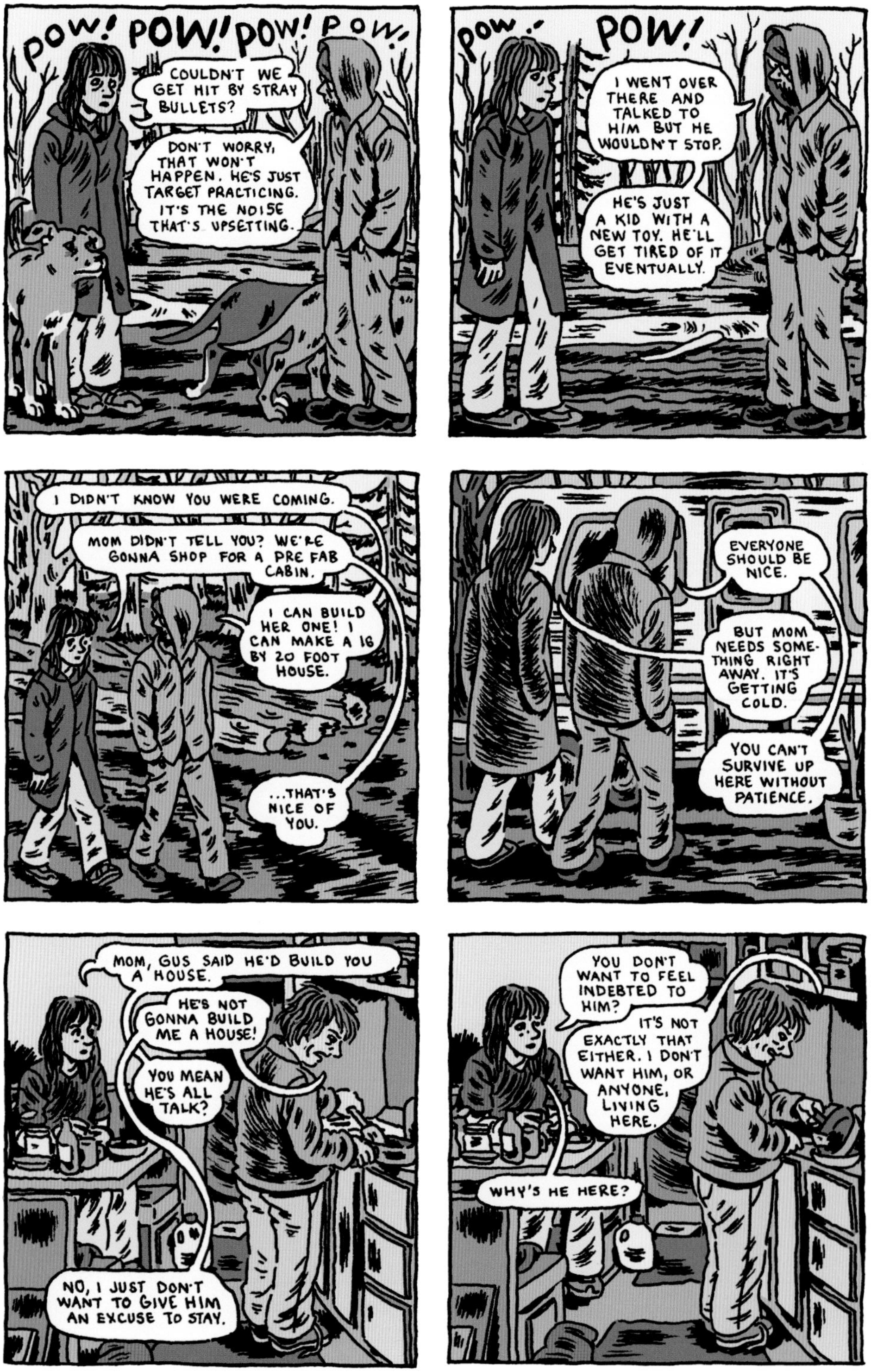
POW! POW! POW! POW!
COULDN'T WE GET HIT BY STRAY BULLETS?
DON'T WORRY, THAT WON'T HAPPEN. HE'S JUST TARGET PRACTICING. IT'S THE NOISE THAT'S UPSETTING.
POW POW!
I WENT OVER THERE AND TALKED TO HIM BUT HE WOULDN'T STOP.
HE'S JUST A KID WITH A NEW TOY. HE'LL GET TIRED OF IT EVENTUALLY.
I DIDN'T KNOW YOU WERE COMING.
MOM DIDN'T TELL YOU? WE'RE GONNA SHOP FOR A PRE FAB CABIN.
I CAN BUILD HER ONE! I CAN MAKE A 16 BY 20 FOOT HOUSE.
...THAT'S NICE OF YOU.
EVERYONE SHOULD BE NICE.
BUT MOM NEEDS SOMETHING RIGHT AWAY. IT'S GETTING COLD.
YOU CAN'T SURVIVE UP HERE WITHOUT PATIENCE.
MOM, GUS SAID HE'D BUILD YOU A HOUSE.
HE'S NOT GONNA BUILD ME A HOUSE!
YOU MEAN HE'S ALL TALK?
NO, I JUST DON'T WANT TO GIVE HIM AN EXCUSE TO STAY.
YOU DON'T WANT TO FEEL INDEBTED TO HIM?
IT'S NOT EXACTLY THAT EITHER. I DON'T WANT HIM, OR ANYONE, LIVING HERE.
WHY'S HE HERE?

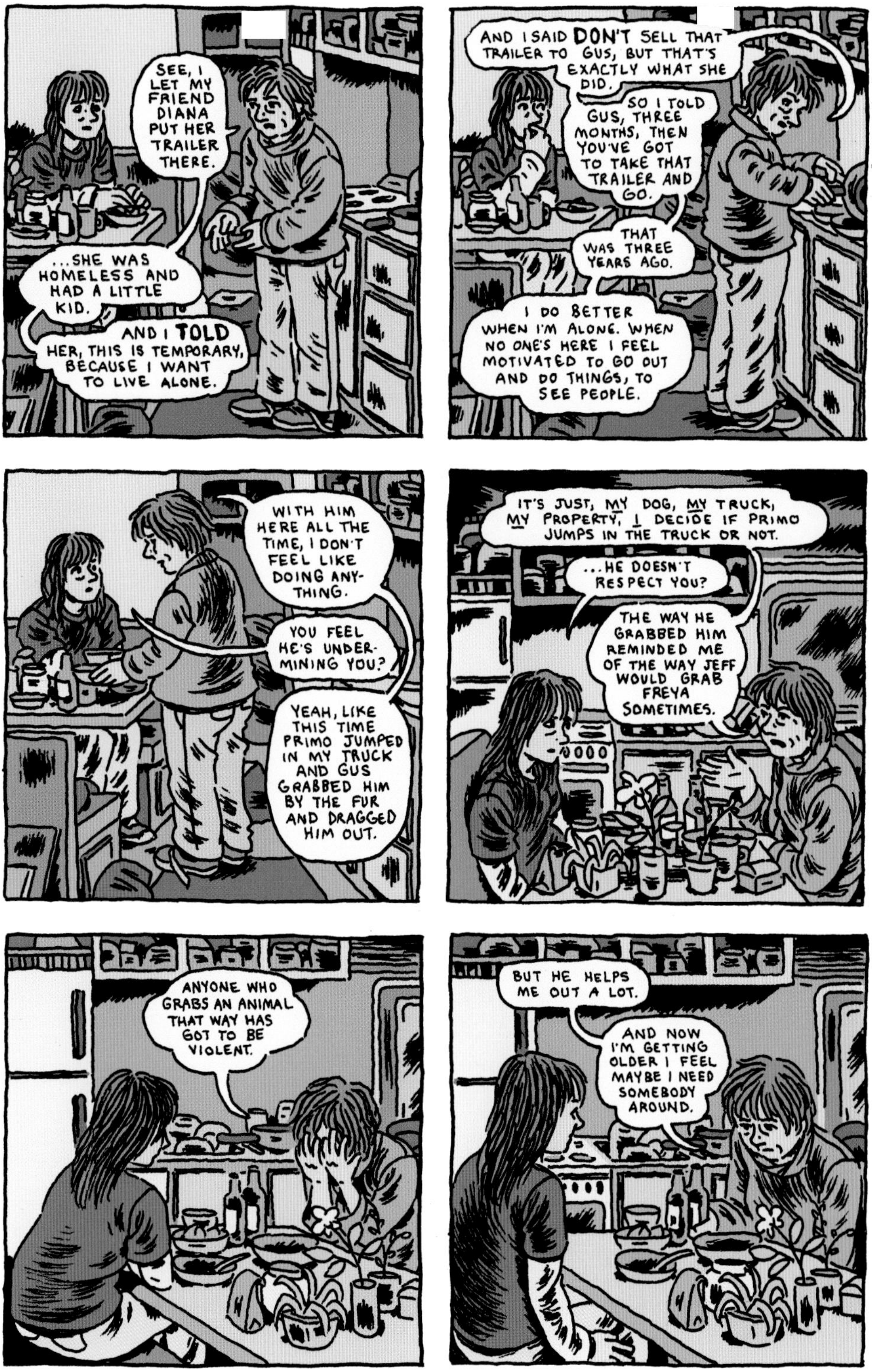
SEE, I LET MY FRIEND DIANA PUT HER TRAILER THERE.
...SHE WAS HOMELESS AND HAD A LITTLE KID.
AND I TOLD HER, THIS IS TEMPORARY, BECAUSE I WANT TO LIVE ALONE.
AND I SAID DON'T SELL THAT TRAILER TO GUS, BUT THAT'S EXACTLY WHAT SHE DID.
SO I TOLD GUS, THREE MONTHS, THEN YOU'VE GOT TO TAKE THAT TRAILER AND GO.
THAT WAS THREE YEARS AGO.
I DO BETTER WHEN I'M ALONE. WHEN NO ONE'S HERE I FEEL MOTIVATED TO GO OUT AND DO THINGS, TO SEE PEOPLE.
WITH HIM HERE ALL THE TIME, I DON'T FEEL LIKE DOING ANY-THING.
YOU FEEL HE'S UNDER-MINING YOU?
YEAH, LIKE THIS TIME PRIMO JUMPED IN MY TRUCK AND GUS GRABBED HIM BY THE FUR AND DRAGGED HIM OUT.
IT'S JUST, MY DOG, MY TRUCK, MY PROPERTY, I DECIDE IF PRIMO JUMPS IN THE TRUCK OR NOT.
...HE DOESN'T RESPECT YOU?
THE WAY HE GRABBED HIM REMINDED ME OF THE WAY JEFF WOULD GRAB FREYA SOMETIMES.
ANYONE WHO GRABS AN ANIMAL THAT WAY HAS GOT TO BE VIOLENT.
BUT HE HELPS ME OUT A LOT.
AND NOW I'M GETTING OLDER I FEEL MAYBE I NEED SOMEBODY AROUND.

Windows

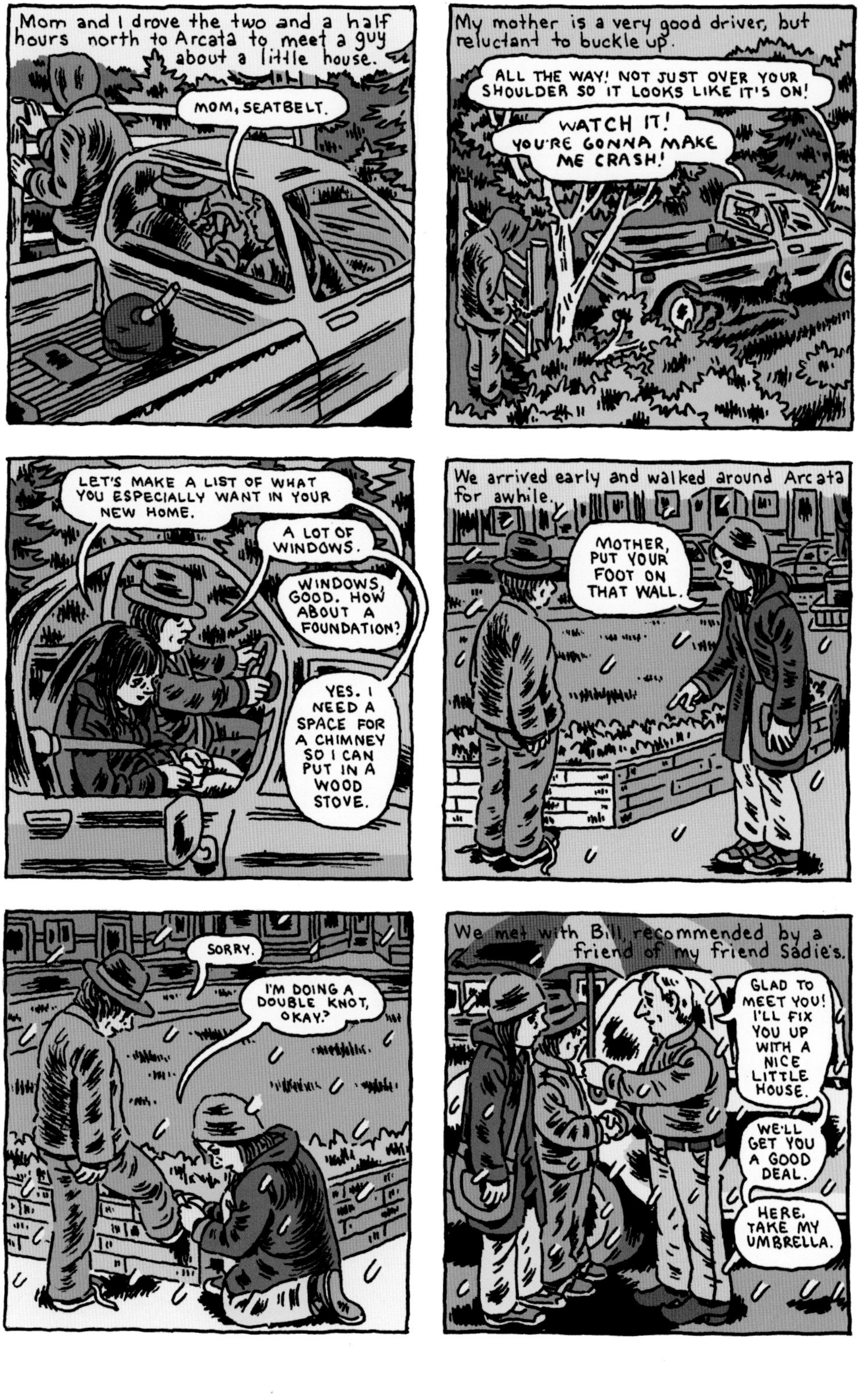
Mom and I drove the two and a half hours north to Arcata to meet a guy about a little house.
MOM, SEATBELT.
My mother is a very good driver, but reluctant to buckle up.
ALL THE WAY! NOT JUST OVER YOUR SHOULDER SO IT LOOKS LIKE IT'S ON!
WATCH IT! YOU'RE GONNA MAKE ME CRASH!
LET'S MAKE A LIST OF WHAT YOU ESPECIALLY WANT IN YOUR NEW HOME.
A LOT OF WINDOWS.
WINDOWS, GOOD. HOW ABOUT A FOUNDATION?
YES. I NEED A SPACE FOR A CHIMNEY SO I CAN PUT IN A WOOD STOVE.
We arrived early and walked around Arcata for awhile.
MOTHER, PUT YOUR FOOT ON THAT WALL.
SORRY.
I'M DOING A DOUBLE KNOT, OKAY?
We met with Bill, recommended by a friend of my friend Sadie's.
GLAD TO MEET YOU! I'LL FIX YOU UP WITH A NICE LITTLE HOUSE.
WE'LL GET YOU A GOOD DEAL.
HERE, TAKE MY UMBRELLA.

THIS ONE'S GOT A GABLED, SHINGLED ROOF, A GOOD SOLID, LOCKABLE DOOR...

YOU'VE GOT PLYWOOD SIDING, DOUBLE BEAMS, A NICE WOOD FLOOR...

HOW BIG IS IT?

EIGHT BY SIXTEEN FEET.

GO AHEAD, IT'S NOT LOCKED.

HOW MUCH IS IT?

FOUR THOUSAND. YOU'VE GOT EXPOSED BEAMS AND EXTRA REINFORCEMENT.

CAN YOU PUT IN A HOLE FOR A CHIMNEY?

ABSOLUTELY. IN FACT I'VE GOT A TILED HEARTH TO PLACE THE STOVE ON THAT I CAN THROW IN.

THIS ONE'S EIGHT BY TWENTY FEET. YOU CAN SEE IT HAS A SLANTED METAL ROOF, GOOD FOR IF YOU GET A LOT OF SNOW IN THE WINTER.

HOW MUCH IS THIS ONE?

IT'S THIRTY-TWO HUNDRED.

SAY, I'VE GOT SOME BOOKSHELVES I CAN GIVE YOU. DO YOU WANT THEM?

OH YES, I NEED BOOKSHELVES.

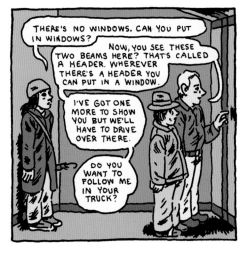

THERE'S NO WINDOWS. CAN YOU PUT IN WINDOWS?

NOW, YOU SEE THESE TWO BEAMS HERE? THAT'S CALLED A HEADER. WHEREVER THERE'S A HEADER YOU CAN PUT IN A WINDOW.

I'VE GOT ONE MORE TO SHOW YOU BUT WE'LL HAVE TO DRIVE OVER THERE.

DO YOU WANT TO FOLLOW ME IN YOUR TRUCK?

WHAT DO YOU THINK? TOO BAD THE BIGGER ONE JUST HAD THE ONE HEADER.

I LIKED THE GABLED ROOF ON THE LITTLE ONE.

THIS ONE'S READY TO GO. IT'S ALL PAINTED AND INSULATED AND YOU'VE GOT THESE BEAMS AT THE BASE FOR EXTRA REINFORCEMENT.

HOW MUCH IS-

EIGHT BY SIXTEEN AND FOUR THOUSAND DOLLARS.

DO YOU NEED A CABINET? I CAN THROW IN A KITCHEN CABINET.

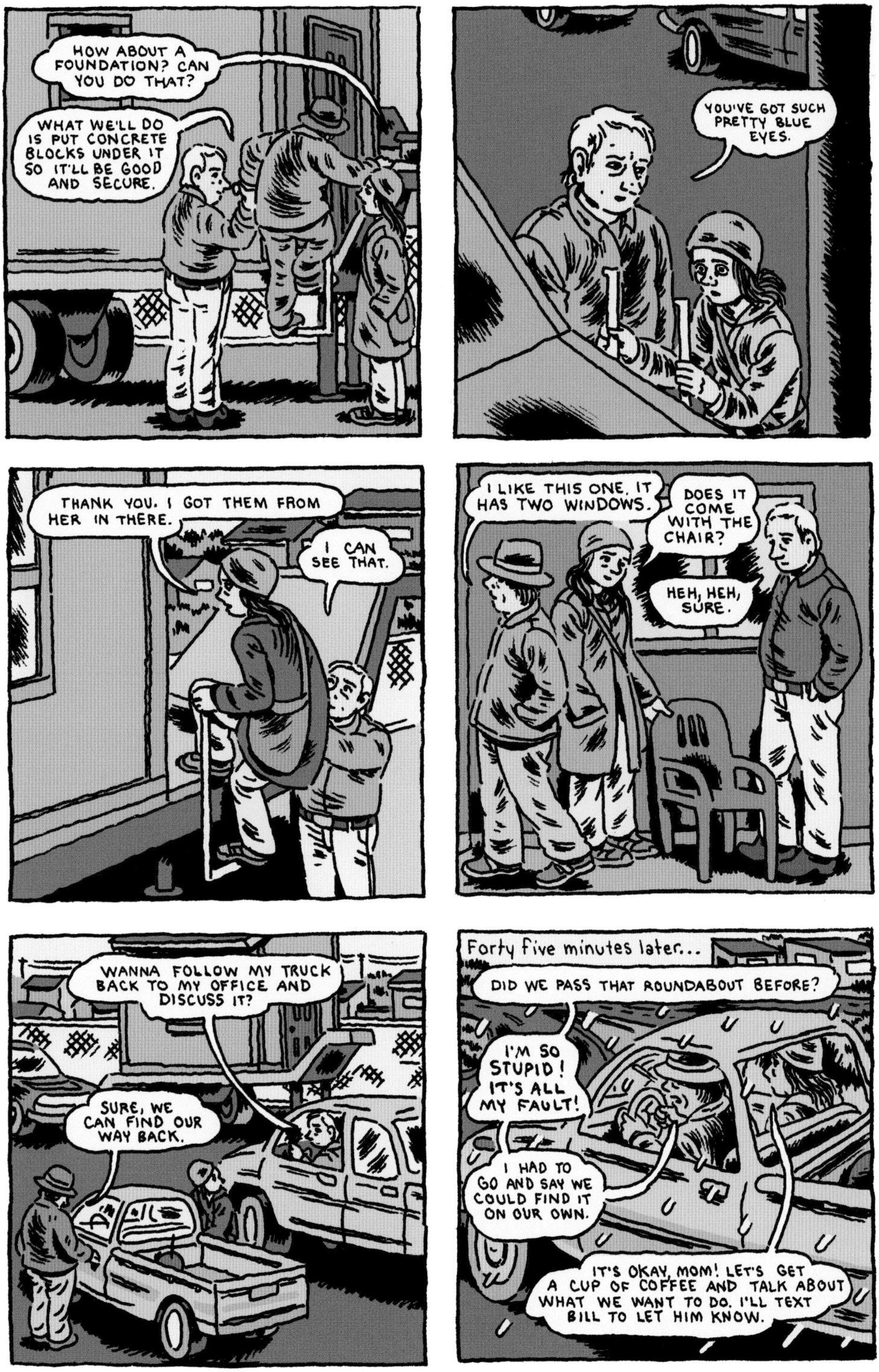
HOW ABOUT A FOUNDATION? CAN YOU DO THAT?
WHAT WE'LL DO IS PUT CONCRETE BLOCKS UNDER IT SO IT'LL BE GOOD AND SECURE.
YOU'VE GOT SUCH PRETTY BLUE EYES.
THANK YOU. I GOT THEM FROM HER IN THERE.
I CAN SEE THAT.
I LIKE THIS ONE. IT HAS TWO WINDOWS.
DOES IT COME WITH THE CHAIR?
HEH, HEH, SURE.
WANNA FOLLOW MY TRUCK BACK TO MY OFFICE AND DISCUSS IT?
SURE, WE CAN FIND OUR WAY BACK.
Forty five minutes later...
DID WE PASS THAT ROUNDABOUT BEFORE?
I'M SO STUPID! IT'S ALL MY FAULT!
I HAD TO GO AND SAY WE COULD FIND IT ON OUR OWN.
IT'S OKAY, MOM! LET'S GET A CUP OF COFFEE AND TALK ABOUT WHAT WE WANT TO DO. I'LL TEXT BILL TO LET HIM KNOW.

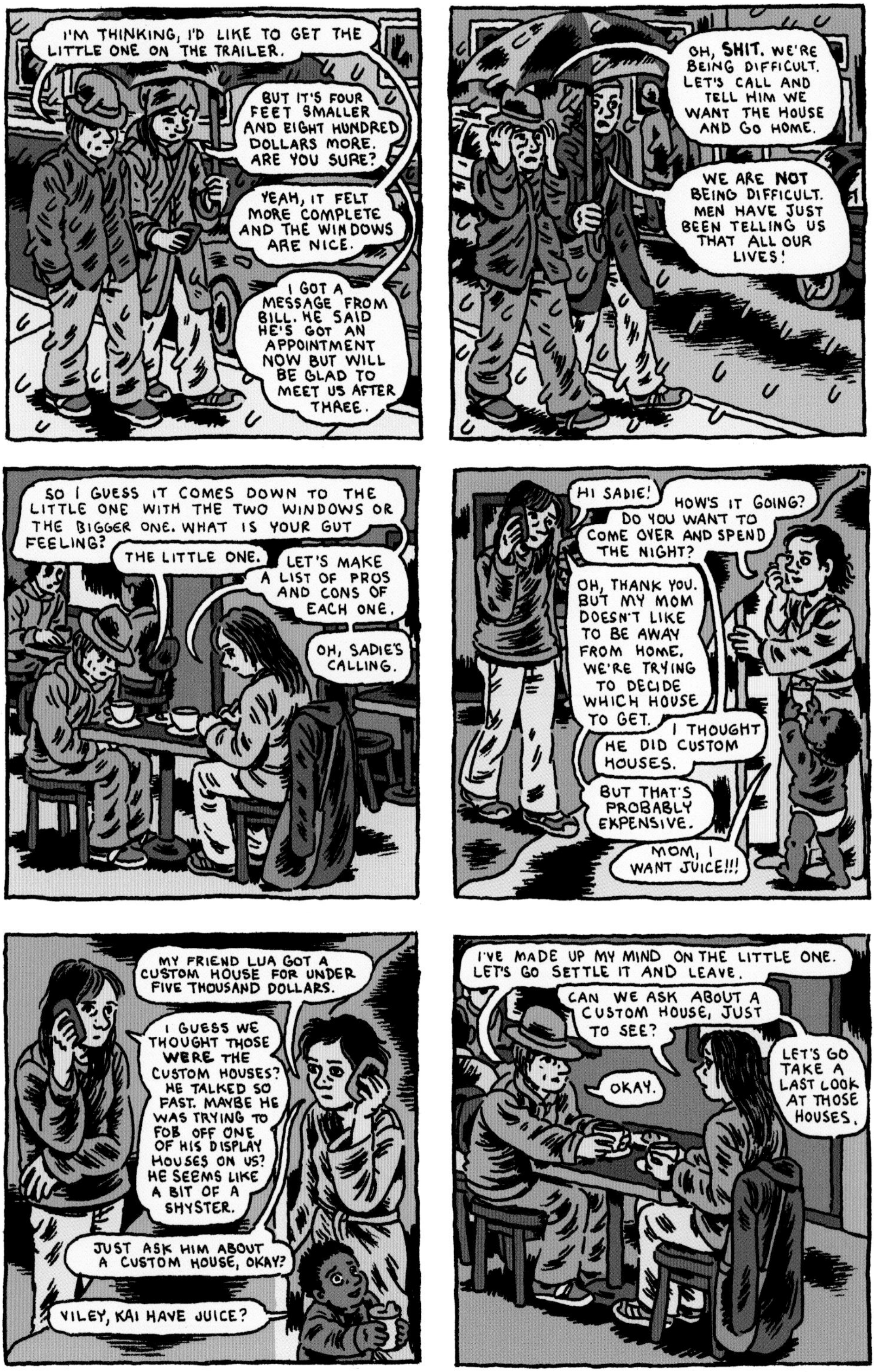
I'M THINKING, I'D LIKE TO GET THE LITTLE ONE ON THE TRAILER.
BUT IT'S FOUR FEET SMALLER AND EIGHT HUNDRED DOLLARS MORE. ARE YOU SURE?
YEAH, IT FELT MORE COMPLETE AND THE WINDOWS ARE NICE.
I GOT A MESSAGE FROM BILL. HE SAID HE'S GOT AN APPOINTMENT NOW BUT WILL BE GLAD TO MEET US AFTER THREE.
OH, SHIT. WE'RE BEING DIFFICULT. LET'S CALL AND TELL HIM WE WANT THE HOUSE AND GO HOME.
WE ARE NOT BEING DIFFICULT. MEN HAVE JUST BEEN TELLING US THAT ALL OUR LIVES!
SO I GUESS IT COMES DOWN TO THE LITTLE ONE WITH THE TWO WINDOWS OR THE BIGGER ONE. WHAT IS YOUR GUT FEELING?
THE LITTLE ONE.
LET'S MAKE A LIST OF PROS AND CONS OF EACH ONE.
OH, SADIE'S CALLING.
HI SADIE!
HOW'S IT GOING? DO YOU WANT TO COME OVER AND SPEND THE NIGHT?
OH, THANK YOU. BUT MY MOM DOESN'T LIKE TO BE AWAY FROM HOME. WE'RE TRYING TO DECIDE WHICH HOUSE TO GET.
I THOUGHT HE DID CUSTOM HOUSES.
BUT THAT'S PROBABLY EXPENSIVE.
MOM, I WANT JUICE!!!
MY FRIEND LUA GOT A CUSTOM HOUSE FOR UNDER FIVE THOUSAND DOLLARS.
I GUESS WE THOUGHT THOSE WERE THE CUSTOM HOUSES? HE TALKED SO FAST. MAYBE HE WAS TRYING TO FOB OFF ONE OF HIS DISPLAY HOUSES ON US? HE SEEMS LIKE A BIT OF A SHYSTER.
JUST ASK HIM ABOUT A CUSTOM HOUSE, OKAY?
VILEY, KAI HAVE JUICE?
I'VE MADE UP MY MIND ON THE LITTLE ONE. LET'S GO SETTLE IT AND LEAVE.
CAN WE ASK ABOUT A CUSTOM HOUSE, JUST TO SEE?
OKAY.
LET'S GO TAKE A LAST LOOK AT THOSE HOUSES.

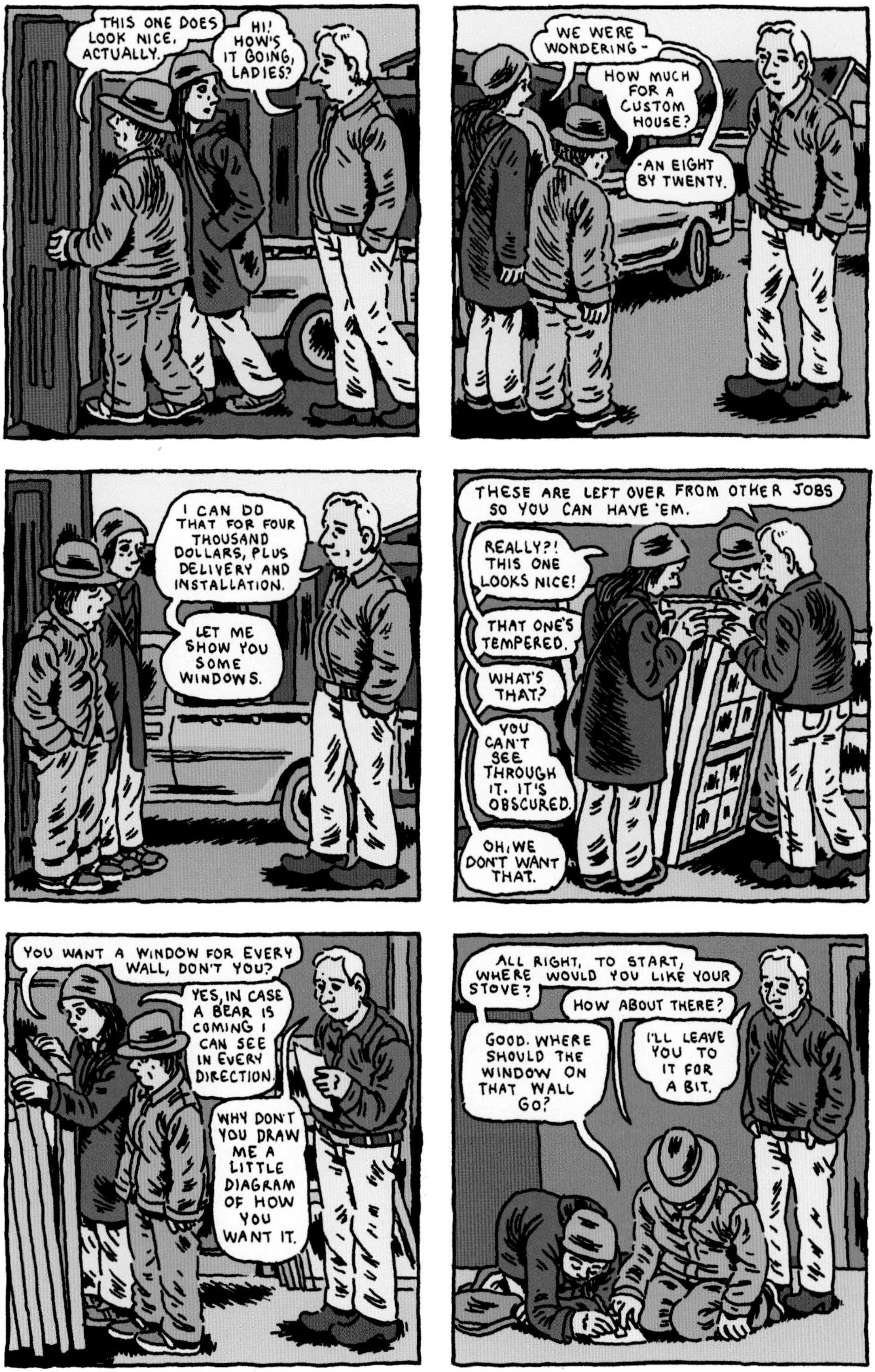
THIS ONE DOES LOOK NICE, ACTUALLY.
HI! HOW'S IT GOING, LADIES?
WE WERE WONDERING -
HOW MUCH FOR A CUSTOM HOUSE?
-AN EIGHT BY TWENTY.
I CAN DO THAT FOR FOUR THOUSAND DOLLARS, PLUS DELIVERY AND INSTALLATION.
LET ME SHOW YOU SOME WINDOWS.
THESE ARE LEFT OVER FROM OTHER JOBS SO YOU CAN HAVE 'EM.
REALLY?! THIS ONE LOOKS NICE!
THAT ONE'S TEMPERED.
WHAT'S THAT?
YOU CAN'T SEE THROUGH IT. IT'S OBSCURED.
OH, WE DON'T WANT THAT.
YOU WANT A WINDOW FOR EVERY WALL, DON'T YOU?
YES, IN CASE A BEAR IS COMING I CAN SEE IN EVERY DIRECTION.
WHY DON'T YOU DRAW ME A LITTLE DIAGRAM OF HOW YOU WANT IT.
ALL RIGHT, TO START, WHERE WOULD YOU LIKE YOUR STOVE?
HOW ABOUT THERE?
GOOD. WHERE SHOULD THE WINDOW ON THAT WALL GO?
I'LL LEAVE YOU TO IT FOR A BIT.

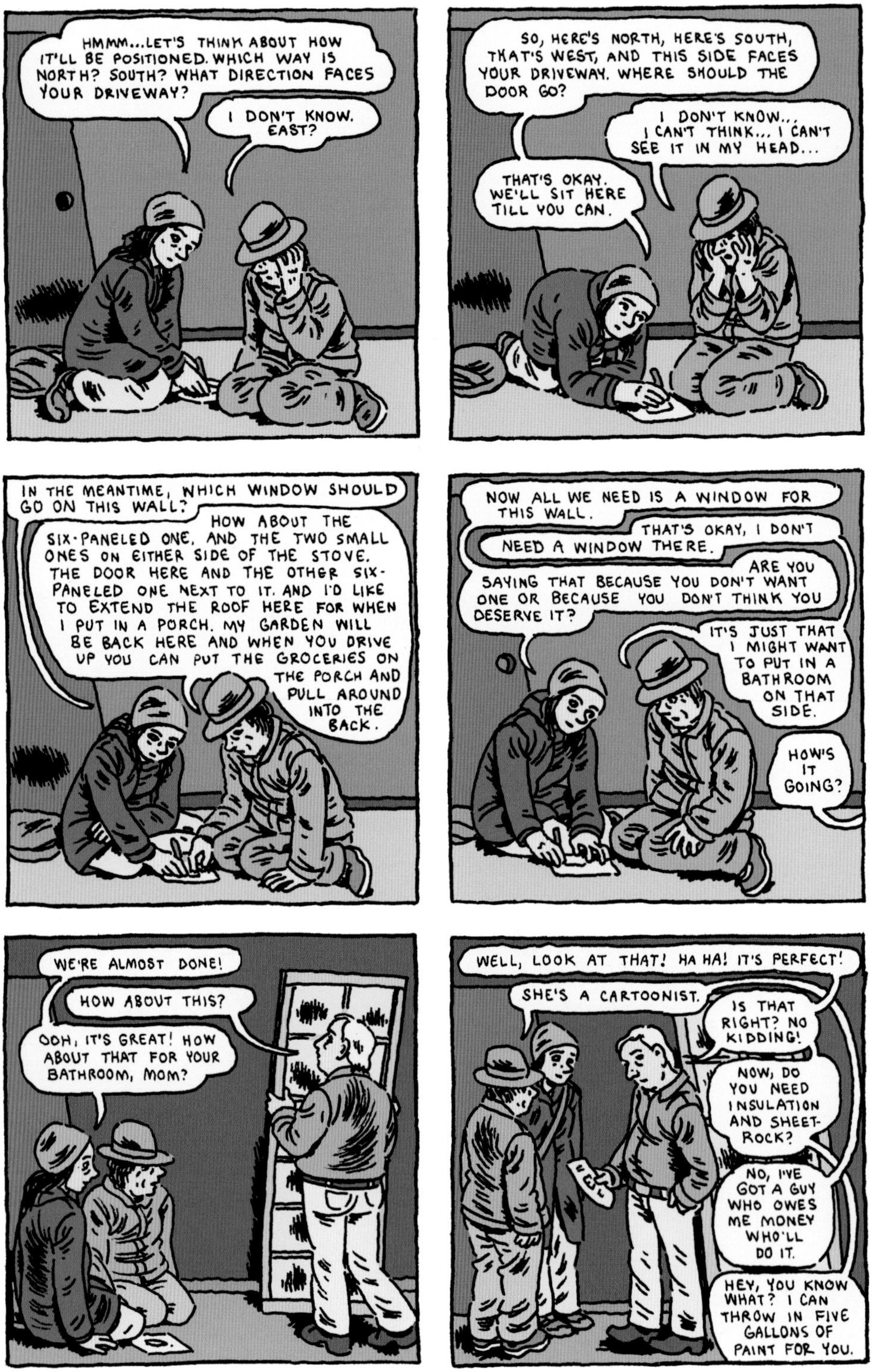
HMMM...LET'S THINK ABOUT HOW IT'LL BE POSITIONED. WHICH WAY IS NORTH? SOUTH? WHAT DIRECTION FACES YOUR DRIVEWAY?
I DON'T KNOW. EAST?
SO, HERE'S NORTH, HERE'S SOUTH, THAT'S WEST, AND THIS SIDE FACES YOUR DRIVEWAY. WHERE SHOULD THE DOOR GO?
I DON'T KNOW... I CAN'T THINK... I CAN'T SEE IT IN MY HEAD...
THAT'S OKAY. WE'LL SIT HERE TILL YOU CAN.
IN THE MEANTIME, WHICH WINDOW SHOULD GO ON THIS WALL?
HOW ABOUT THE SIX-PANELED ONE, AND THE TWO SMALL ONES ON EITHER SIDE OF THE STOVE. THE DOOR HERE AND THE OTHER SIX-PANELED ONE NEXT TO IT. AND I'D LIKE TO EXTEND THE ROOF HERE FOR WHEN I PUT IN A PORCH. MY GARDEN WILL BE BACK HERE AND WHEN YOU DRIVE UP YOU CAN PUT THE GROCERIES ON THE PORCH AND PULL AROUND INTO THE BACK.
NOW ALL WE NEED IS A WINDOW FOR THIS WALL.
THAT'S OKAY, I DON'T NEED A WINDOW THERE.
ARE YOU SAYING THAT BECAUSE YOU DON'T WANT ONE OR BECAUSE YOU DON'T THINK YOU DESERVE IT?
IT'S JUST THAT I MIGHT WANT TO PUT IN A BATHROOM ON THAT SIDE.
HOW'S IT GOING?
WE'RE ALMOST DONE!
HOW ABOUT THIS?
OOH, IT'S GREAT! HOW ABOUT THAT FOR YOUR BATHROOM, MOM?
WELL, LOOK AT THAT! HA HA! IT'S PERFECT!
SHE'S A CARTOONIST.
IS THAT RIGHT? NO KIDDING!
NOW, DO YOU NEED INSULATION AND SHEET-ROCK?
NO, I'VE GOT A GUY WHO OWES ME MONEY WHO'LL DO IT.
HEY, YOU KNOW WHAT? I CAN THROW IN FIVE GALLONS OF PAINT FOR YOU.

CAN YOU GIVE US AN ESTIMATE FOR HOW MUCH THIS WILL COST?

WELL, WITH INSTALLATION AND DELIVERY WE'RE TALKING 45, 46, 47, 48...

SHE DOESN'T HAVE A LOT OF MONEY.

47... 46... 45... 44.

BUT I'LL NEED A FIFTY PERCENT DEPOSIT.

HEY, BILL!

HI!

MARGARET, GABRIELLE, THIS IS MY FIANCÉE, DEBORAH! AND HER BROTHER ADAM.

We stayed with Sadie after all, to finish the deal the next morning.

IS THAT BUHNE STREET? WHAT DOES IT SAY? I CAN'T SEE A THING.

I FORG MY GLASSES.

THERE'S NO WAY WE'RE GONNA DRIVE HOME TONIGHT!

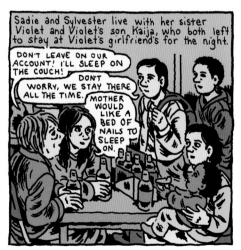

Sadie and Sylvester live with her sister Violet and Violet's son Kaija, who both left to stay at Violet's girlfriend's for the night.

DON'T LEAVE ON OUR ACCOUNT! I'LL SLEEP ON THE COUCH!

DON'T WORRY, WE STAY THERE ALL THE TIME.

MOTHER WOULD LIKE A BED OF NAILS TO SLEEP ON.

That night I got the shame attacks.

I'M SUCH A JERK.

I SHOULD STOP CALLING MYSELF A JERK.

STOP CALLING YOURSELF A JERK, YOU JERK!

YOU'RE NOT A JERK!

BUT ISN'T THAT WHAT A JERK WOULD BELIEVE, THAT HE'S NOT A JERK?

MAYBE THINKING I'M A JERK IS WHAT KEEPS ME FROM BEING A JERK?

YOU POOR JERK.

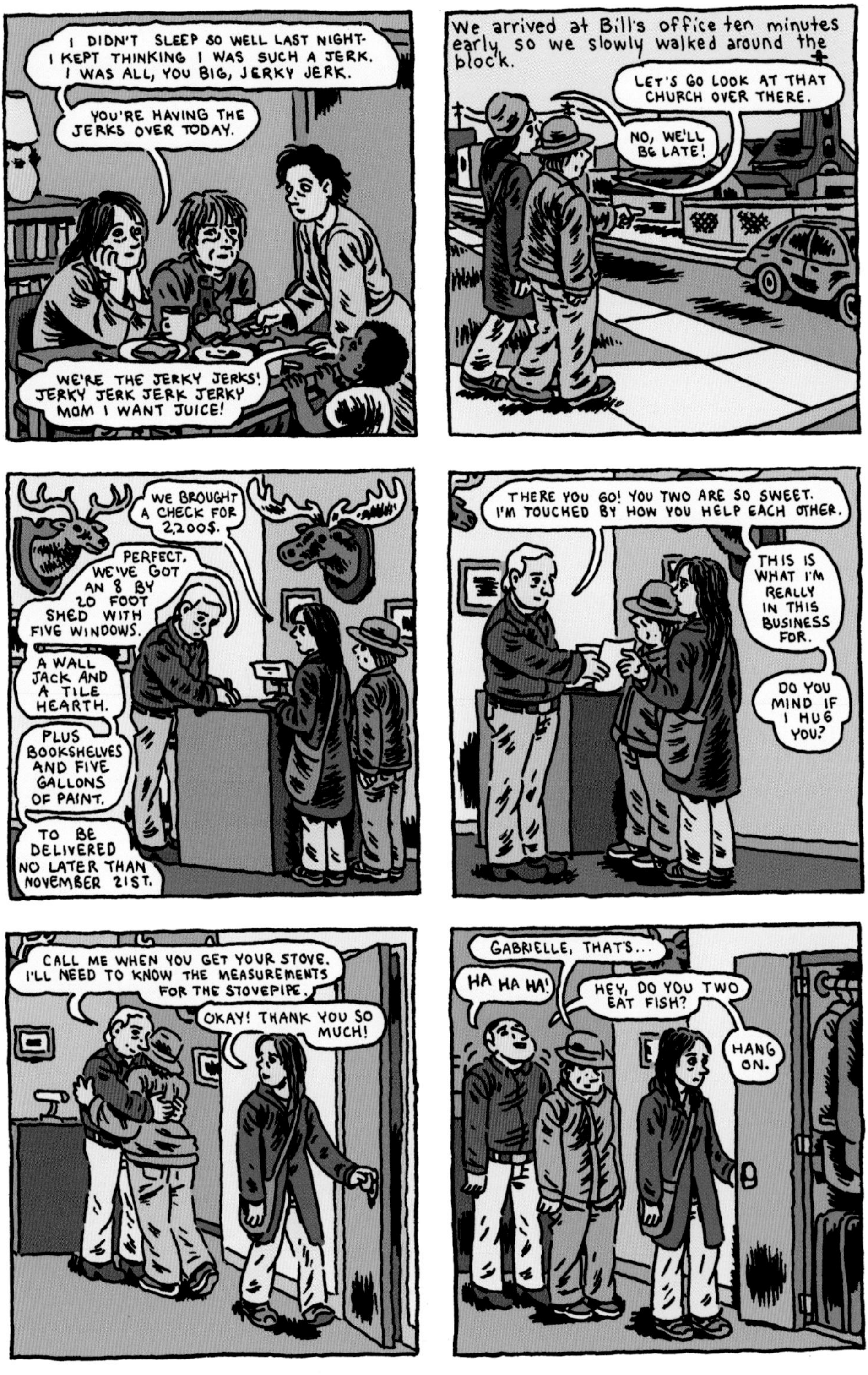
I DIDN'T SLEEP SO WELL LAST NIGHT- I KEPT THINKING I WAS SUCH A JERK. I WAS ALL, YOU BIG, JERKY JERK.
YOU'RE HAVING THE JERKS OVER TODAY.
WE'RE THE JERKY JERKS! JERKY JERK JERK JERKY MOM I WANT JUICE!
We arrived at Bill's office ten minutes early, so we slowly walked around the block.
LET'S GO LOOK AT THAT CHURCH OVER THERE.
NO, WE'LL BE LATE!
WE BROUGHT A CHECK FOR 2,200$.
PERFECT. WE'VE GOT AN 8 BY 20 FOOT SHED WITH FIVE WINDOWS.
A WALL JACK AND A TILE HEARTH.
PLUS BOOKSHELVES AND FIVE GALLONS OF PAINT.
TO BE DELIVERED NO LATER THAN NOVEMBER 21ST.
THERE YOU GO! YOU TWO ARE SO SWEET. I'M TOUCHED BY HOW YOU HELP EACH OTHER.
THIS IS WHAT I'M REALLY IN THIS BUSINESS FOR.
DO YOU MIND IF I HUG YOU?
CALL ME WHEN YOU GET YOUR STOVE. I'LL NEED TO KNOW THE MEASUREMENTS FOR THE STOVEPIPE.
OKAY! THANK YOU SO MUCH!
GABRIELLE, THAT'S...
HA HA HA!
HEY, DO YOU TWO EAT FISH?
HANG ON.

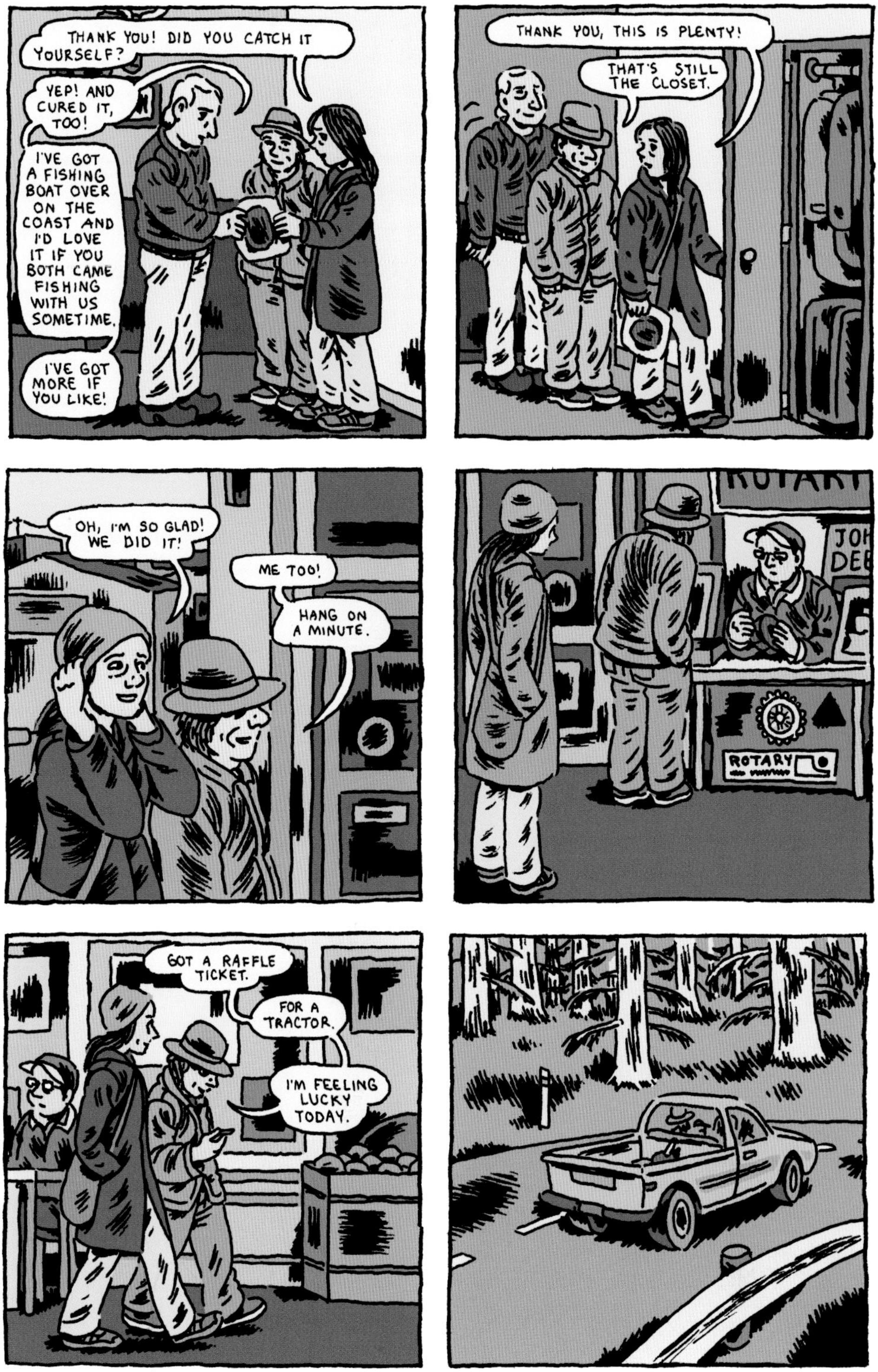
THANK YOU! DID YOU CATCH IT YOURSELF?
YEP! AND CURED IT, TOO!
I'VE GOT A FISHING BOAT OVER ON THE COAST AND I'D LOVE IT IF YOU BOTH CAME FISHING WITH US SOMETIME.
I'VE GOT MORE IF YOU LIKE!
THANK YOU, THIS IS PLENTY!
THAT'S STILL THE CLOSET.
OH, I'M SO GLAD! WE DID IT!
ME TOO!
HANG ON A MINUTE.
ROTARY
GOT A RAFFLE TICKET.
FOR A TRACTOR.
I'M FEELING LUCKY TODAY.

Stove Shopping

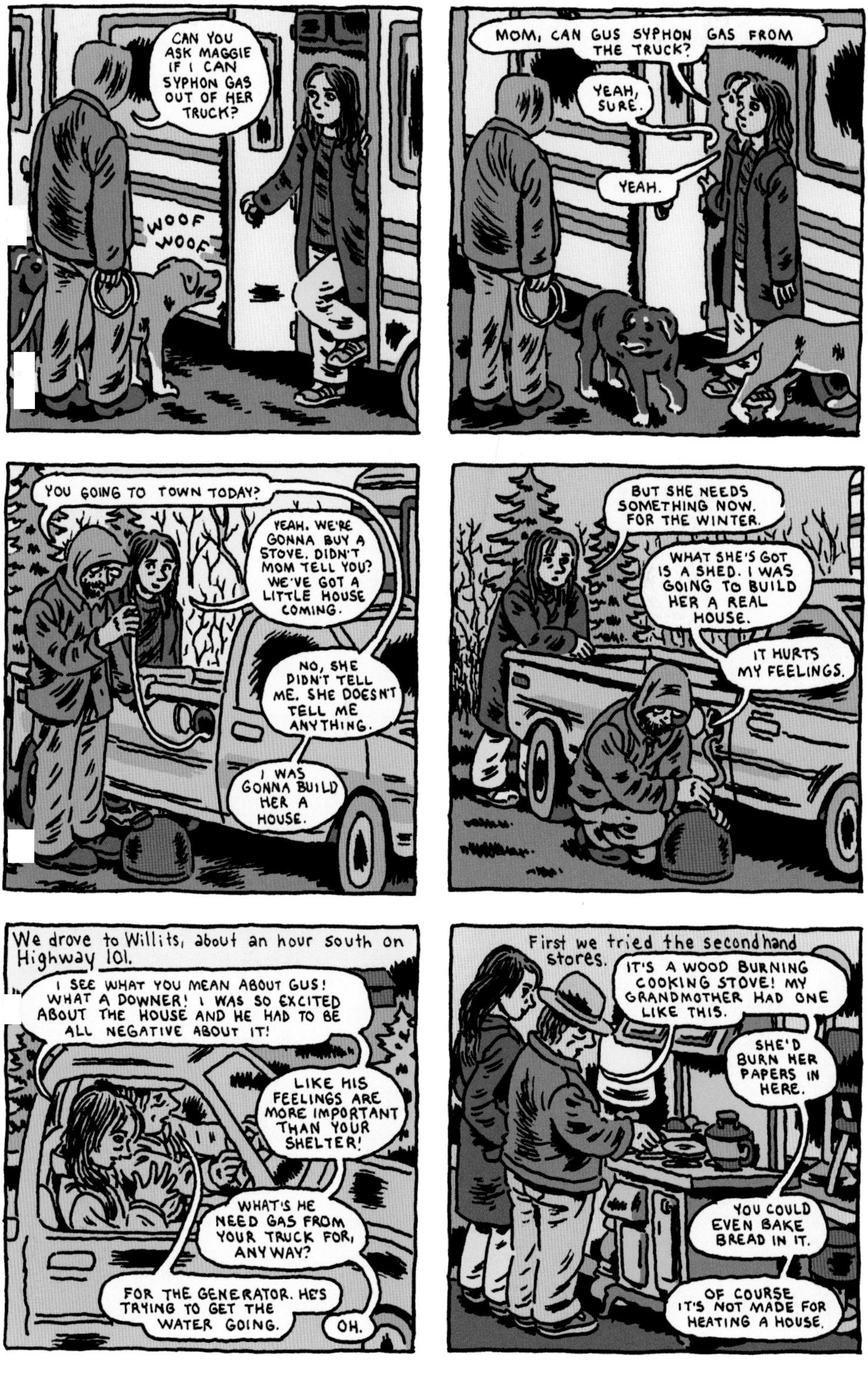
CAN YOU ASK MAGGIE IF I CAN SYPHON GAS OUT OF HER TRUCK?
WOOF WOOF
MOM, CAN GUS SYPHON GAS FROM THE TRUCK?
YEAH, SURE.
YEAH.
YOU GOING TO TOWN TODAY?
YEAH. WE'RE GONNA BUY A STOVE. DIDN'T MOM TELL YOU? WE'VE GOT A LITTLE HOUSE COMING.
NO, SHE DIDN'T TELL ME. SHE DOESN'T TELL ME ANYTHING.
I WAS GONNA BUILD HER A HOUSE.
BUT SHE NEEDS SOMETHING NOW. FOR THE WINTER.
WHAT SHE'S GOT IS A SHED. I WAS GOING TO BUILD HER A REAL HOUSE.
IT HURTS MY FEELINGS.
We drove to Willits, about an hour south on Highway 101.
I SEE WHAT YOU MEAN ABOUT GUS! WHAT A DOWNER! I WAS SO EXCITED ABOUT THE HOUSE AND HE HAD TO BE ALL NEGATIVE ABOUT IT!
LIKE HIS FEELINGS ARE MORE IMPORTANT THAN YOUR SHELTER!
WHAT'S HE NEED GAS FROM YOUR TRUCK FOR, ANYWAY?
FOR THE GENERATOR. HE'S TRYING TO GET THE WATER GOING.
OH.
First we tried the secondhand stores.
IT'S A WOOD BURNING COOKING STOVE! MY GRANDMOTHER HAD ONE LIKE THIS.
SHE'D BURN HER PAPERS IN HERE.
YOU COULD EVEN BAKE BREAD IN IT.
OF COURSE IT'S NOT MADE FOR HEATING A HOUSE.

We tried the Internet.

HERE'S ONE IN GRANTS PASS FOR 150$. WHERE'S GRANTS PASS?

THAT'S IN OREGON.

MAYBE I SHOULD GET THAT COOKING STOVE. IT WOULDN'T TAKE MUCH TO HEAT THAT LITTLE ROOM. AND I COULD COOK AND BAKE, TOO.

HERE'S ONE ON AMAZON FOR 250$. BUT HOW COULD WE GET IT DELIVERED UP THERE?

We tried the fancy stove store.

HOW COME THOSE ONES ON AMAZON WERE 250$ AND THESE ONES ARE 2000$? THEY LOOK THE SAME.

THOSE ONES WEREN'T AIRTIGHT.

WHAT'S THE DIFFERENCE?

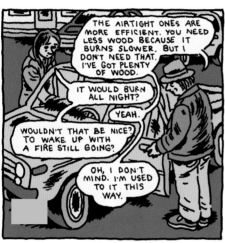

THE AIRTIGHT ONES ARE MORE EFFICIENT. YOU NEED LESS WOOD BECAUSE IT BURNS SLOWER. BUT I DON'T NEED THAT. I'VE GOT PLENTY OF WOOD.

IT WOULD BURN ALL NIGHT?

YEAH.

WOULDN'T THAT BE NICE? TO WAKE UP WITH A FIRE STILL GOING?

OH, I DON'T MIND. I'M USED TO IT THIS WAY.

I THINK I WANT THE COOKING STOVE. 450$ IS A GOOD PRICE.

DO YOU THINK IT MIGHT BE TOO BIG FOR YOUR HOUSE?

IT'S WHAT, TWO BY TWO? I'VE GOT EIGHT BY TWENTY FEET. THAT'S... 160 SQUARE FEET? SO I'D STILL HAVE 158 LEFTOVER FEET.

I THINK IT WAS CLOSER TO THREE BY THREE?

I'D LIKE TO BUY THIS.

SURE. BUT IT'S HEAVY. I WON'T BE ABLE TO HELP LIFT IT. YOU'LL NEED A COUPLE GUYS.

CAN I GIVE YOU A DEPOSIT AND PICK IT UP LATER?

OKAY.

I THINK I'VE GOT 200$...

CAN YOU JUST WRITE A RECEIPT FOR "A PILE OF CRUMPLED BILLS"?

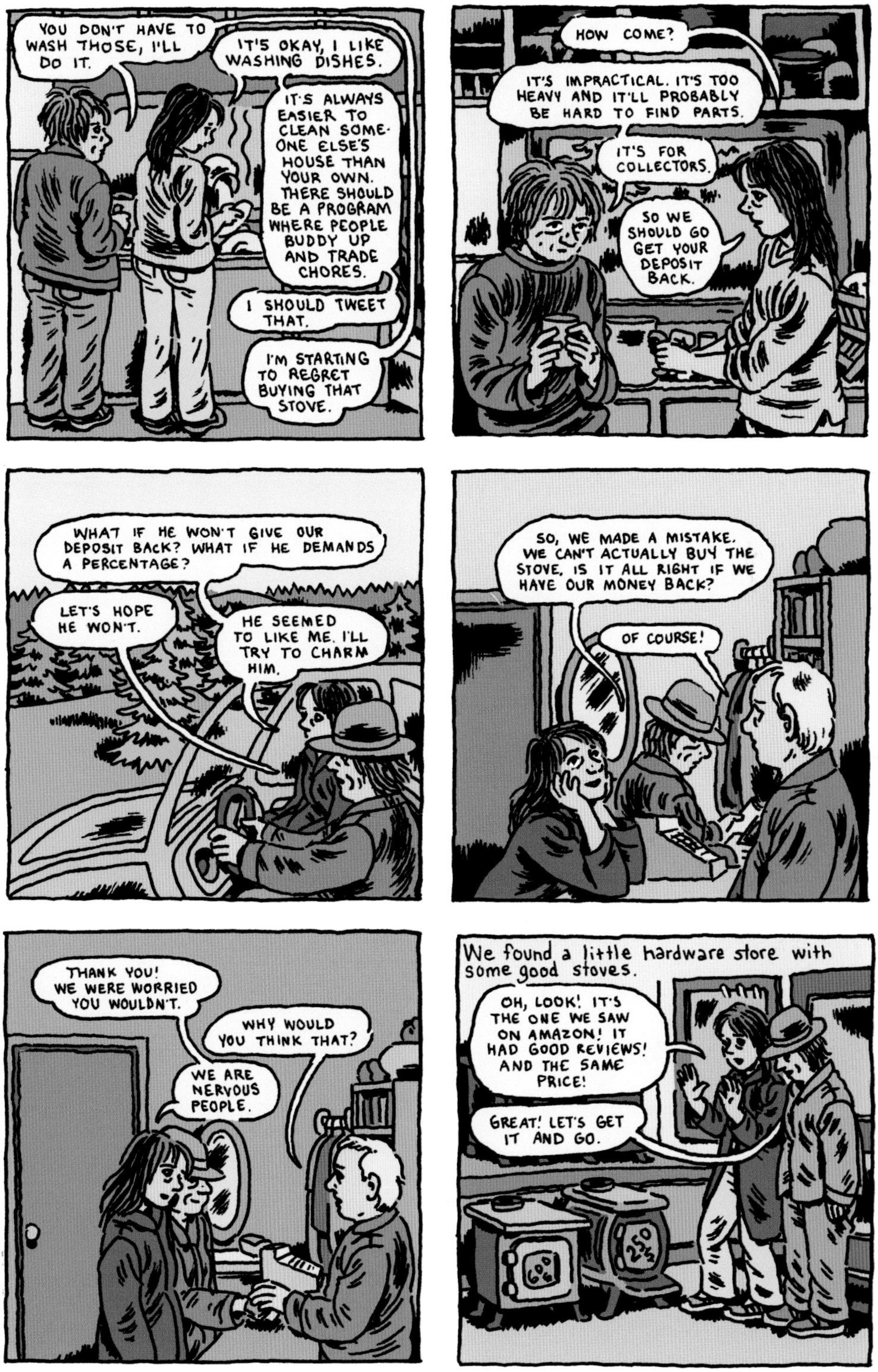
YOU DON'T HAVE TO WASH THOSE, I'LL DO IT.
IT'S OKAY, I LIKE WASHING DISHES.
IT'S ALWAYS EASIER TO CLEAN SOME-ONE ELSE'S HOUSE THAN YOUR OWN. THERE SHOULD BE A PROGRAM WHERE PEOPLE BUDDY UP AND TRADE CHORES.
I SHOULD TWEET THAT.
I'M STARTING TO REGRET BUYING THAT STOVE.
HOW COME?
IT'S IMPRACTICAL. IT'S TOO HEAVY AND IT'LL PROBABLY BE HARD TO FIND PARTS.
IT'S FOR COLLECTORS.
SO WE SHOULD GO GET YOUR DEPOSIT BACK.
WHAT IF HE WON'T GIVE OUR DEPOSIT BACK? WHAT IF HE DEMANDS A PERCENTAGE?
LET'S HOPE HE WON'T.
HE SEEMED TO LIKE ME. I'LL TRY TO CHARM HIM.
SO, WE MADE A MISTAKE. WE CAN'T ACTUALLY BUY THE STOVE. IS IT ALL RIGHT IF WE HAVE OUR MONEY BACK?
OF COURSE!
THANK YOU! WE WERE WORRIED YOU WOULDN'T.
WHY WOULD YOU THINK THAT?
WE ARE NERVOUS PEOPLE.
We found a little hardware store with some good stoves.
OH, LOOK! IT'S THE ONE WE SAW ON AMAZON! IT HAD GOOD REVIEWS! AND THE SAME PRICE!
GREAT! LET'S GET IT AND GO.

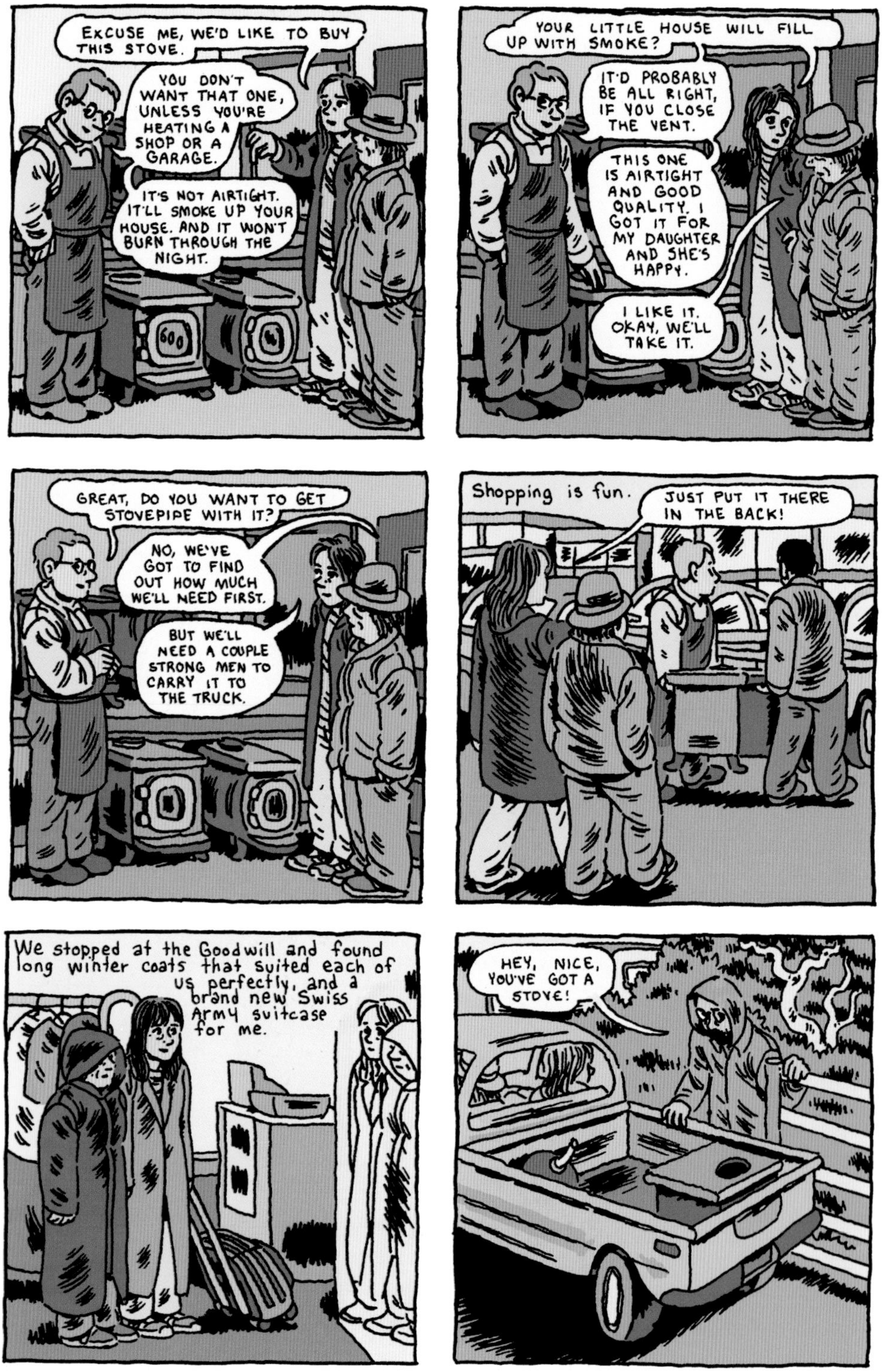
EXCUSE ME, WE'D LIKE TO BUY THIS STOVE.
YOU DON'T WANT THAT ONE, UNLESS YOU'RE HEATING A SHOP OR A GARAGE.
IT'S NOT AIRTIGHT. IT'LL SMOKE UP YOUR HOUSE. AND IT WON'T BURN THROUGH THE NIGHT.
YOUR LITTLE HOUSE WILL FILL UP WITH SMOKE?
IT'D PROBABLY BE ALL RIGHT, IF YOU CLOSE THE VENT.
THIS ONE IS AIRTIGHT AND GOOD QUALITY. I GOT IT FOR MY DAUGHTER AND SHE'S HAPPY.
I LIKE IT. OKAY, WE'LL TAKE IT.
GREAT, DO YOU WANT TO GET STOVEPIPE WITH IT?
NO, WE'VE GOT TO FIND OUT HOW MUCH WE'LL NEED FIRST.
BUT WE'LL NEED A COUPLE STRONG MEN TO CARRY IT TO THE TRUCK.
Shopping is fun.
JUST PUT IT THERE IN THE BACK!
We stopped at the Goodwill and found long winter coats that suited each of us perfectly, and a brand new Swiss Army suitcase for me.
HEY, NICE, YOU'VE GOT A STOVE!

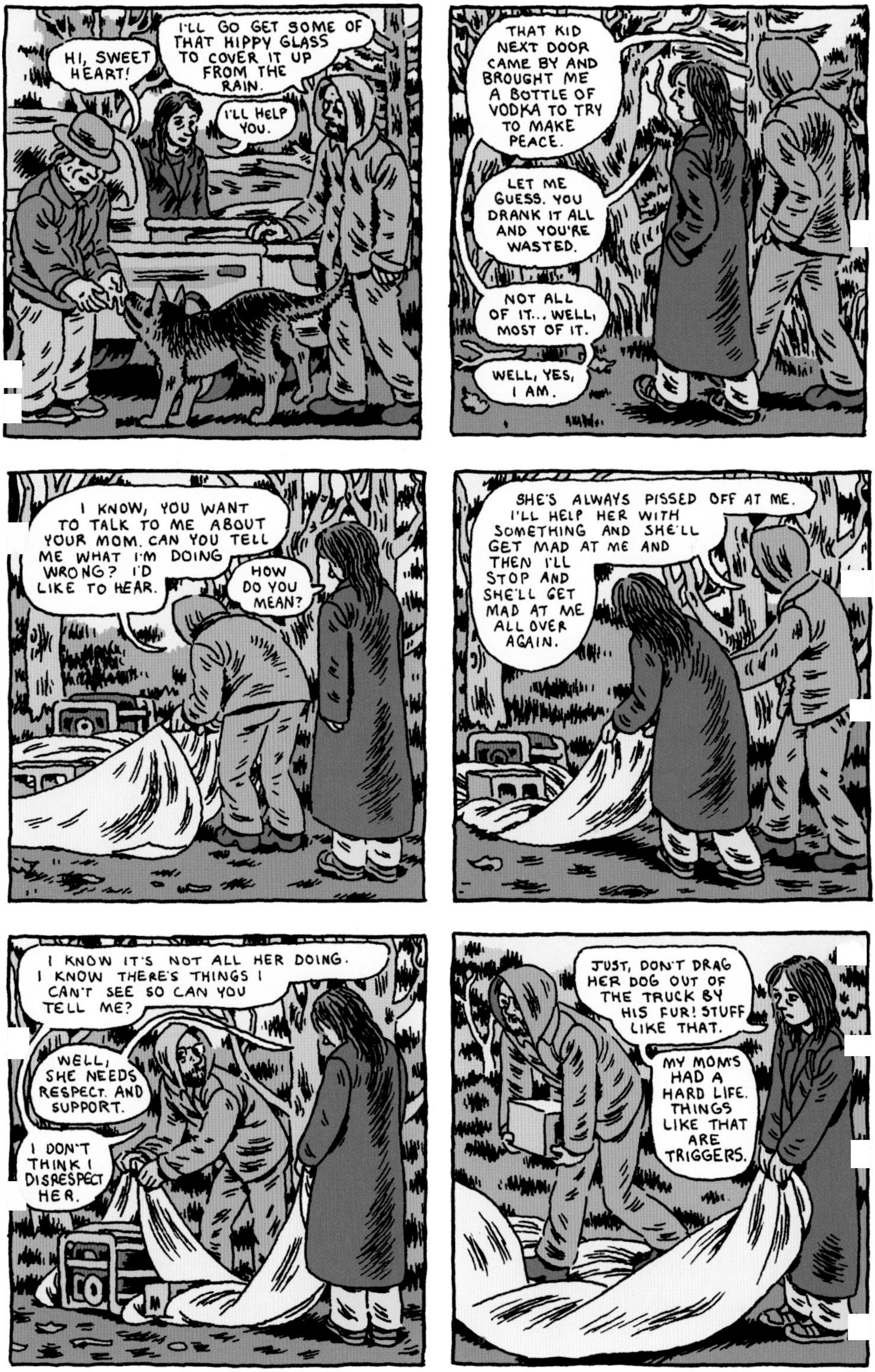
HI, SWEET HEART!
I'LL GO GET SOME OF THAT HIPPY GLASS TO COVER IT UP FROM THE RAIN.
I'LL HELP YOU.
THAT KID NEXT DOOR CAME BY AND BROUGHT ME A BOTTLE OF VODKA TO TRY TO MAKE PEACE.
LET ME GUESS. YOU DRANK IT ALL AND YOU'RE WASTED.
NOT ALL OF IT... WELL, MOST OF IT.
WELL, YES, I AM.
I KNOW, YOU WANT TO TALK TO ME ABOUT YOUR MOM. CAN YOU TELL ME WHAT I'M DOING WRONG? I'D LIKE TO HEAR.
HOW DO YOU MEAN?
SHE'S ALWAYS PISSED OFF AT ME. I'LL HELP HER WITH SOMETHING AND SHE'LL GET MAD AT ME AND THEN I'LL STOP AND SHE'LL GET MAD AT ME ALL OVER AGAIN.
I KNOW IT'S NOT ALL HER DOING. I KNOW THERE'S THINGS I CAN'T SEE SO CAN YOU TELL ME?
WELL, SHE NEEDS RESPECT. AND SUPPORT.
I DON'T THINK I DISRESPECT HER.
JUST, DON'T DRAG HER DOG OUT OF THE TRUCK BY HIS FUR! STUFF LIKE THAT.
MY MOM'S HAD A HARD LIFE. THINGS LIKE THAT ARE TRIGGERS.

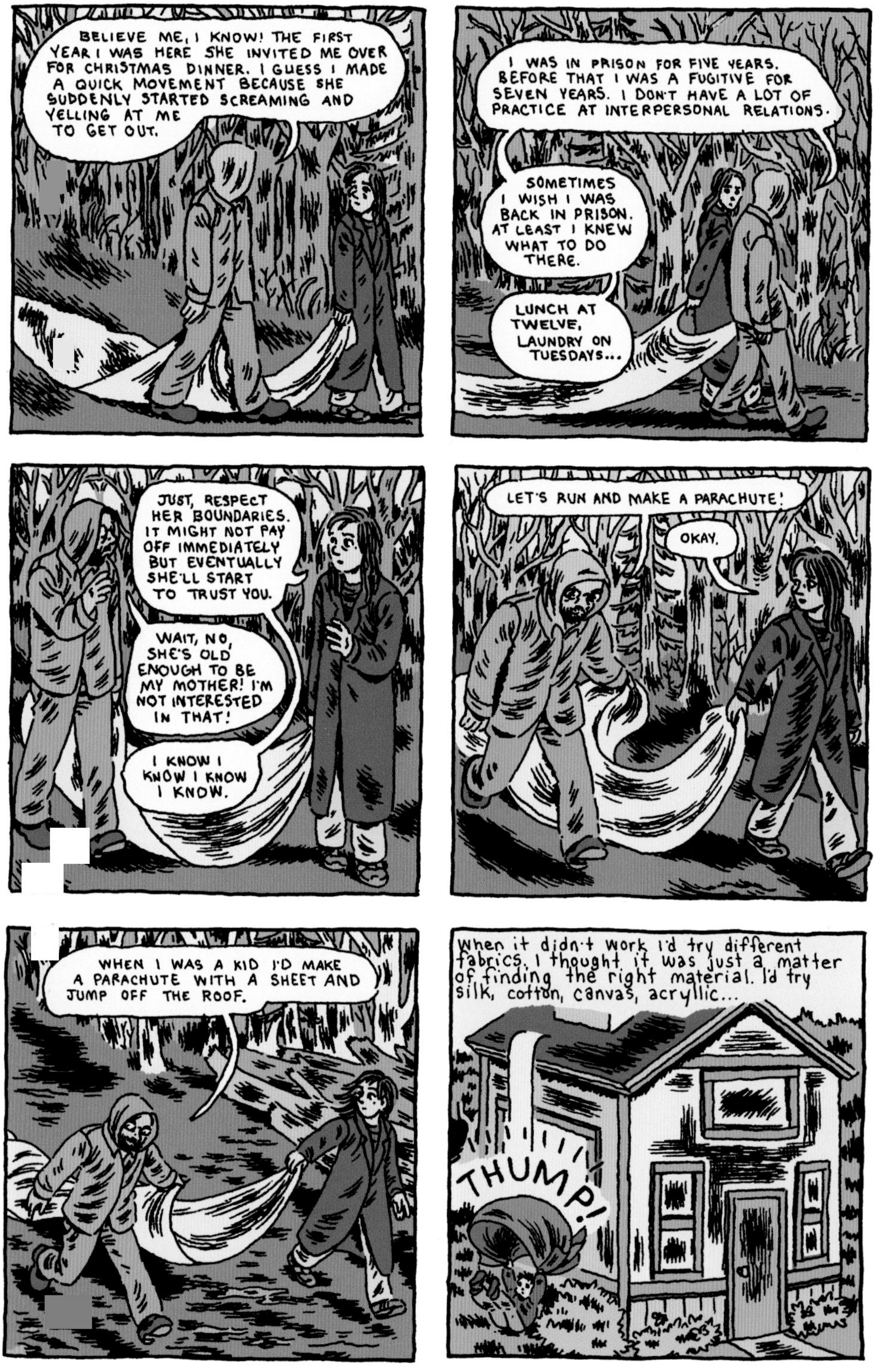
BELIEVE ME, I KNOW! THE FIRST YEAR I WAS HERE SHE INVITED ME OVER FOR CHRISTMAS DINNER. I GUESS I MADE A QUICK MOVEMENT BECAUSE SHE SUDDENLY STARTED SCREAMING AND YELLING AT ME TO GET OUT.
I WAS IN PRISON FOR FIVE YEARS. BEFORE THAT I WAS A FUGITIVE FOR SEVEN YEARS. I DON'T HAVE A LOT OF PRACTICE AT INTERPERSONAL RELATIONS.
SOMETIMES I WISH I WAS BACK IN PRISON. AT LEAST I KNEW WHAT TO DO THERE.
LUNCH AT TWELVE, LAUNDRY ON TUESDAYS...
JUST, RESPECT HER BOUNDARIES. IT MIGHT NOT PAY OFF IMMEDIATELY BUT EVENTUALLY SHE'LL START TO TRUST YOU.
WAIT, NO, SHE'S OLD ENOUGH TO BE MY MOTHER! I'M NOT INTERESTED IN THAT!
I KNOW I KNOW I KNOW I KNOW.
LET'S RUN AND MAKE A PARACHUTE!
OKAY.
WHEN I WAS A KID I'D MAKE A PARACHUTE WITH A SHEET AND JUMP OFF THE ROOF.
When it didn't work I'd try different fabrics. I thought it was just a matter of finding the right material. I'd try silk, cotton, canvas, acryllic...
THUMP!

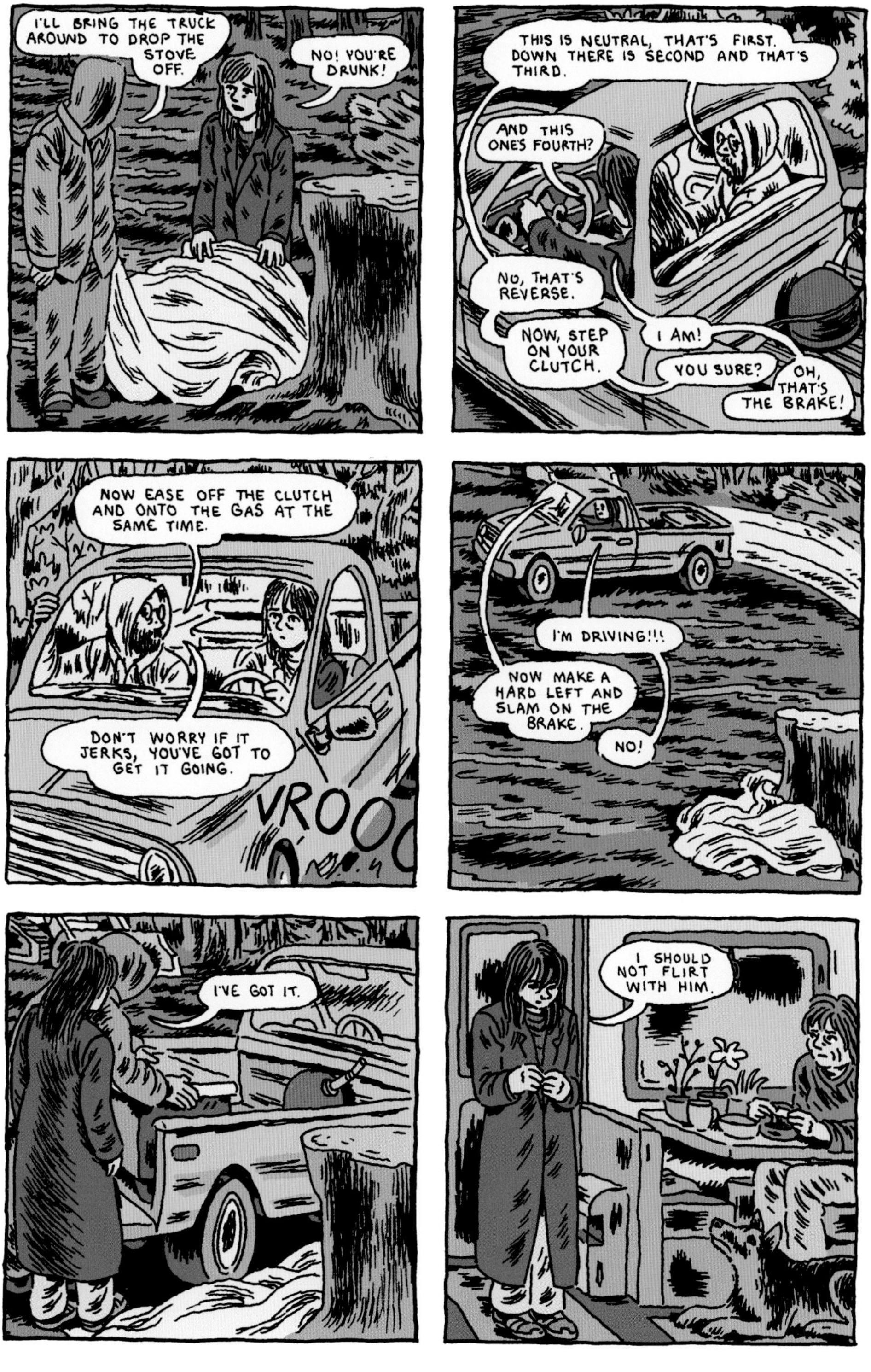
I'LL BRING THE TRUCK AROUND TO DROP THE STOVE OFF.
NO! YOU'RE DRUNK!
THIS IS NEUTRAL, THAT'S FIRST. DOWN THERE IS SECOND AND THAT'S THIRD.
AND THIS ONE'S FOURTH?
NO, THAT'S REVERSE.
NOW, STEP ON YOUR CLUTCH.
I AM!
YOU SURE?
OH, THAT'S THE BRAKE!
NOW EASE OFF THE CLUTCH AND ONTO THE GAS AT THE SAME TIME.
DON'T WORRY IF IT JERKS, YOU'VE GOT TO GET IT GOING.
VROOO
I'M DRIVING!!!
NOW MAKE A HARD LEFT AND SLAM ON THE BRAKE.
NO!
I'VE GOT IT.
I SHOULD NOT FLIRT WITH HIM.

Nice and Clean

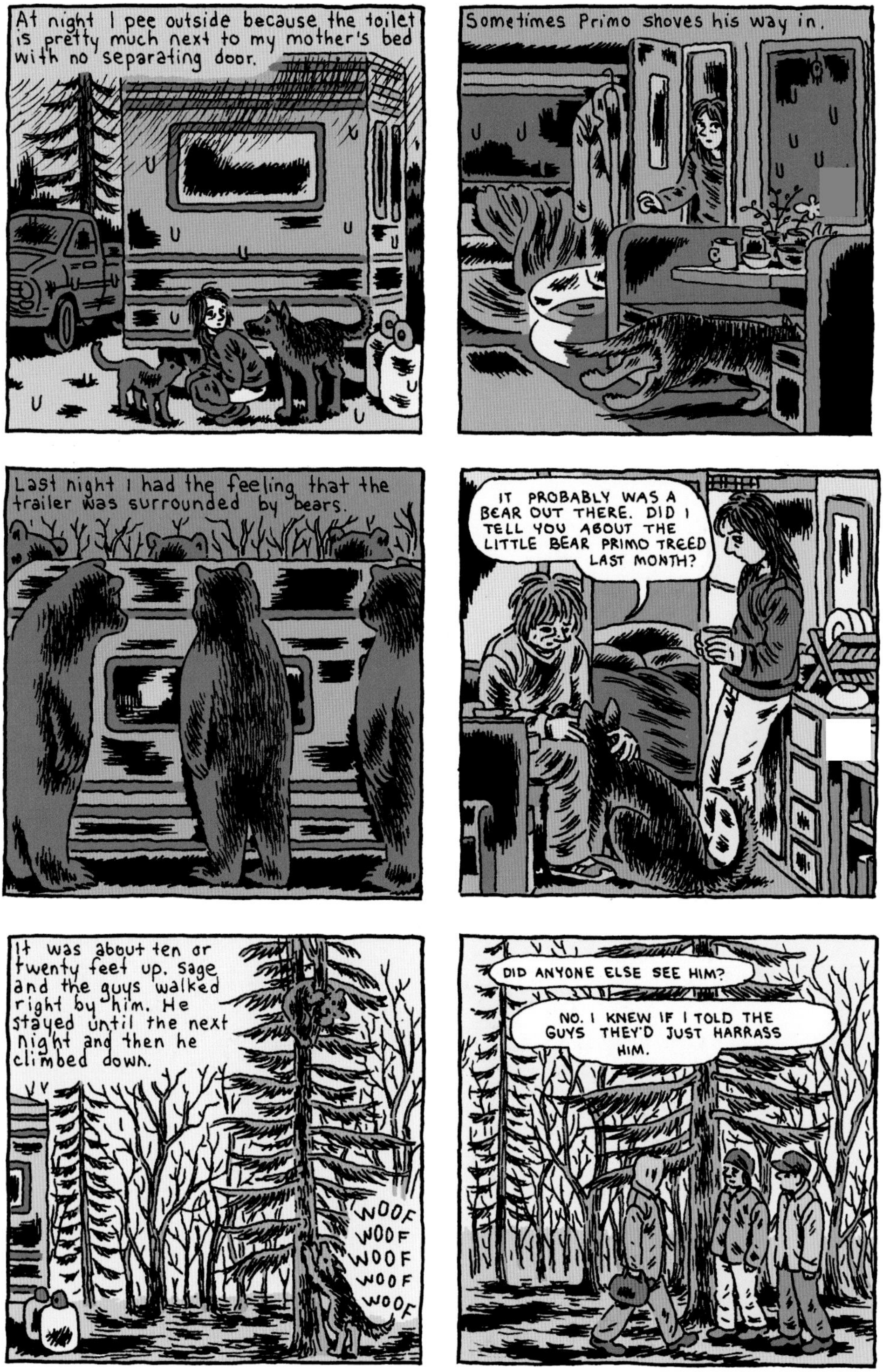
At night I pee outside because the toilet is pretty much next to my mother's bed with no separating door.
Sometimes Primo shoves his way in.
Last night I had the feeling that the trailer was surrounded by bears.
IT PROBABLY WAS A BEAR OUT THERE. DID I TELL YOU ABOUT THE LITTLE BEAR PRIMO TREED LAST MONTH?
It was about ten or twenty feet up. Sage and the guys walked right by him. He stayed until the next night and then he climbed down.
WOOF WOOF WOOF WOOF WOOF
DID ANYONE ELSE SEE HIM?
NO. I KNEW IF I TOLD THE GUYS THEY'D JUST HARRASS HIM.

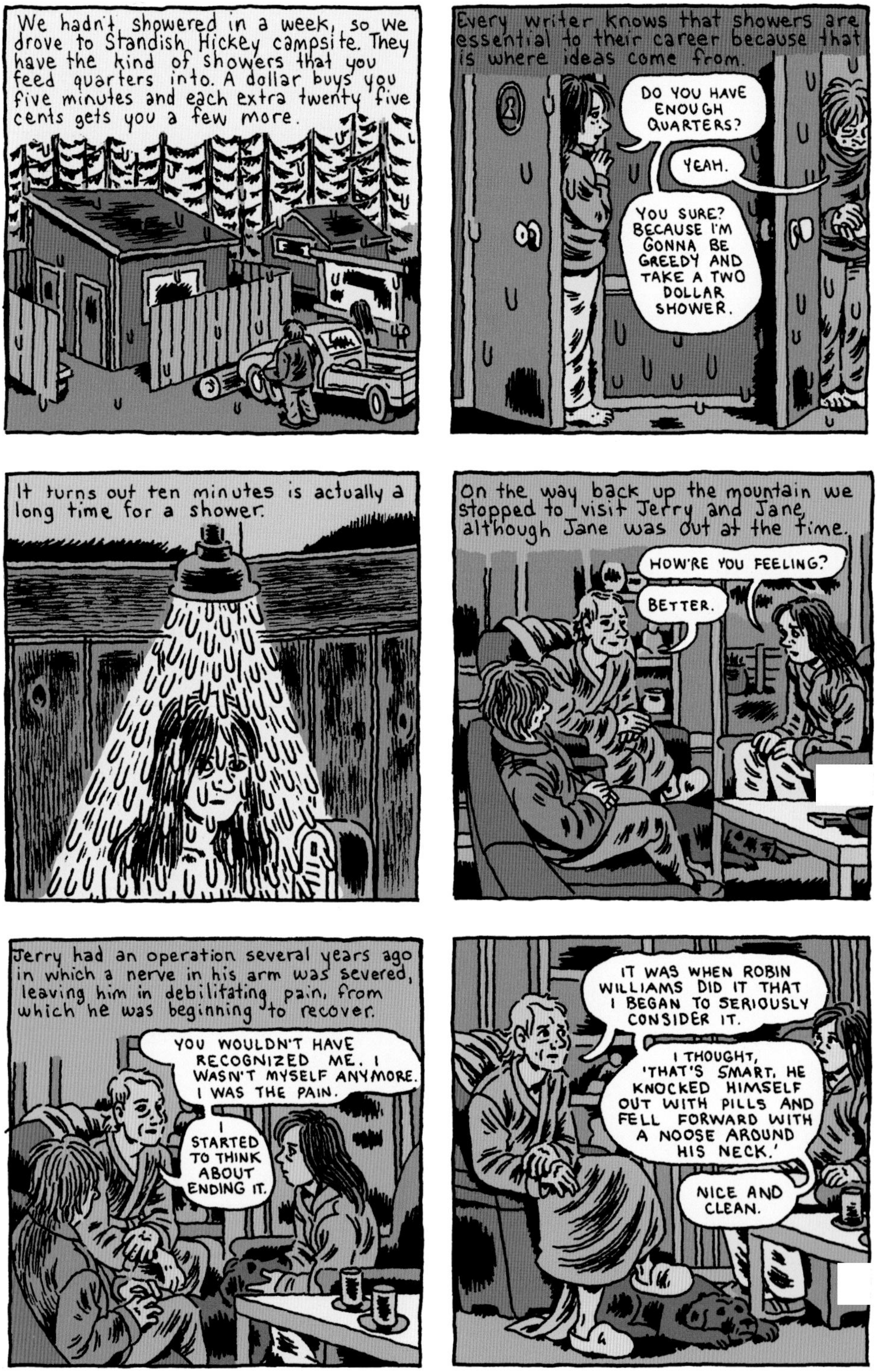
We hadn't showered in a week, so we drove to Standish Hickey campsite. They have the kind of showers that you feed quarters into. A dollar buys you five minutes and each extra twenty five cents gets you a few more.
Every writer knows that showers are essential to their career because that is where ideas come from.
DO YOU HAVE ENOUGH QUARTERS?
YEAH.
YOU SURE? BECAUSE I'M GONNA BE GREEDY AND TAKE A TWO DOLLAR SHOWER.
It turns out ten minutes is actually a long time for a shower.
On the way back up the mountain we stopped to visit Jerry and Jane, although Jane was out at the time.
HOW'RE YOU FEELING?
BETTER.
Jerry had an operation several years ago in which a nerve in his arm was severed, leaving him in debilitating pain, from which he was beginning to recover.
YOU WOULDN'T HAVE RECOGNIZED ME. I WASN'T MYSELF ANYMORE. I WAS THE PAIN.
I STARTED TO THINK ABOUT ENDING IT.
IT WAS WHEN ROBIN WILLIAMS DID IT THAT I BEGAN TO SERIOUSLY CONSIDER IT.
I THOUGHT, 'THAT'S SMART. HE KNOCKED HIMSELF OUT WITH PILLS AND FELL FORWARD WITH A NOOSE AROUND HIS NECK.'
NICE AND CLEAN.

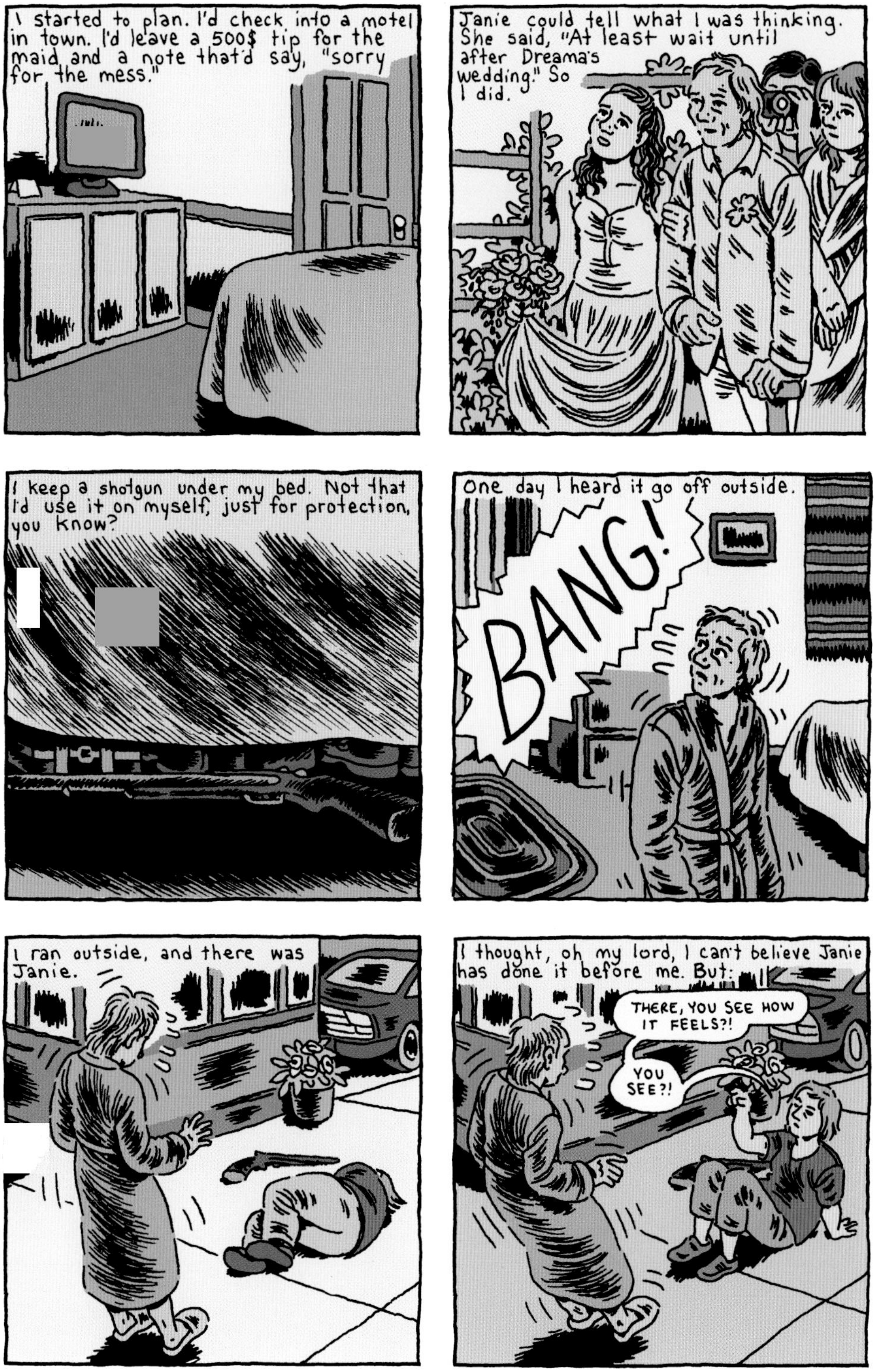
I started to plan. I'd check into a motel in town. I'd leave a 500$ tip for the maid and a note that'd say, "sorry for the mess."
Janie could tell what I was thinking. She said, "At least wait until after Dreama's wedding." So I did.
I keep a shotgun under my bed. Not that I'd use it on myself, just for protection, you know?
One day I heard it go off outside.
BANG!
I ran outside, and there was Janie.
I thought, oh my lord, I can't believe Janie has done it before me. But:
THERE, YOU SEE HOW IT FEELS?!
YOU SEE?!

Waiting

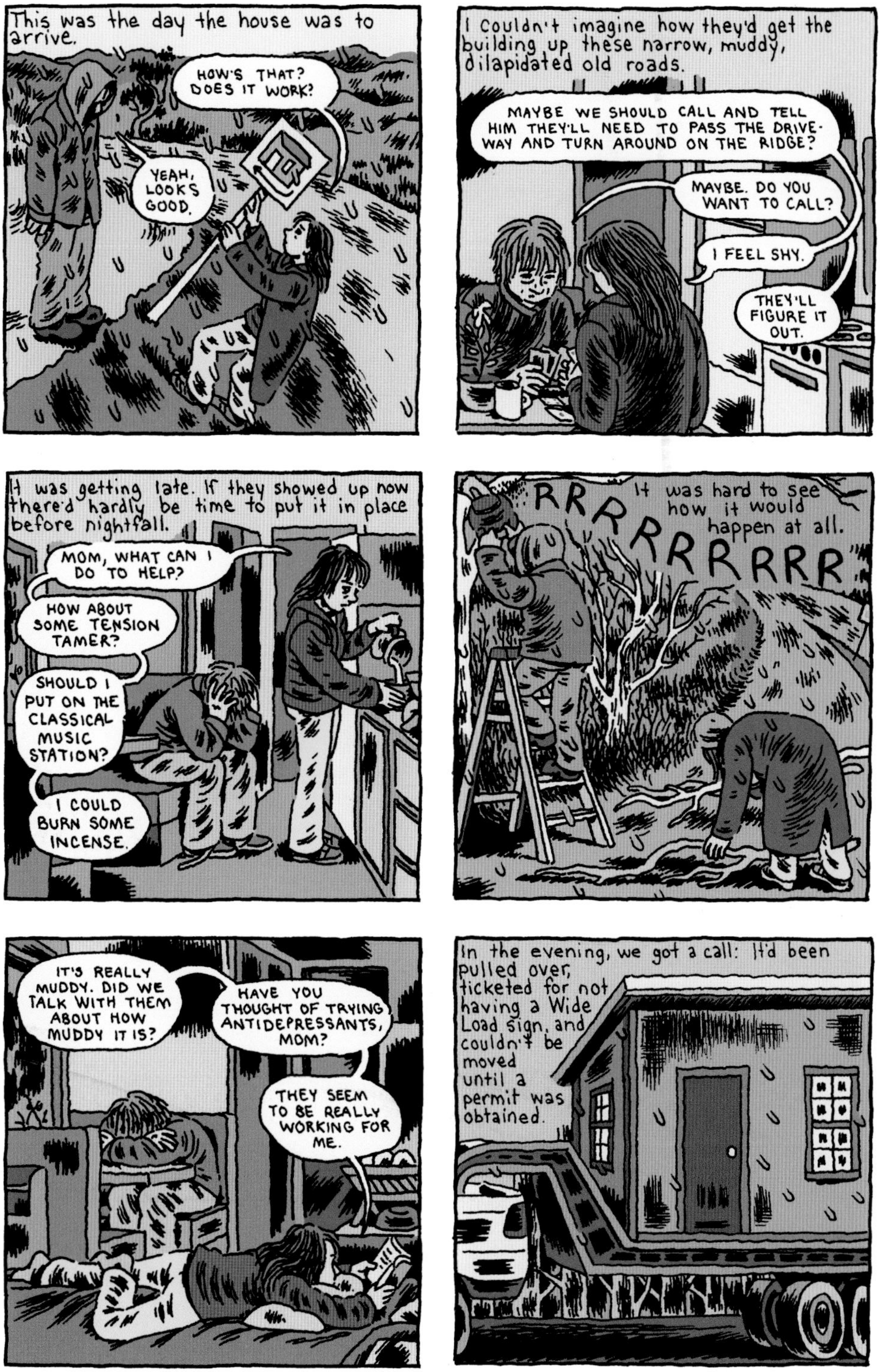
This was the day the house was to arrive.
HOW'S THAT? DOES IT WORK?
YEAH, LOOKS GOOD.
I couldn't imagine how they'd get the building up these narrow, muddy, dilapidated old roads.
MAYBE WE SHOULD CALL AND TELL HIM THEY'LL NEED TO PASS THE DRIVE-WAY AND TURN AROUND ON THE RIDGE?
MAYBE. DO YOU WANT TO CALL?
I FEEL SHY.
THEY'LL FIGURE IT OUT.
It was getting late. If they showed up now there'd hardly be time to put it in place before nightfall.
MOM, WHAT CAN I DO TO HELP?
HOW ABOUT SOME TENSION TAMER?
SHOULD I PUT ON THE CLASSICAL MUSIC STATION?
I COULD BURN SOME INCENSE.
RRRRRRRRR
It was hard to see how it would happen at all.
IT'S REALLY MUDDY. DID WE TALK WITH THEM ABOUT HOW MUDDY IT IS?
HAVE YOU THOUGHT OF TRYING ANTIDEPRESSANTS, MOM?
THEY SEEM TO BE REALLY WORKING FOR ME.
In the evening, we got a call: It'd been pulled over, ticketed for not having a Wide Load sign, and couldn't be moved until a permit was obtained.

The Interview

Another day of waiting. I had the idea to ask Gus if I could interview him in the greenhouse.

I DON'T UNDERSTAND.

THE ONLY TIMES I'VE BEEN INTERVIEWED HAVE BEEN BY THE POLICE OR BY PSYCHIATRISTS.

CAN YOU TELL ME WHY YOU WERE IN PRISON?

IT WAS FOR GROWING POT. BUT THEY GOT ME FOR SOME EARLIER ASSAULT CHARGES.

CAN YOU TELL ME ABOUT THOSE?

I WAS DEALING COKE AND HEROIN IN THE CITY. I HAD SOME PROBLEMS... I GOT BEAT UP. I GOT ROBBED, SO I HIRED SOME GUYS TO DO SOMETHING FOR ME.

GO HOME, JUNIOR!

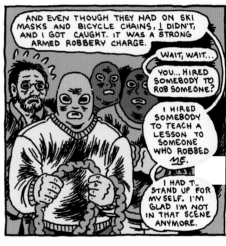

AND EVEN THOUGH THEY HAD ON SKI MASKS AND BICYCLE CHAINS, I DIDN'T, AND I GOT CAUGHT. IT WAS A STRONG ARMED ROBBERY CHARGE.

WAIT, WAIT...

YOU... HIRED SOMEBODY TO ROB SOMEONE?

I HIRED SOMEBODY TO TEACH A LESSON TO SOMEONE WHO ROBBED ME.

I HAD T- STAND UP FOR MYSELF. I'M GLAD I'M NOT IN THAT SCENE ANYMORE.

I JUMPED ON A FREIGHT TRAIN THE NEXT DAY.

YOU WENT ON THE LAM?

After six months or so of getting lost, I landed in New Mexico. I got to know the area, I bought a donkey and a couple of mules and started growing pot in the wilderness area.

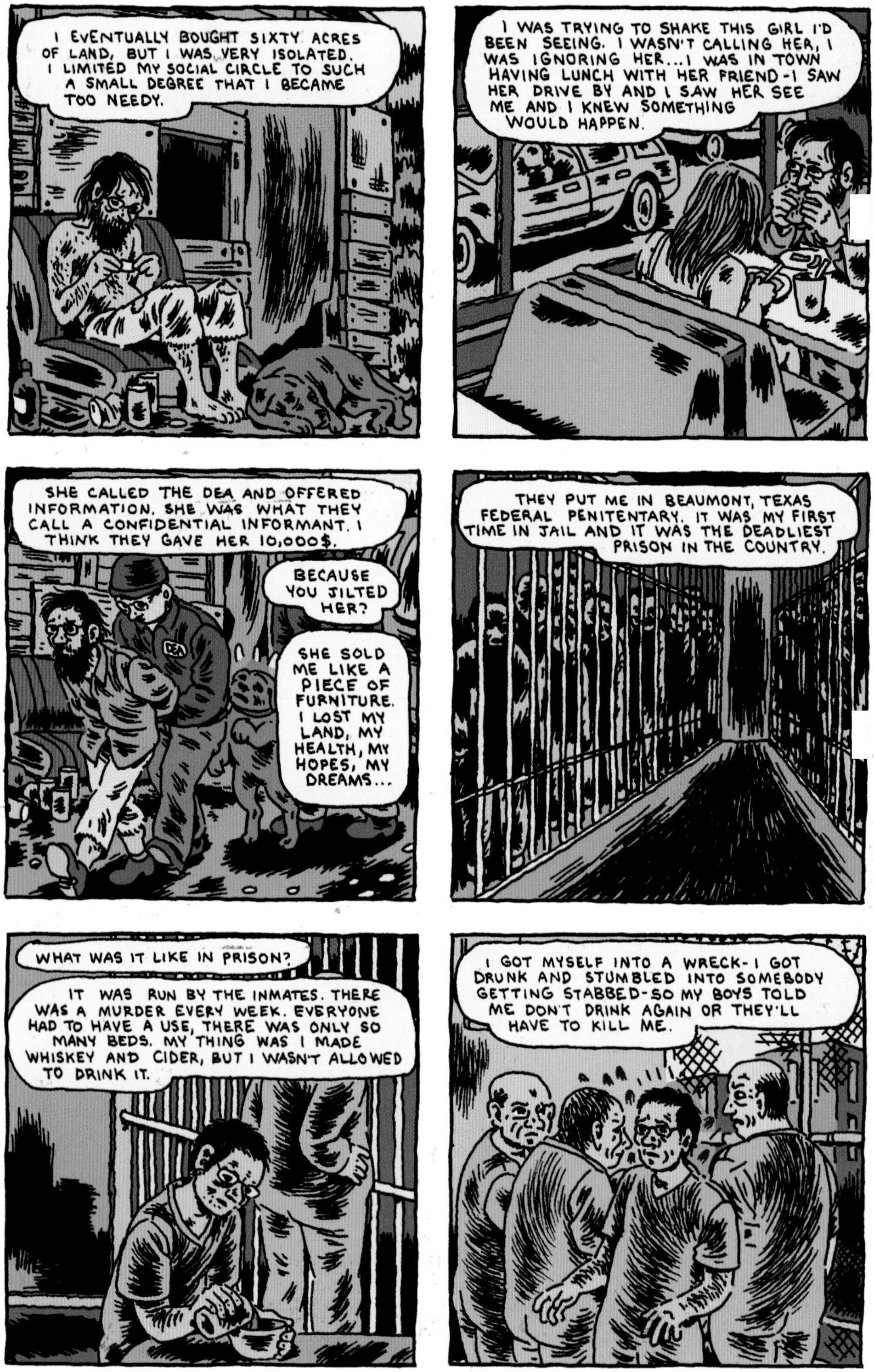

I EVENTUALLY BOUGHT SIXTY ACRES OF LAND, BUT I WAS VERY ISOLATED. I LIMITED MY SOCIAL CIRCLE TO SUCH A SMALL DEGREE THAT I BECAME TOO NEEDY.
I WAS TRYING TO SHAKE THIS GIRL I'D BEEN SEEING. I WASN'T CALLING HER, I WAS IGNORING HER... I WAS IN TOWN HAVING LUNCH WITH HER FRIEND - I SAW HER DRIVE BY AND I SAW HER SEE ME AND I KNEW SOMETHING WOULD HAPPEN.
SHE CALLED THE DEA AND OFFERED INFORMATION. SHE WAS WHAT THEY CALL A CONFIDENTIAL INFORMANT. I THINK THEY GAVE HER 10,000$.
BECAUSE YOU JILTED HER?
SHE SOLD ME LIKE A PIECE OF FURNITURE. I LOST MY LAND, MY HEALTH, MY HOPES, MY DREAMS...
DEA
THEY PUT ME IN BEAUMONT, TEXAS FEDERAL PENITENTARY. IT WAS MY FIRST TIME IN JAIL AND IT WAS THE DEADLIEST PRISON IN THE COUNTRY.
WHAT WAS IT LIKE IN PRISON?
IT WAS RUN BY THE INMATES. THERE WAS A MURDER EVERY WEEK. EVERYONE HAD TO HAVE A USE, THERE WAS ONLY SO MANY BEDS. MY THING WAS I MADE WHISKEY AND CIDER, BUT I WASN'T ALLOWED TO DRINK IT.
I GOT MYSELF INTO A WRECK - I GOT DRUNK AND STUMBLED INTO SOMEBODY GETTING STABBED - SO MY BOYS TOLD ME DON'T DRINK AGAIN OR THEY'LL HAVE TO KILL ME.

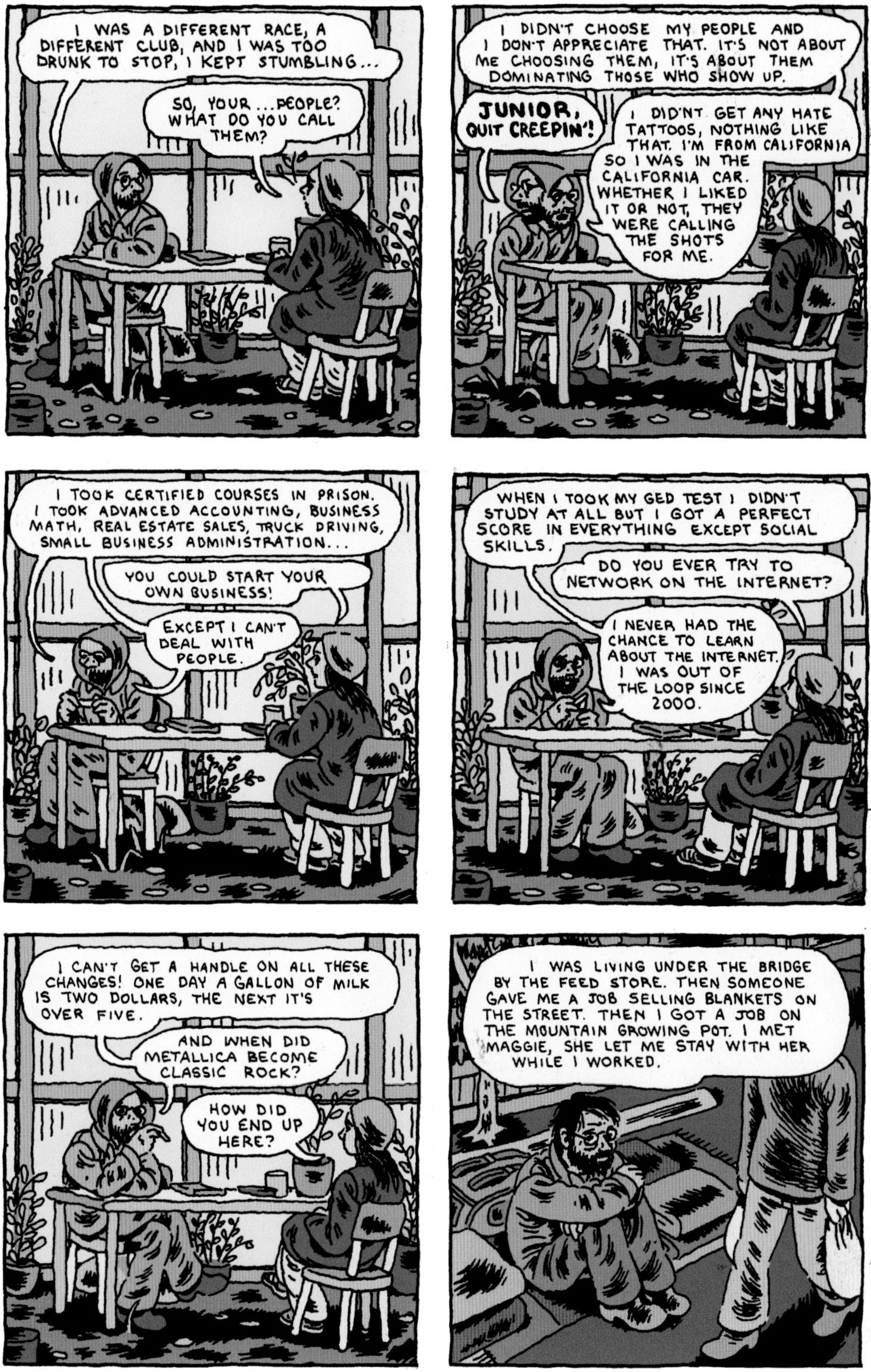
I WAS A DIFFERENT RACE, A DIFFERENT CLUB, AND I WAS TOO DRUNK TO STOP, I KEPT STUMBLING...
SO, YOUR ...PEOPLE? WHAT DO YOU CALL THEM?
I DIDN'T CHOOSE MY PEOPLE AND I DON'T APPRECIATE THAT. IT'S NOT ABOUT ME CHOOSING THEM, IT'S ABOUT THEM DOMINATING THOSE WHO SHOW UP.
JUNIOR, QUIT CREEPIN'!
I DIDN'T GET ANY HATE TATTOOS, NOTHING LIKE THAT. I'M FROM CALIFORNIA SO I WAS IN THE CALIFORNIA CAR. WHETHER I LIKED IT OR NOT, THEY WERE CALLING THE SHOTS FOR ME.
I TOOK CERTIFIED COURSES IN PRISON. I TOOK ADVANCED ACCOUNTING, BUSINESS MATH, REAL ESTATE SALES, TRUCK DRIVING, SMALL BUSINESS ADMINISTRATION...
YOU COULD START YOUR OWN BUSINESS!
EXCEPT I CAN'T DEAL WITH PEOPLE.
WHEN I TOOK MY GED TEST I DIDN'T STUDY AT ALL BUT I GOT A PERFECT SCORE IN EVERYTHING EXCEPT SOCIAL SKILLS.
DO YOU EVER TRY TO NETWORK ON THE INTERNET?
I NEVER HAD THE CHANCE TO LEARN ABOUT THE INTERNET. I WAS OUT OF THE LOOP SINCE 2000.
I CAN'T GET A HANDLE ON ALL THESE CHANGES! ONE DAY A GALLON OF MILK IS TWO DOLLARS, THE NEXT IT'S OVER FIVE.
AND WHEN DID METALLICA BECOME CLASSIC ROCK?
HOW DID YOU END UP HERE?
I WAS LIVING UNDER THE BRIDGE BY THE FEED STORE. THEN SOMEONE GAVE ME A JOB SELLING BLANKETS ON THE STREET. THEN I GOT A JOB ON THE MOUNTAIN GROWING POT. I MET MAGGIE, SHE LET ME STAY WITH HER WHILE I WORKED.

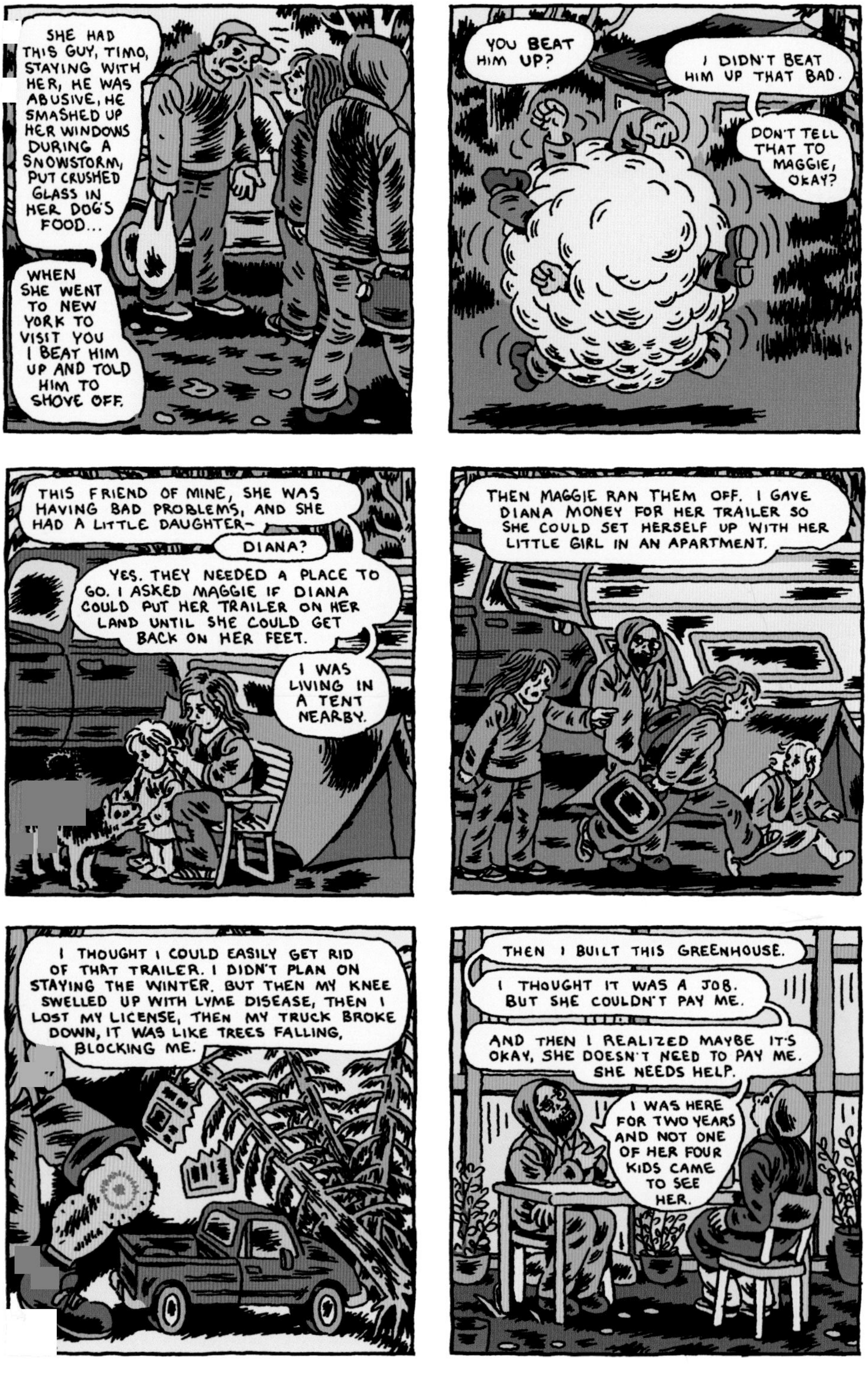
SHE HAD THIS GUY, TIMO, STAYING WITH HER, HE WAS ABUSIVE, HE SMASHED UP HER WINDOWS DURING A SNOWSTORM, PUT CRUSHED GLASS IN HER DOG'S FOOD...
WHEN SHE WENT TO NEW YORK TO VISIT YOU I BEAT HIM UP AND TOLD HIM TO SHOVE OFF.
YOU BEAT HIM UP?
I DIDN'T BEAT HIM UP THAT BAD.
DON'T TELL THAT TO MAGGIE, OKAY?
THIS FRIEND OF MINE, SHE WAS HAVING BAD PROBLEMS, AND SHE HAD A LITTLE DAUGHTER~
DIANA?
YES. THEY NEEDED A PLACE TO GO. I ASKED MAGGIE IF DIANA COULD PUT HER TRAILER ON HER LAND UNTIL SHE COULD GET BACK ON HER FEET.
I WAS LIVING IN A TENT NEARBY.
THEN MAGGIE RAN THEM OFF. I GAVE DIANA MONEY FOR HER TRAILER SO SHE COULD SET HERSELF UP WITH HER LITTLE GIRL IN AN APARTMENT.
I THOUGHT I COULD EASILY GET RID OF THAT TRAILER. I DIDN'T PLAN ON STAYING THE WINTER. BUT THEN MY KNEE SWELLED UP WITH LYME DISEASE, THEN I LOST MY LICENSE, THEN MY TRUCK BROKE DOWN, IT WAS LIKE TREES FALLING, BLOCKING ME.
THEN I BUILT THIS GREENHOUSE.
I THOUGHT IT WAS A JOB. BUT SHE COULDN'T PAY ME.
AND THEN I REALIZED MAYBE IT'S OKAY, SHE DOESN'T NEED TO PAY ME. SHE NEEDS HELP.
I WAS HERE FOR TWO YEARS AND NOT ONE OF HER FOUR KIDS CAME TO SEE HER.

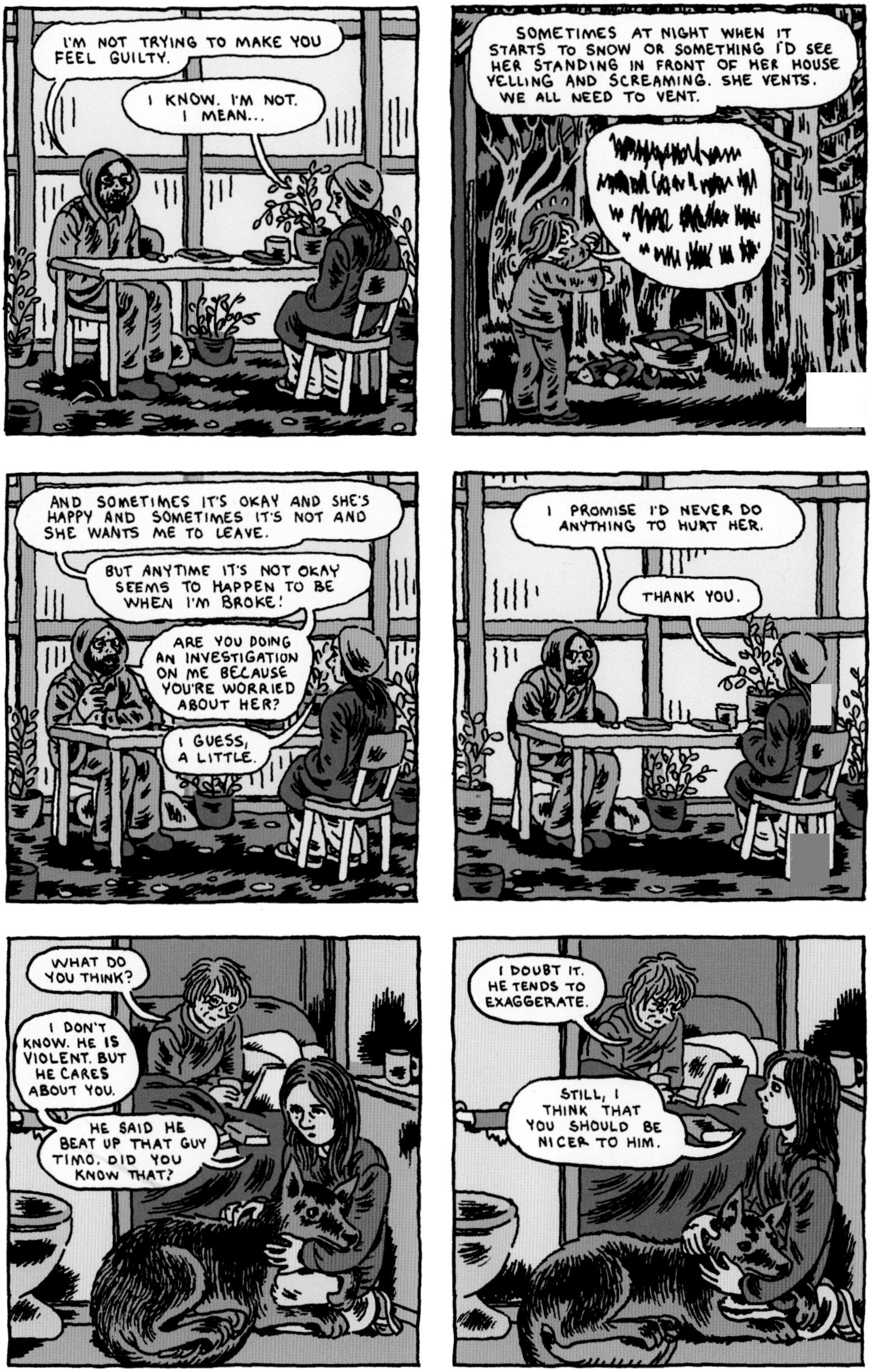
I'M NOT TRYING TO MAKE YOU FEEL GUILTY.
I KNOW. I'M NOT. I MEAN...
SOMETIMES AT NIGHT WHEN IT STARTS TO SNOW OR SOMETHING I'D SEE HER STANDING IN FRONT OF HER HOUSE YELLING AND SCREAMING. SHE VENTS. WE ALL NEED TO VENT.
AND SOMETIMES IT'S OKAY AND SHE'S HAPPY AND SOMETIMES IT'S NOT AND SHE WANTS ME TO LEAVE.
BUT ANYTIME IT'S NOT OKAY SEEMS TO HAPPEN TO BE WHEN I'M BROKE!
ARE YOU DOING AN INVESTIGATION ON ME BECAUSE YOU'RE WORRIED ABOUT HER?
I GUESS, A LITTLE.
I PROMISE I'D NEVER DO ANYTHING TO HURT HER.
THANK YOU.
WHAT DO YOU THINK?
I DON'T KNOW. HE IS VIOLENT. BUT HE CARES ABOUT YOU.
HE SAID HE BEAT UP THAT GUY TIMO. DID YOU KNOW THAT?
I DOUBT IT. HE TENDS TO EXAGGERATE.
STILL, I THINK THAT YOU SHOULD BE NICER TO HIM.

A Solitary
Form of Reassurance

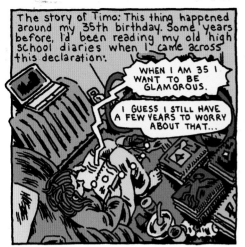

The story of Timo: This thing happened around my 35th birthday. Some years before, I'd been reading my old high school diaries when I came across this declaration:

WHEN I AM 35 I WANT TO BE GLAMOROUS.

I GUESS I STILL HAVE A FEW YEARS TO WORRY ABOUT THAT...

Next thing I knew, I was turning 35. I threw a party and requested that everyone dress as glamorously as possible.

It was so cold then, however, that nobody could take off their coats.

HAPPY BIRTHDAY!

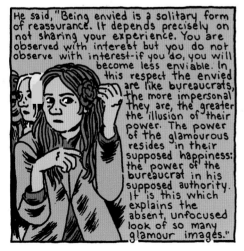

At the time I was reading Ways of Seeing. There's a whole chapter on glamour. John Berger says glamour didn't exist before the industrial revolution, that it was created by advertising. He said, "The state of being envied is what constitutes glamour.."

He said, "Being envied is a solitary form of reassurance. It depends precisely on not sharing your experience. You are observed with interest but you do not observe with interest-if you do, you will become less enviable. In this respect the envied are like bureaucrats, the more impersonal they are, the greater the illusion of their power. The power of the glamourous resides in their supposed happiness: the power of the bureaucrat in his supposed authority. It is this which explains the absent, unfocused look of so many glamour images."

It was at this party that I got a distressing phone call.

UH-OH, MY BOOT IS VIBRATING...

I'VE GOT NO POCKETS IN THIS OUTFIT...

It was Jerry.

GABBY, YOU SHOULD CALL YOUR MAMA, SHE'S NOT DOING SO WELL. IF YOU WANT TO SEND HER SOME MONEY YOU CAN USE OUR ADDRESS.

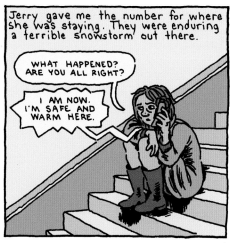

Jerry gave me the number for where she was staying. They were enduring a terrible snowstorm out there.

WHAT HAPPENED? ARE YOU ALL RIGHT?

I AM NOW. I'M SAFE AND WARM HERE.

She'd been snowed in with her two unruly dogs and a guy staying with her who was wigging out.

WHAT IS WRONG WITH YOU, YOU FUCKIN' STUPID WOMAN

WOOF WOOF!

WOOF WOOF

He went berserk and started to smash all the windows.

SMASH!!!

He scooped up the broken glass and put it in the dogs' food, so that eating it would kill them.

WHAT ARE YOU DOING?!

He continued to run amok until she whacked him on the head with a mag-light.

WHACK!!!

WOOF WOOF!

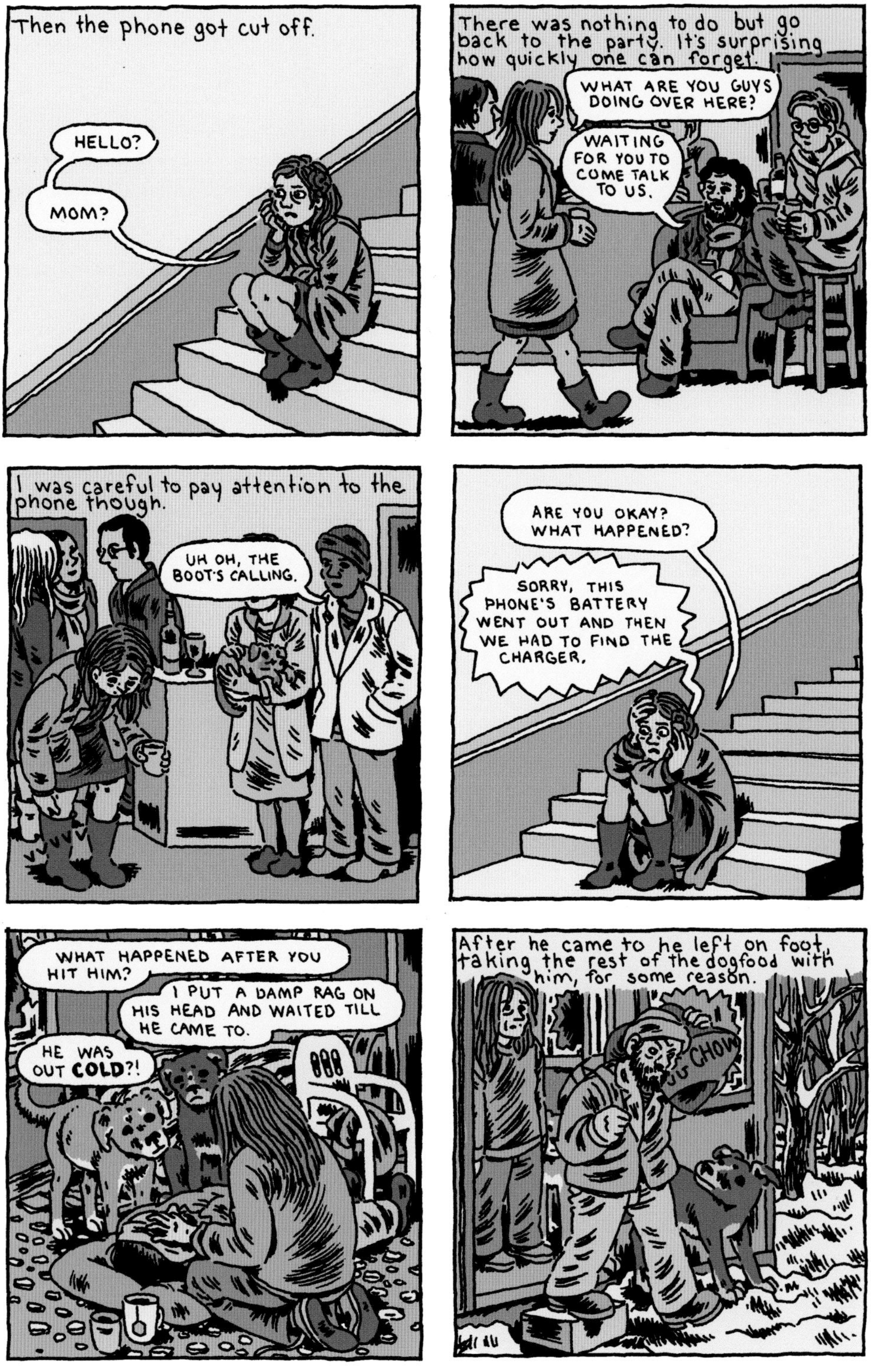
Then the phone got cut off.
HELLO?
MOM?
There was nothing to do but go back to the party. It's surprising how quickly one can forget.
WHAT ARE YOU GUYS DOING OVER HERE?
WAITING FOR YOU TO COME TALK TO US.
I was careful to pay attention to the phone though.
UH OH, THE BOOT'S CALLING.
ARE YOU OKAY? WHAT HAPPENED?
SORRY, THIS PHONE'S BATTERY WENT OUT AND THEN WE HAD TO FIND THE CHARGER.
WHAT HAPPENED AFTER YOU HIT HIM?
I PUT A DAMP RAG ON HIS HEAD AND WAITED TILL HE CAME TO.
HE WAS OUT **COLD**?!
After he came to he left on foot, taking the rest of the dogfood with him, for some reason.
CHOW

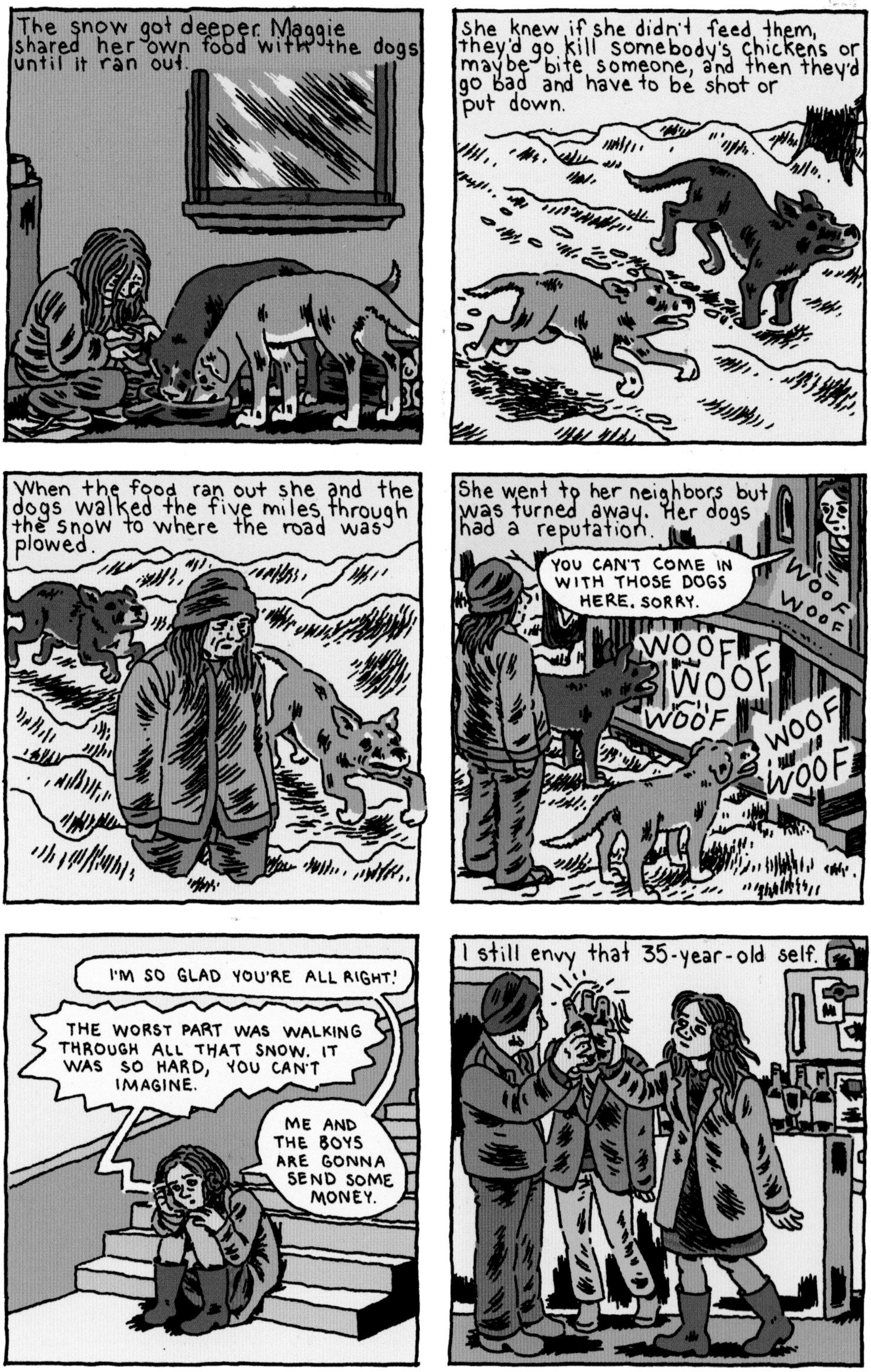

The snow got deeper. Maggie shared her own food with the dogs until it ran out.
She knew if she didn't feed them, they'd go kill somebody's chickens or maybe bite someone, and then they'd go bad and have to be shot or put down.
When the food ran out she and the dogs walked the five miles through the snow to where the road was plowed.
She went to her neighbors but was turned away. Her dogs had a reputation.
YOU CAN'T COME IN WITH THOSE DOGS HERE. SORRY.
WOOF WOOF
WOOF WOOF WOOF
WOOF WOOF
I'M SO GLAD YOU'RE ALL RIGHT!
THE WORST PART WAS WALKING THROUGH ALL THAT SNOW. IT WAS SO HARD, YOU CAN'T IMAGINE.
ME AND THE BOYS ARE GONNA SEND SOME MONEY.
I still envy that 35-year-old self.

The Arrival

The house finally arrived the next afternoon, accompanied by a caravan of crew and equipment.

YOU'VE GOTTA GO UP ON THE RIDGE BECAUSE THE TURN'S TOO SHARP HERE.

WE'VE GOT THAT, SWEETIE.

UH OH, CAR'S COMING, WE'VE GOTTA MOVE!

I hopped into the truck that towed the bobcat with a guy named Ryan.

UH OH. THAT LOOKS DANGEROUSLY TILTED.

I'LL FILM IT IN CASE IT FALLS OVER.

THAT WOULD NOT BE GOOD.

YEAH, BUT THINK OF ALL THE HITS ON YOUTUBE YOU'D GET!

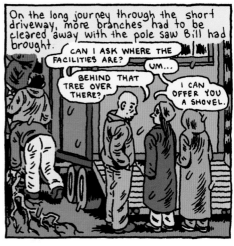

On the long journey through the short driveway, more branches had to be cleared away with the pole saw Bill had brought.

CAN I ASK WHERE THE FACILITIES ARE?

UM...

BEHIND THAT TREE OVER THERE?

I CAN OFFER YOU A SHOVEL.

We watched for hours.

When he'd described the foundation, I had not understood that the concrete blocks he'd referred to were the same kind you'd use to prop up bookshelves.

DO YOU LIKE IT?

YEAH. IT'S GREAT.

THERE ARE GAPS BETWEEN THE ROOF AND THE WALLS.

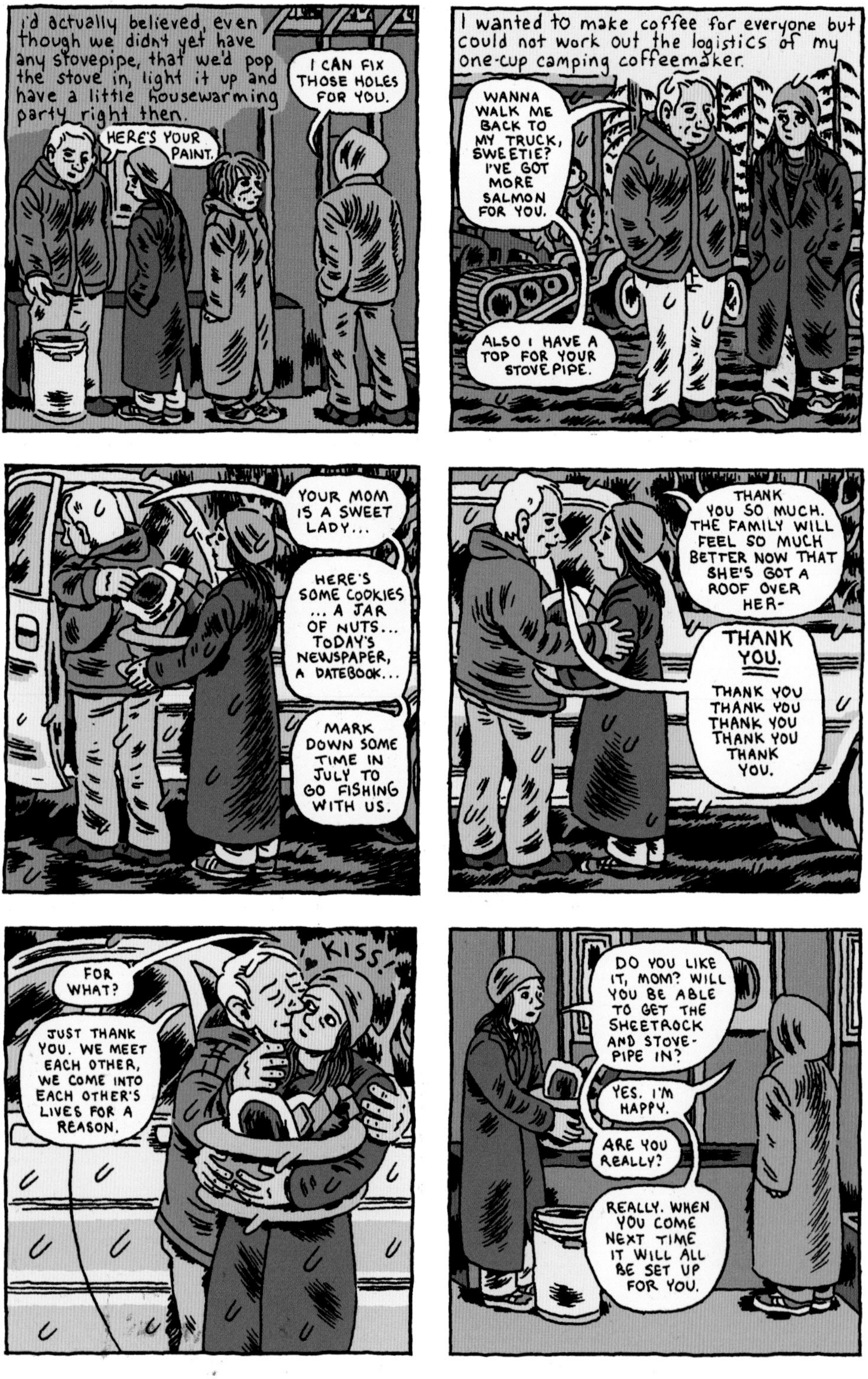
i'd actually believed, even though we didn't yet have any stovepipe, that we'd pop the stove in, light it up and have a little housewarming party right then.
HERE'S YOUR PAINT.
I CAN FIX THOSE HOLES FOR YOU.
I wanted to make coffee for everyone but could not work out the logistics of my one-cup camping coffeemaker.
WANNA WALK ME BACK TO MY TRUCK, SWEETIE? I'VE GOT MORE SALMON FOR YOU.
ALSO I HAVE A TOP FOR YOUR STOVEPIPE.
YOUR MOM IS A SWEET LADY...
HERE'S SOME COOKIES ... A JAR OF NUTS... TODAY'S NEWSPAPER, A DATEBOOK...
MARK DOWN SOME TIME IN JULY TO GO FISHING WITH US.
THANK YOU SO MUCH. THE FAMILY WILL FEEL SO MUCH BETTER NOW THAT SHE'S GOT A ROOF OVER HER-
THANK YOU.
THANK YOU THANK YOU THANK YOU THANK YOU THANK YOU.
FOR WHAT?
JUST THANK YOU. WE MEET EACH OTHER, WE COME INTO EACH OTHER'S LIVES FOR A REASON.
KISS!
DO YOU LIKE IT, MOM? WILL YOU BE ABLE TO GET THE SHEETROCK AND STOVE-PIPE IN?
YES. I'M HAPPY.
ARE YOU REALLY?
REALLY. WHEN YOU COME NEXT TIME IT WILL ALL BE SET UP FOR YOU.

Mothers

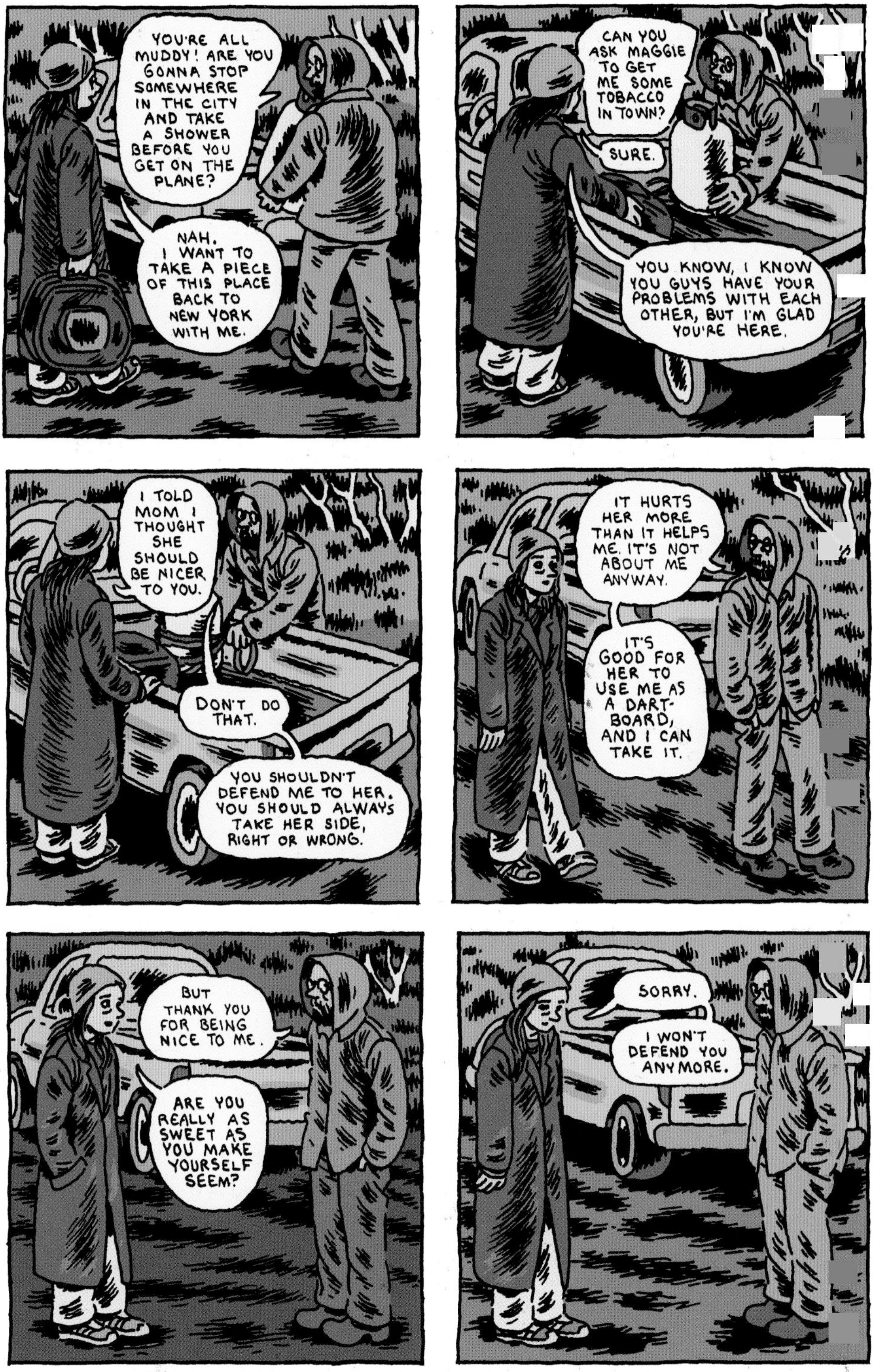
YOU'RE ALL MUDDY! ARE YOU GONNA STOP SOMEWHERE IN THE CITY AND TAKE A SHOWER BEFORE YOU GET ON THE PLANE?
NAH. I WANT TO TAKE A PIECE OF THIS PLACE BACK TO NEW YORK WITH ME.
CAN YOU ASK MAGGIE TO GET ME SOME TOBACCO IN TOWN?
SURE.
YOU KNOW, I KNOW YOU GUYS HAVE YOUR PROBLEMS WITH EACH OTHER, BUT I'M GLAD YOU'RE HERE.
I TOLD MOM I THOUGHT SHE SHOULD BE NICER TO YOU.
DON'T DO THAT.
YOU SHOULDN'T DEFEND ME TO HER. YOU SHOULD ALWAYS TAKE HER SIDE, RIGHT OR WRONG.
IT HURTS HER MORE THAN IT HELPS ME. IT'S NOT ABOUT ME ANYWAY.
IT'S GOOD FOR HER TO USE ME AS A DART-BOARD, AND I CAN TAKE IT.
BUT THANK YOU FOR BEING NICE TO ME.
ARE YOU REALLY AS SWEET AS YOU MAKE YOURSELF SEEM?
SORRY.
I WON'T DEFEND YOU ANYMORE.

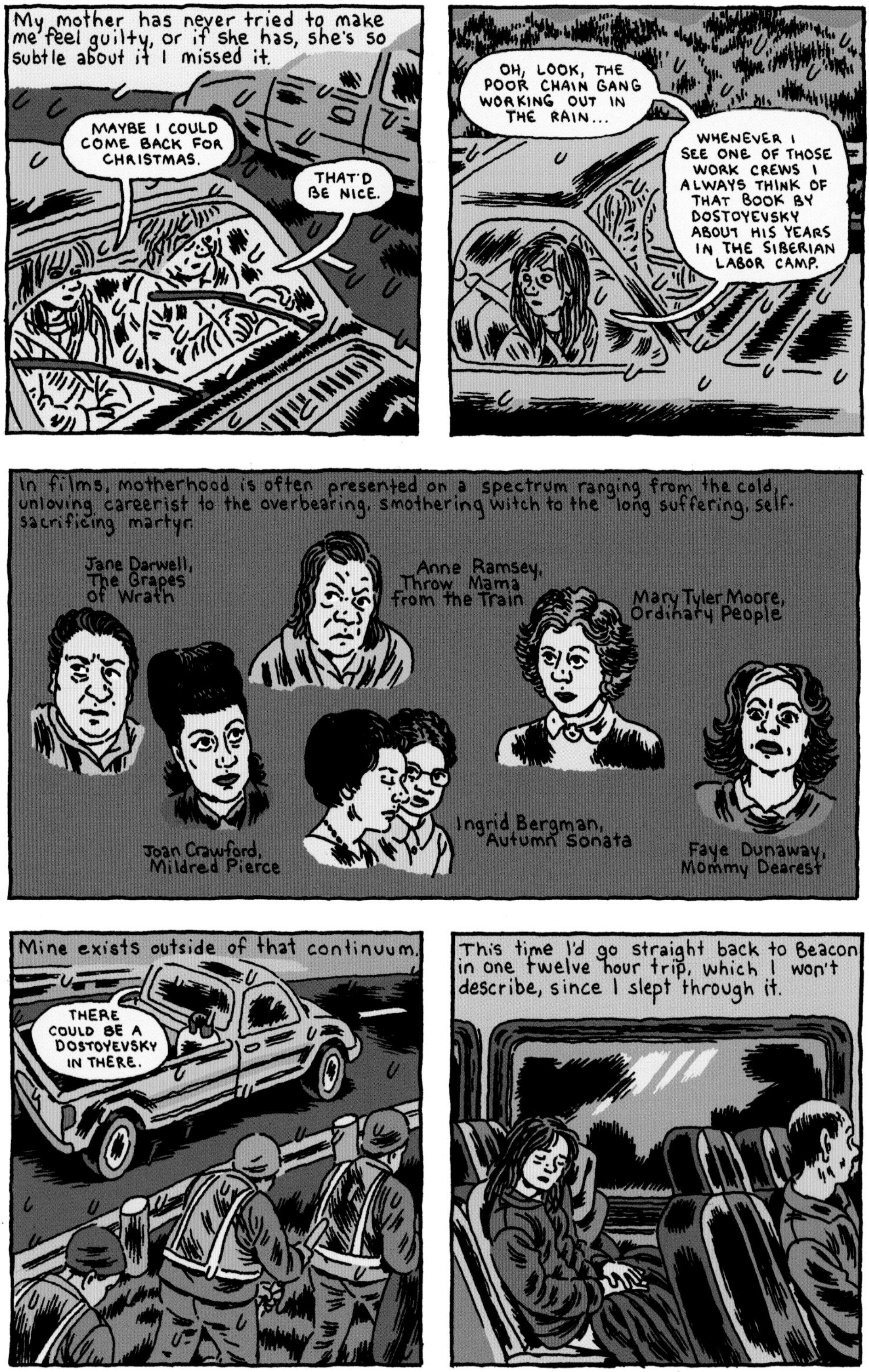
My mother has never tried to make me feel guilty, or if she has, she's so subtle about it I missed it.
MAYBE I COULD COME BACK FOR CHRISTMAS.
THAT'D BE NICE.
OH, LOOK, THE POOR CHAIN GANG WORKING OUT IN THE RAIN...
WHENEVER I SEE ONE OF THOSE WORK CREWS I ALWAYS THINK OF THAT BOOK BY DOSTOYEVSKY ABOUT HIS YEARS IN THE SIBERIAN LABOR CAMP.
In films, motherhood is often presented on a spectrum ranging from the cold, unloving careerist to the overbearing, smothering witch to the long suffering, self-sacrificing martyr.
Jane Darwell, The Grapes of Wrath
Anne Ramsey, Throw Mama from the Train
Mary Tyler Moore, Ordinary People
Joan Crawford, Mildred Pierce
Ingrid Bergman, Autumn Sonata
Faye Dunaway, Mommy Dearest
Mine exists outside of that continuum.
THERE COULD BE A DOSTOYEVSKY IN THERE.
This time I'd go straight back to Beacon in one twelve hour trip, which I won't describe, since I slept through it.

I'd Appreciate it
if you didn't

In Martinez it was 95 degrees. I'd just come from frigid Upstate New York and was overdressed.

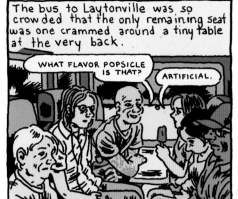

The bus to Laytonville was so crowded that the only remaining seat was one crammed around a tiny table at the very back.

WHAT FLAVOR POPSICLE IS THAT?

ARTIFICIAL.

We had a troublemaker among us.

HOW'S THE BOOK? IS IT GOOD?

IT'S ALL RIGHT.

I LIKE TO READ. I'VE READ TOM CLANCY, DEAN KOONTZ, STEPHEN KING...

I'VE READ THE BIBLE EIGHT TIMES.

THAT'S HOW MANY TIMES I'VE BEEN LOCKED UP.

YOU EVER READ THE SHACK?

I ONLY READ BOOKS BY WOMEN.

YOU LIKE WOMEN?

YES. BOOKS BY AND ABOUT WOMEN.

YOU LIKE PATRICIA CORNWALL?

NO.

Luckily we seemed to understand how to deal with him.

ANYONE WANNA TRACK DOWN A BITCH WITH ME AND FUCKIN' GIT ER?

HEY, MAN, CAN I USE YOUR PHONE?

Don't ignore him, don't encourage him.

HEY, MAN.

HMM?

CAN I USE YOUR PHONE?

SORRY, THIS IS JUST AN IPOD.

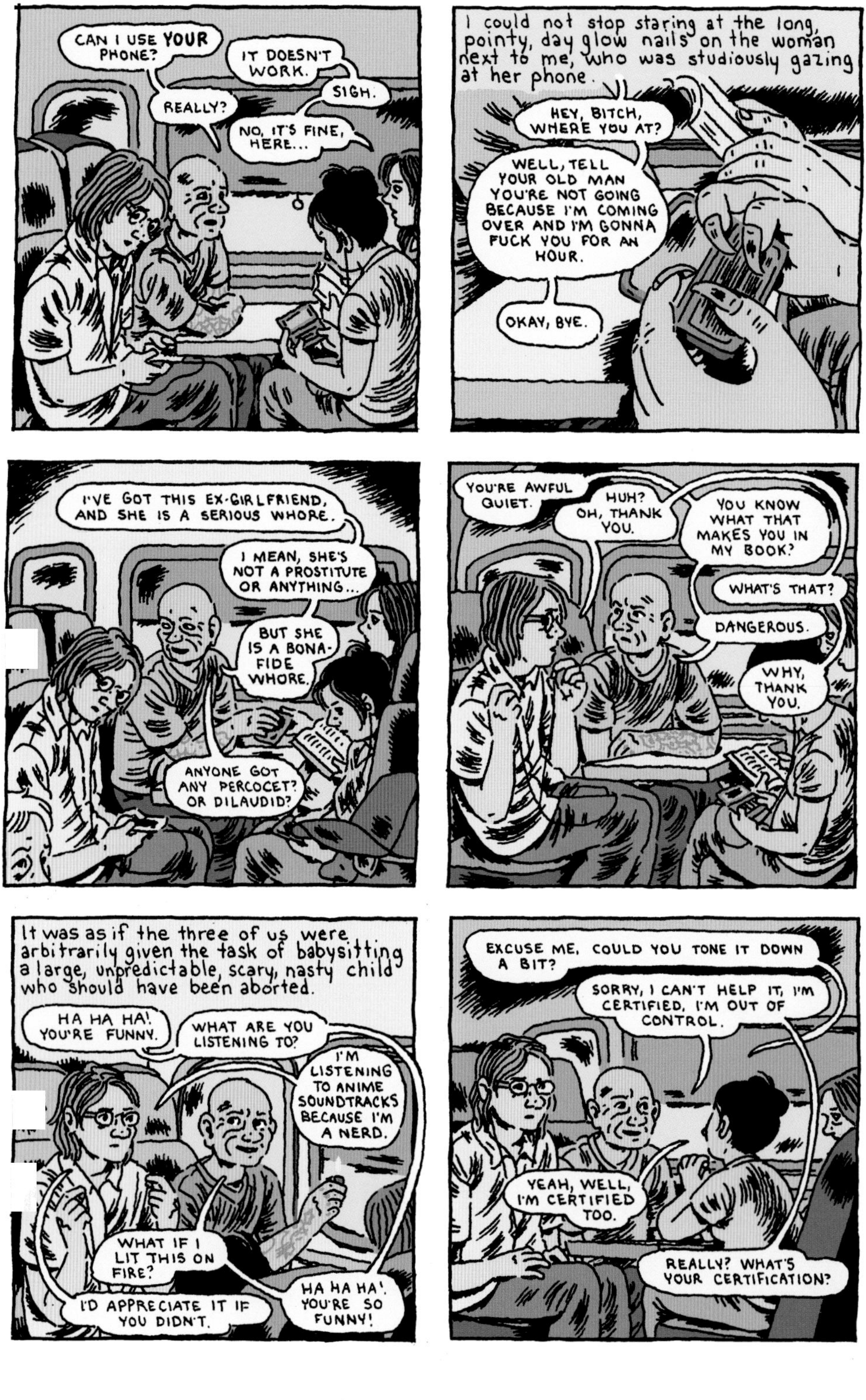
CAN I USE YOUR PHONE?
IT DOESN'T WORK.
SIGH.
REALLY?
NO, IT'S FINE, HERE...
I could not stop staring at the long, pointy, day glow nails on the woman next to me, who was studiously gazing at her phone.
HEY, BITCH, WHERE YOU AT?
WELL, TELL YOUR OLD MAN YOU'RE NOT GOING BECAUSE I'M COMING OVER AND I'M GONNA FUCK YOU FOR AN HOUR.
OKAY, BYE.
I'VE GOT THIS EX-GIRLFRIEND, AND SHE IS A SERIOUS WHORE.
I MEAN, SHE'S NOT A PROSTITUTE OR ANYTHING...
BUT SHE IS A BONA-FIDE WHORE.
ANYONE GOT ANY PERCOCET? OR DILAUDID?
YOU'RE AWFUL QUIET.
HUH? OH, THANK YOU.
YOU KNOW WHAT THAT MAKES YOU IN MY BOOK?
WHAT'S THAT?
DANGEROUS.
WHY, THANK YOU.
It was as if the three of us were arbitrarily given the task of babysitting a large, unpredictable, scary, nasty child who should have been aborted.
HA HA HA! YOU'RE FUNNY.
WHAT ARE YOU LISTENING TO?
I'M LISTENING TO ANIME SOUNDTRACKS BECAUSE I'M A NERD.
WHAT IF I LIT THIS ON FIRE?
I'D APPRECIATE IT IF YOU DIDN'T.
HA HA HA! YOU'RE SO FUNNY!
EXCUSE ME, COULD YOU TONE IT DOWN A BIT?
SORRY, I CAN'T HELP IT, I'M CERTIFIED, I'M OUT OF CONTROL.
YEAH, WELL, I'M CERTIFIED TOO.
REALLY? WHAT'S YOUR CERTIFICATION?

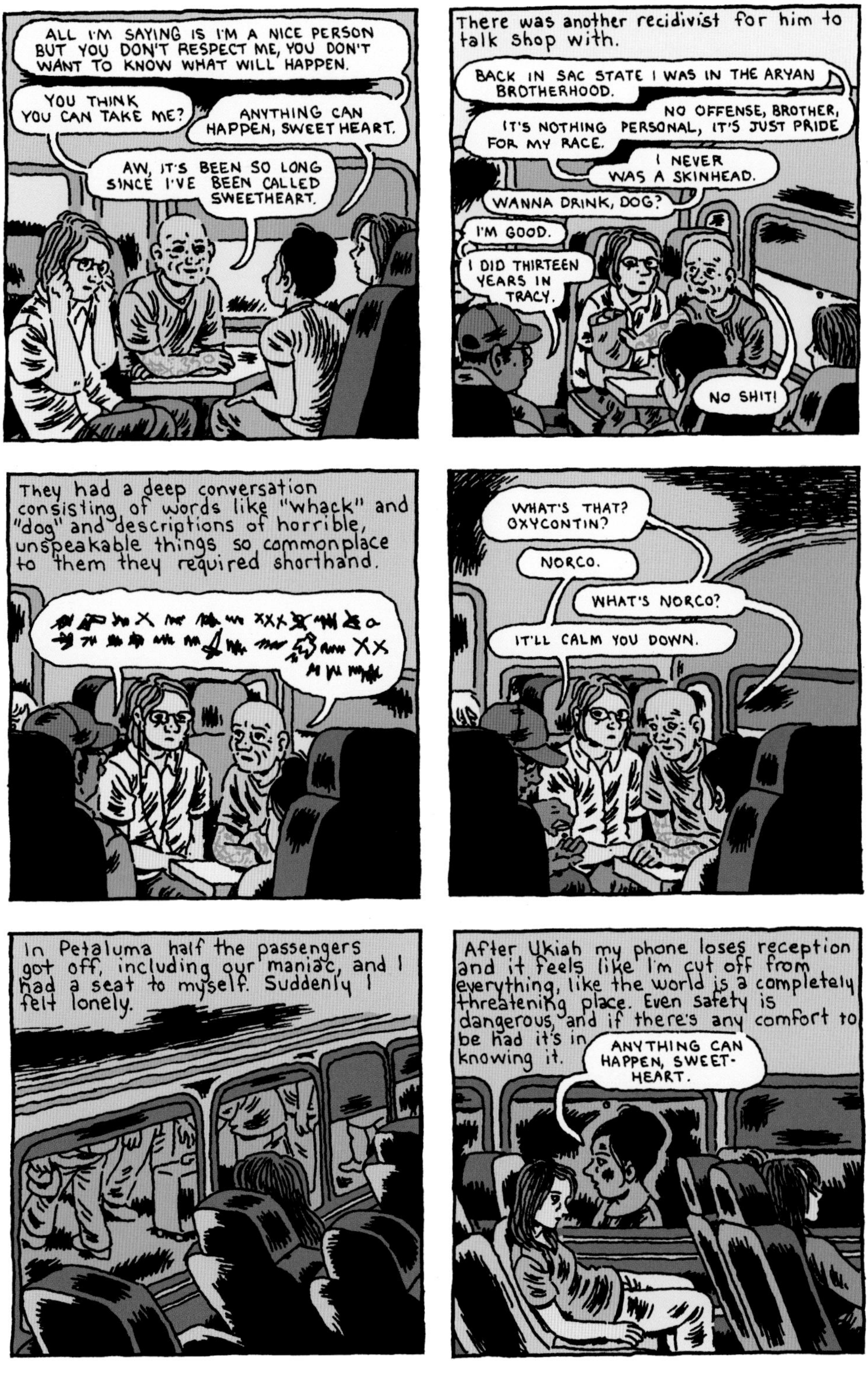
ALL I'M SAYING IS I'M A NICE PERSON BUT YOU DON'T RESPECT ME, YOU DON'T WANT TO KNOW WHAT WILL HAPPEN.
YOU THINK YOU CAN TAKE ME?
ANYTHING CAN HAPPEN, SWEET HEART.
AW, IT'S BEEN SO LONG SINCE I'VE BEEN CALLED SWEETHEART.
There was another recidivist for him to talk shop with.
BACK IN SAC STATE I WAS IN THE ARYAN BROTHERHOOD.
NO OFFENSE, BROTHER, IT'S NOTHING PERSONAL, IT'S JUST PRIDE FOR MY RACE.
I NEVER WAS A SKINHEAD.
WANNA DRINK, DOG?
I'M GOOD.
I DID THIRTEEN YEARS IN TRACY.
NO SHIT!
They had a deep conversation consisting of words like "whack" and "dog" and descriptions of horrible, unspeakable things so commonplace to them they required shorthand.
WHAT'S THAT? OXYCONTIN?
NORCO.
WHAT'S NORCO?
IT'LL CALM YOU DOWN.
In Petaluma half the passengers got off, including our maniac, and I had a seat to myself. Suddenly I felt lonely.
After Ukiah my phone loses reception and it feels like I'm cut off from everything, like the world is a completely threatening place. Even safety is dangerous, and if there's any comfort to be had it's in knowing it.
ANYTHING CAN HAPPEN, SWEET-HEART.

Tannerite

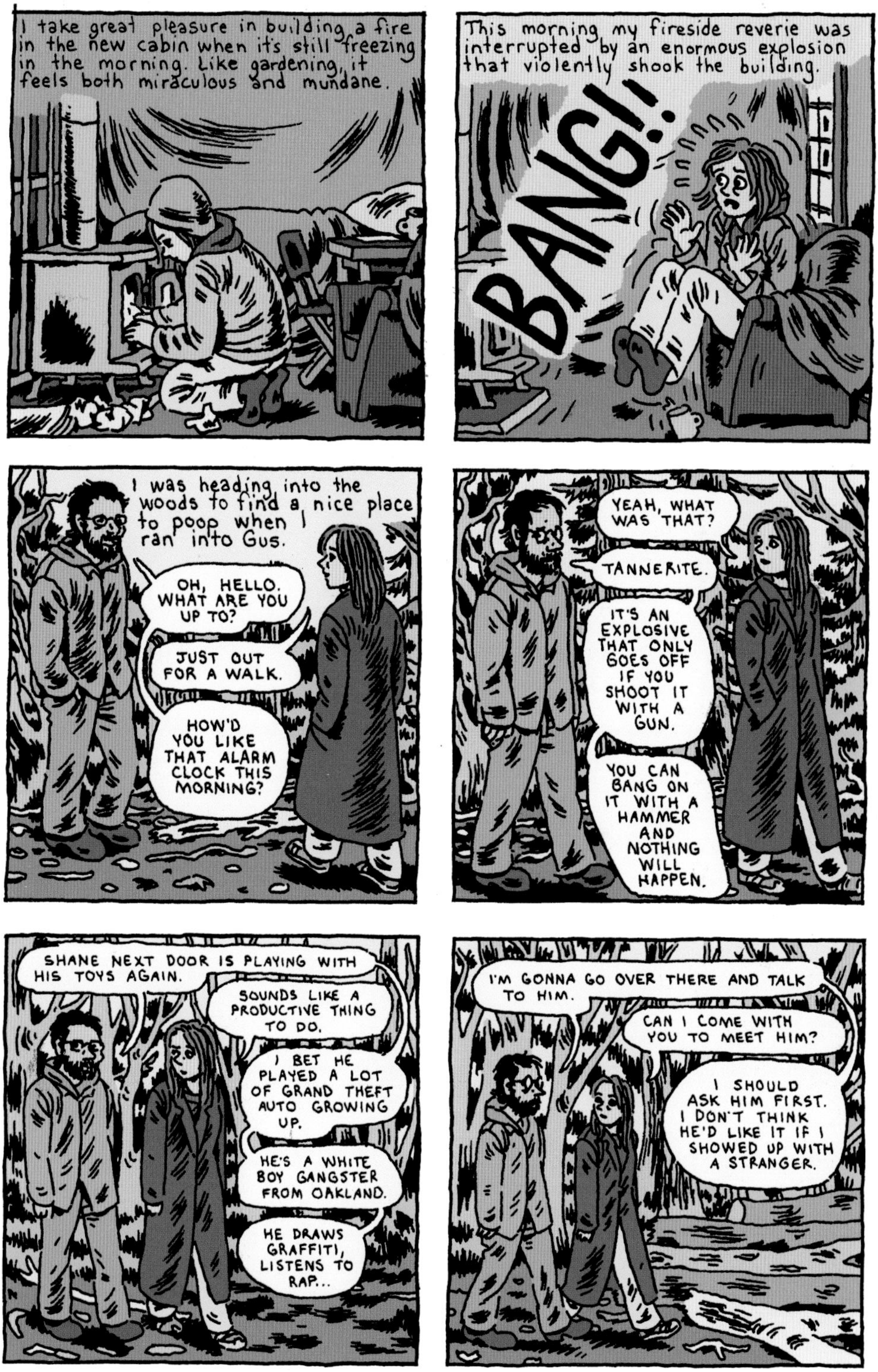

I take great pleasure in building a fire in the new cabin when it's still freezing in the morning. Like gardening, it feels both miraculous and mundane.
This morning my fireside reverie was interrupted by an enormous explosion that violently shook the building.
BANG!!
I was heading into the woods to find a nice place to poop when I ran into Gus.
OH, HELLO. WHAT ARE YOU UP TO?
JUST OUT FOR A WALK.
HOW'D YOU LIKE THAT ALARM CLOCK THIS MORNING?
YEAH, WHAT WAS THAT?
TANNERITE.
IT'S AN EXPLOSIVE THAT ONLY GOES OFF IF YOU SHOOT IT WITH A GUN.
YOU CAN BANG ON IT WITH A HAMMER AND NOTHING WILL HAPPEN.
SHANE NEXT DOOR IS PLAYING WITH HIS TOYS AGAIN.
SOUNDS LIKE A PRODUCTIVE THING TO DO.
I BET HE PLAYED A LOT OF GRAND THEFT AUTO GROWING UP.
HE'S A WHITE BOY GANGSTER FROM OAKLAND.
HE DRAWS GRAFFITI, LISTENS TO RAP...
I'M GONNA GO OVER THERE AND TALK TO HIM.
CAN I COME WITH YOU TO MEET HIM?
I SHOULD ASK HIM FIRST. I DON'T THINK HE'D LIKE IT IF I SHOWED UP WITH A STRANGER.

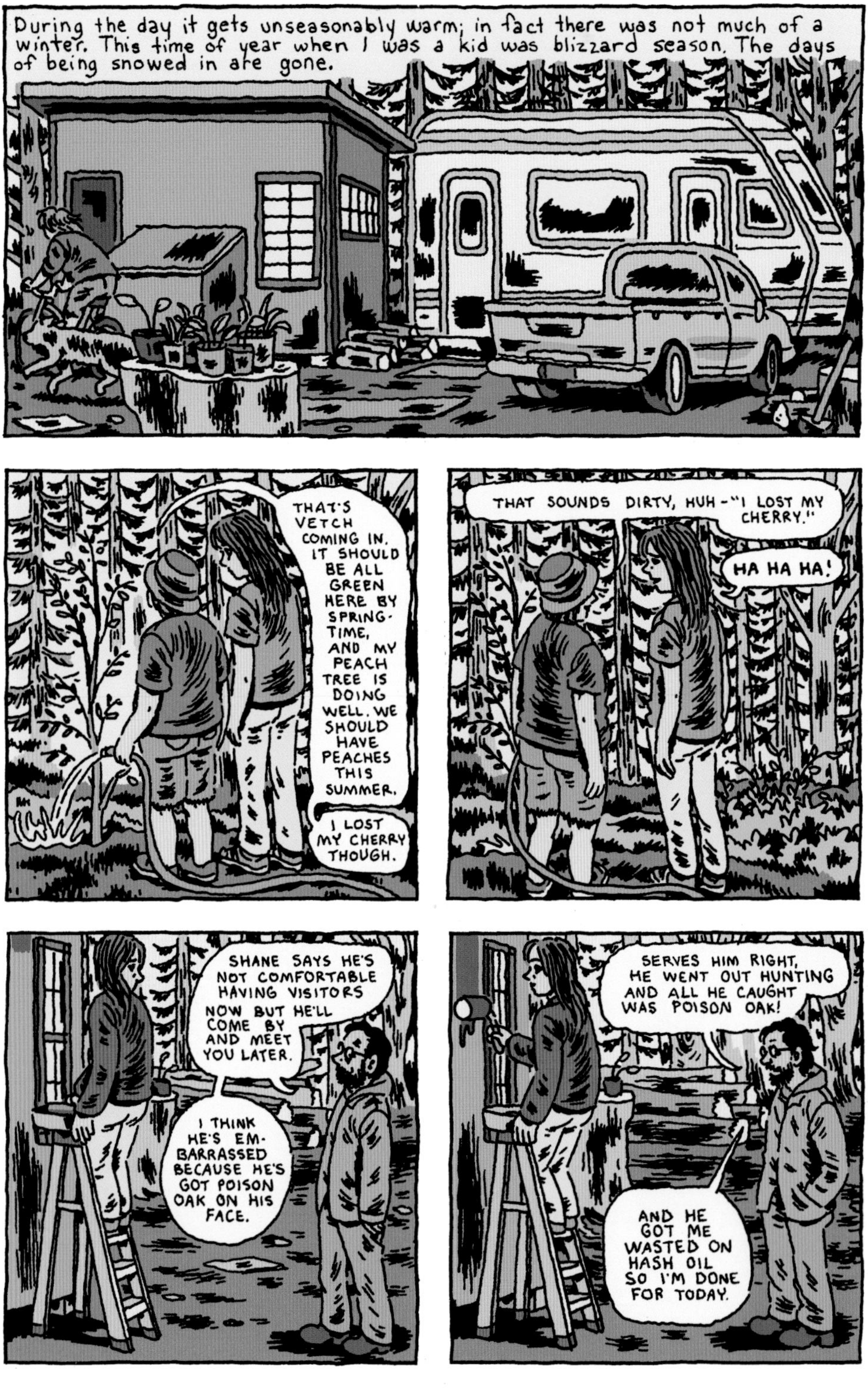
During the day it gets unseasonably warm; in fact there was not much of a winter. This time of year when I was a kid was blizzard season. The days of being snowed in are gone.
THAT'S VETCH COMING IN. IT SHOULD BE ALL GREEN HERE BY SPRING-TIME, AND MY PEACH TREE IS DOING WELL. WE SHOULD HAVE PEACHES THIS SUMMER.
I LOST MY CHERRY THOUGH.
THAT SOUNDS DIRTY, HUH - "I LOST MY CHERRY."
HA HA HA!
SHANE SAYS HE'S NOT COMFORTABLE HAVING VISITORS NOW BUT HE'LL COME BY AND MEET YOU LATER.
I THINK HE'S EM-BARRASSED BECAUSE HE'S GOT POISON OAK ON HIS FACE.
SERVES HIM RIGHT, HE WENT OUT HUNTING AND ALL HE CAUGHT WAS POISON OAK!
AND HE GOT ME WASTED ON HASH OIL SO I'M DONE FOR TODAY.

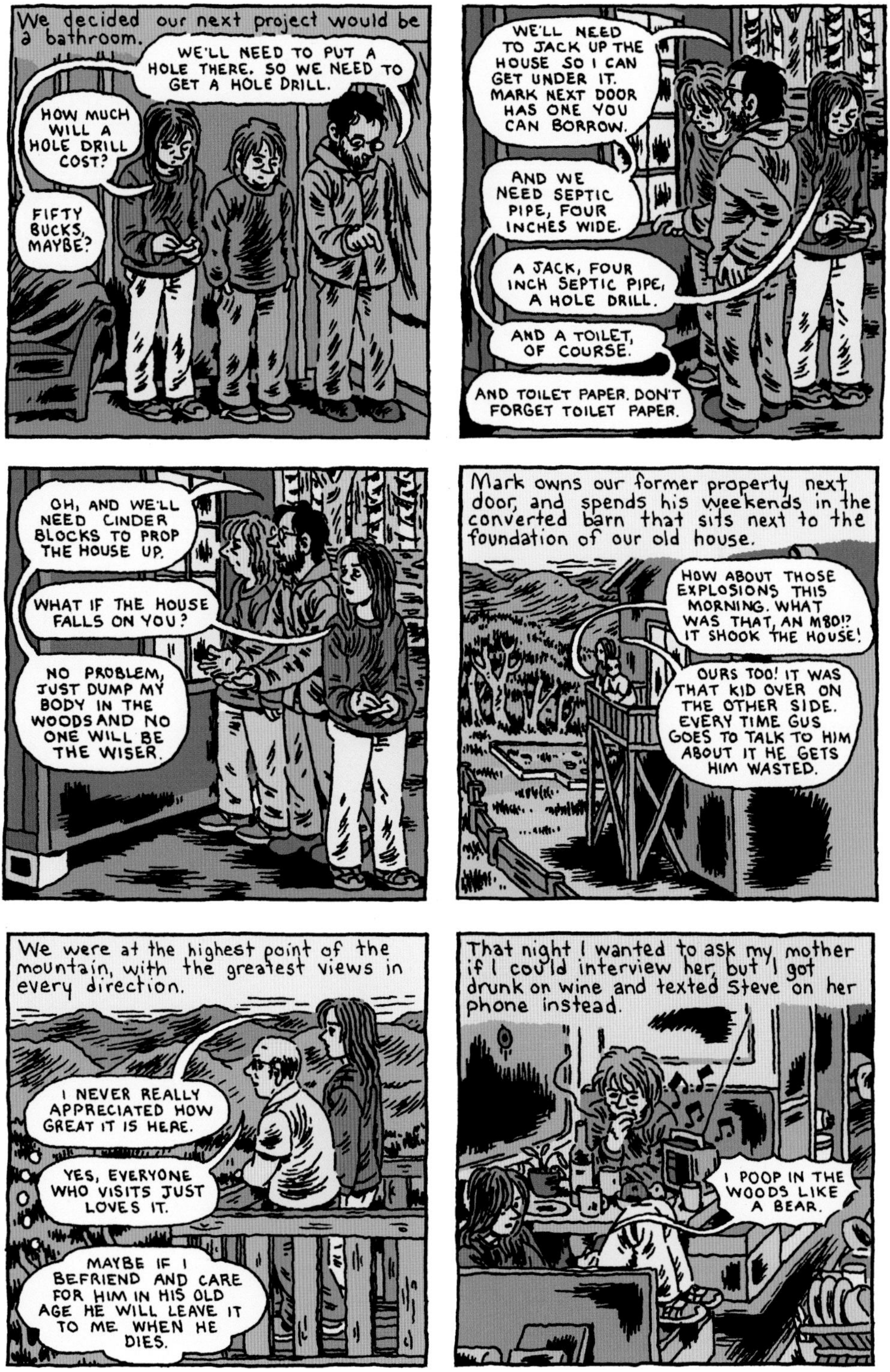
We decided our next project would be a bathroom.
WE'LL NEED TO PUT A HOLE THERE. SO WE NEED TO GET A HOLE DRILL.
HOW MUCH WILL A HOLE DRILL COST?
FIFTY BUCKS, MAYBE?
WE'LL NEED TO JACK UP THE HOUSE SO I CAN GET UNDER IT. MARK NEXT DOOR HAS ONE YOU CAN BORROW.
AND WE NEED SEPTIC PIPE, FOUR INCHES WIDE.
A JACK, FOUR INCH SEPTIC PIPE, A HOLE DRILL.
AND A TOILET, OF COURSE.
AND TOILET PAPER. DON'T FORGET TOILET PAPER.
OH, AND WE'LL NEED CINDER BLOCKS TO PROP THE HOUSE UP.
WHAT IF THE HOUSE FALLS ON YOU?
NO PROBLEM, JUST DUMP MY BODY IN THE WOODS AND NO ONE WILL BE THE WISER.
Mark owns our former property next door, and spends his weekends in the converted barn that sits next to the foundation of our old house.
HOW ABOUT THOSE EXPLOSIONS THIS MORNING. WHAT WAS THAT, AN M80!? IT SHOOK THE HOUSE!
OURS TOO! IT WAS THAT KID OVER ON THE OTHER SIDE. EVERY TIME GUS GOES TO TALK TO HIM ABOUT IT HE GETS HIM WASTED.
We were at the highest point of the mountain, with the greatest views in every direction.
I NEVER REALLY APPRECIATED HOW GREAT IT IS HERE.
YES, EVERYONE WHO VISITS JUST LOVES IT.
MAYBE IF I BEFRIEND AND CARE FOR HIM IN HIS OLD AGE HE WILL LEAVE IT TO ME WHEN HE DIES.
That night I wanted to ask my mother if I could interview her, but I got drunk on wine and texted Steve on her phone instead.
I POOP IN THE WOODS LIKE A BEAR.

Talk to the Caulk

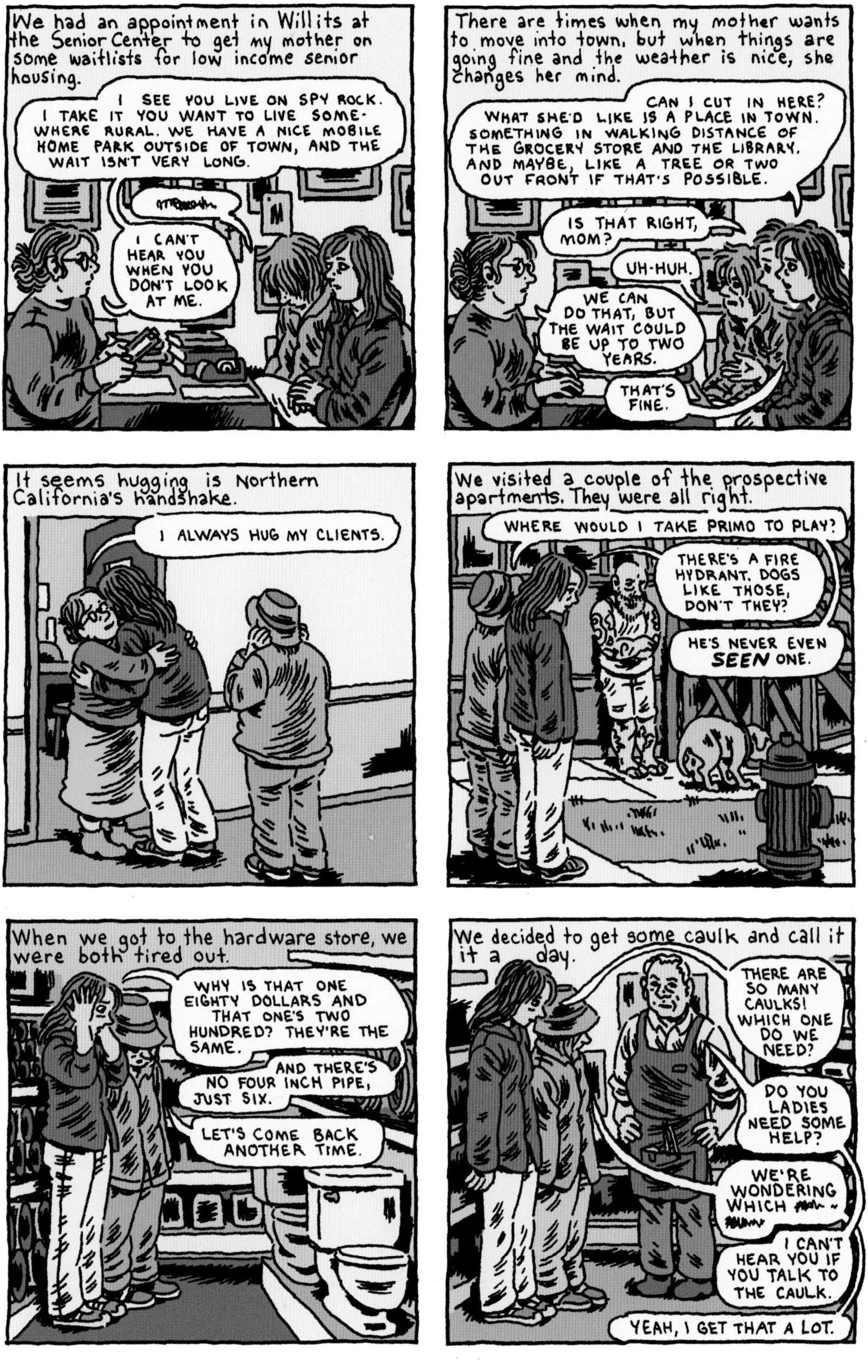

We had an appointment in Willits at the Senior Center to get my mother on some waitlists for low income senior housing.
I SEE YOU LIVE ON SPY ROCK. I TAKE IT YOU WANT TO LIVE SOMEWHERE RURAL. WE HAVE A NICE MOBILE HOME PARK OUTSIDE OF TOWN, AND THE WAIT ISN'T VERY LONG.
I CAN'T HEAR YOU WHEN YOU DON'T LOOK AT ME.
There are times when my mother wants to move into town, but when things are going fine and the weather is nice, she changes her mind.
CAN I CUT IN HERE? WHAT SHE'D LIKE IS A PLACE IN TOWN. SOMETHING IN WALKING DISTANCE OF THE GROCERY STORE AND THE LIBRARY. AND MAYBE, LIKE A TREE OR TWO OUT FRONT IF THAT'S POSSIBLE.
IS THAT RIGHT, MOM?
UH-HUH.
WE CAN DO THAT, BUT THE WAIT COULD BE UP TO TWO YEARS.
THAT'S FINE.
It seems hugging is Northern California's handshake.
I ALWAYS HUG MY CLIENTS.
We visited a couple of the prospective apartments. They were all right.
WHERE WOULD I TAKE PRIMO TO PLAY?
THERE'S A FIRE HYDRANT. DOGS LIKE THOSE, DON'T THEY?
HE'S NEVER EVEN SEEN ONE.
When we got to the hardware store, we were both tired out.
WHY IS THAT ONE EIGHTY DOLLARS AND THAT ONE'S TWO HUNDRED? THEY'RE THE SAME.
AND THERE'S NO FOUR INCH PIPE, JUST SIX.
LET'S COME BACK ANOTHER TIME.
We decided to get some caulk and call it it a day.
THERE ARE SO MANY CAULKS! WHICH ONE DO WE NEED?
DO YOU LADIES NEED SOME HELP?
WE'RE WONDERING WHICH
I CAN'T HEAR YOU IF YOU TALK TO THE CAULK.
YEAH, I GET THAT A LOT.

Graffiti Artist

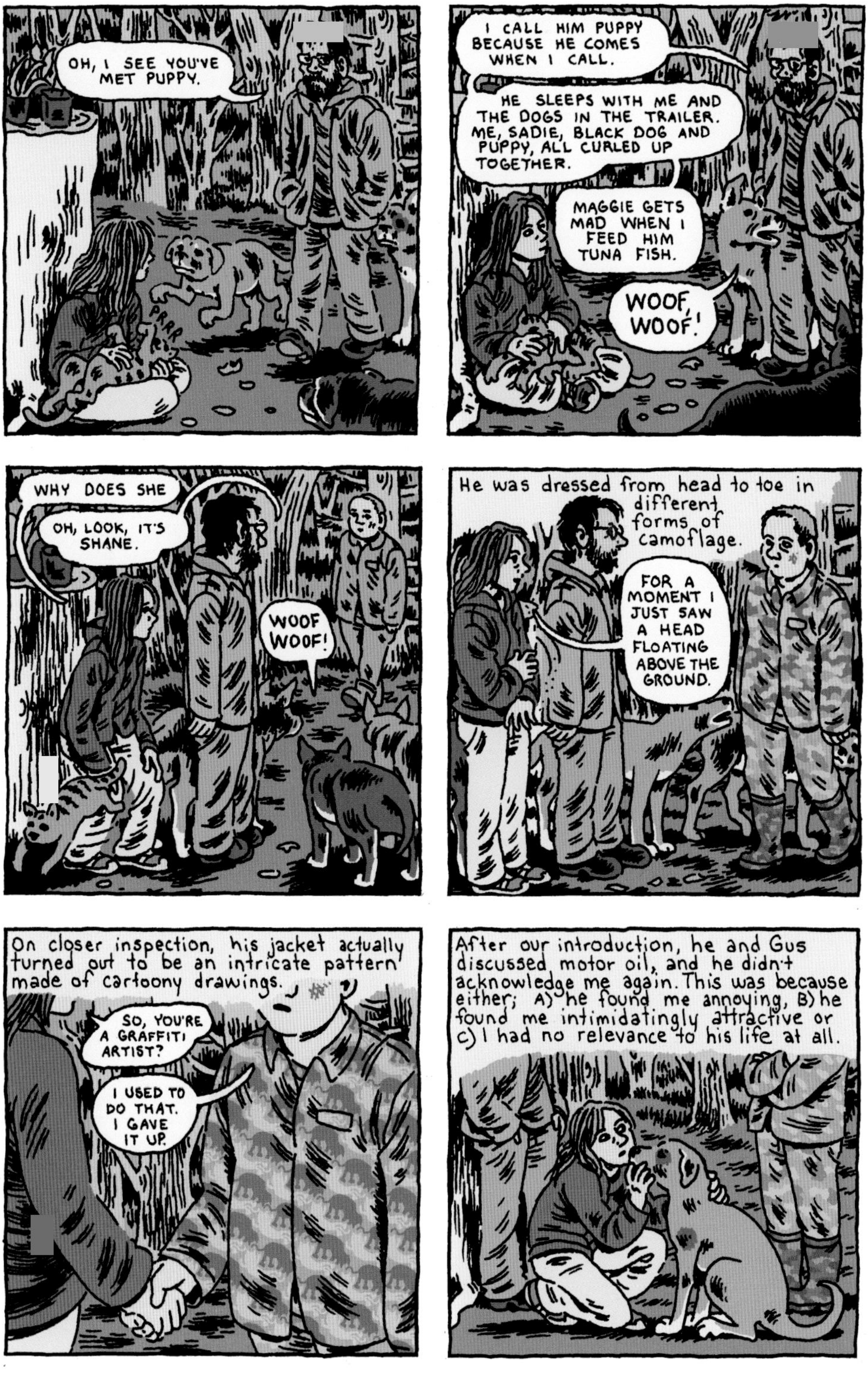
OH, I SEE YOU'VE MET PUPPY.
PRRR
I CALL HIM PUPPY BECAUSE HE COMES WHEN I CALL.
HE SLEEPS WITH ME AND THE DOGS IN THE TRAILER. ME, SADIE, BLACK DOG AND PUPPY, ALL CURLED UP TOGETHER.
MAGGIE GETS MAD WHEN I FEED HIM TUNA FISH.
WOOF, WOOF!
WHY DOES SHE
OH, LOOK, IT'S SHANE.
WOOF WOOF!
He was dressed from head to toe in different forms of camoflage.
FOR A MOMENT I JUST SAW A HEAD FLOATING ABOVE THE GROUND.
On closer inspection, his jacket actually turned out to be an intricate pattern made of cartoony drawings.
SO, YOU'RE A GRAFFITI ARTIST?
I USED TO DO THAT. I GAVE IT UP.
After our introduction, he and Gus discussed motor oil, and he didn't acknowledge me again. This was because either; A) he found me annoying, B) he found me intimidatingly attractive or c) I had no relevance to his life at all.

The Interview, Part two

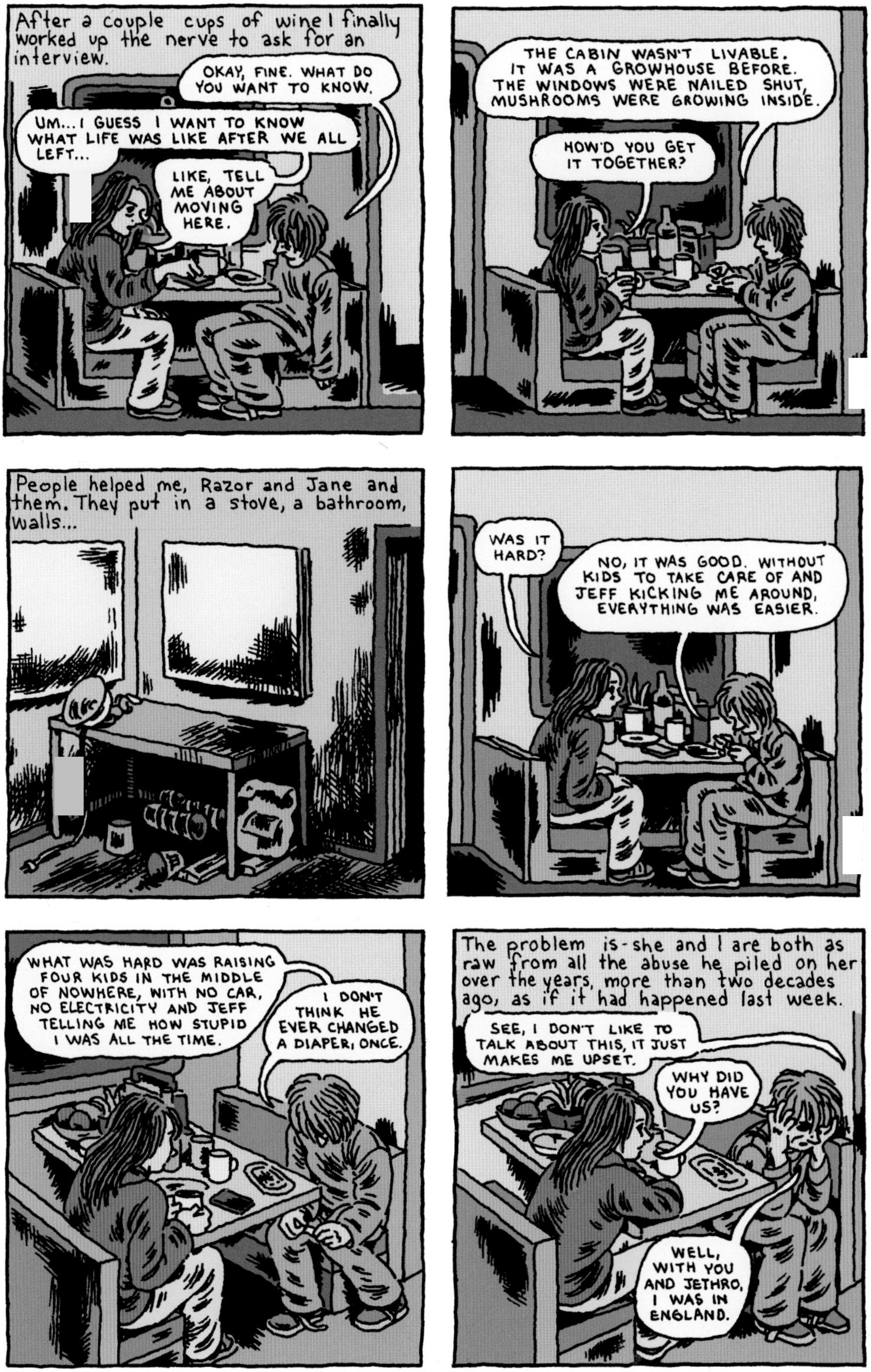

After a couple cups of wine I finally worked up the nerve to ask for an interview.
OKAY, FINE. WHAT DO YOU WANT TO KNOW.
UM...I GUESS I WANT TO KNOW WHAT LIFE WAS LIKE AFTER WE ALL LEFT...
LIKE, TELL ME ABOUT MOVING HERE.
THE CABIN WASN'T LIVABLE. IT WAS A GROWHOUSE BEFORE. THE WINDOWS WERE NAILED SHUT, MUSHROOMS WERE GROWING INSIDE.
HOW'D YOU GET IT TOGETHER?
People helped me, Razor and Jane and them. They put in a stove, a bathroom, walls...
WAS IT HARD?
NO, IT WAS GOOD. WITHOUT KIDS TO TAKE CARE OF AND JEFF KICKING ME AROUND, EVERYTHING WAS EASIER.
WHAT WAS HARD WAS RAISING FOUR KIDS IN THE MIDDLE OF NOWHERE, WITH NO CAR, NO ELECTRICITY AND JEFF TELLING ME HOW STUPID I WAS ALL THE TIME.
I DON'T THINK HE EVER CHANGED A DIAPER, ONCE.
The problem is-she and I are both as raw from all the abuse he piled on her over the years, more than two decades ago, as if it had happened last week.
SEE, I DON'T LIKE TO TALK ABOUT THIS, IT JUST MAKES ME UPSET.
WHY DID YOU HAVE US?
WELL, WITH YOU AND JETHRO, I WAS IN ENGLAND.

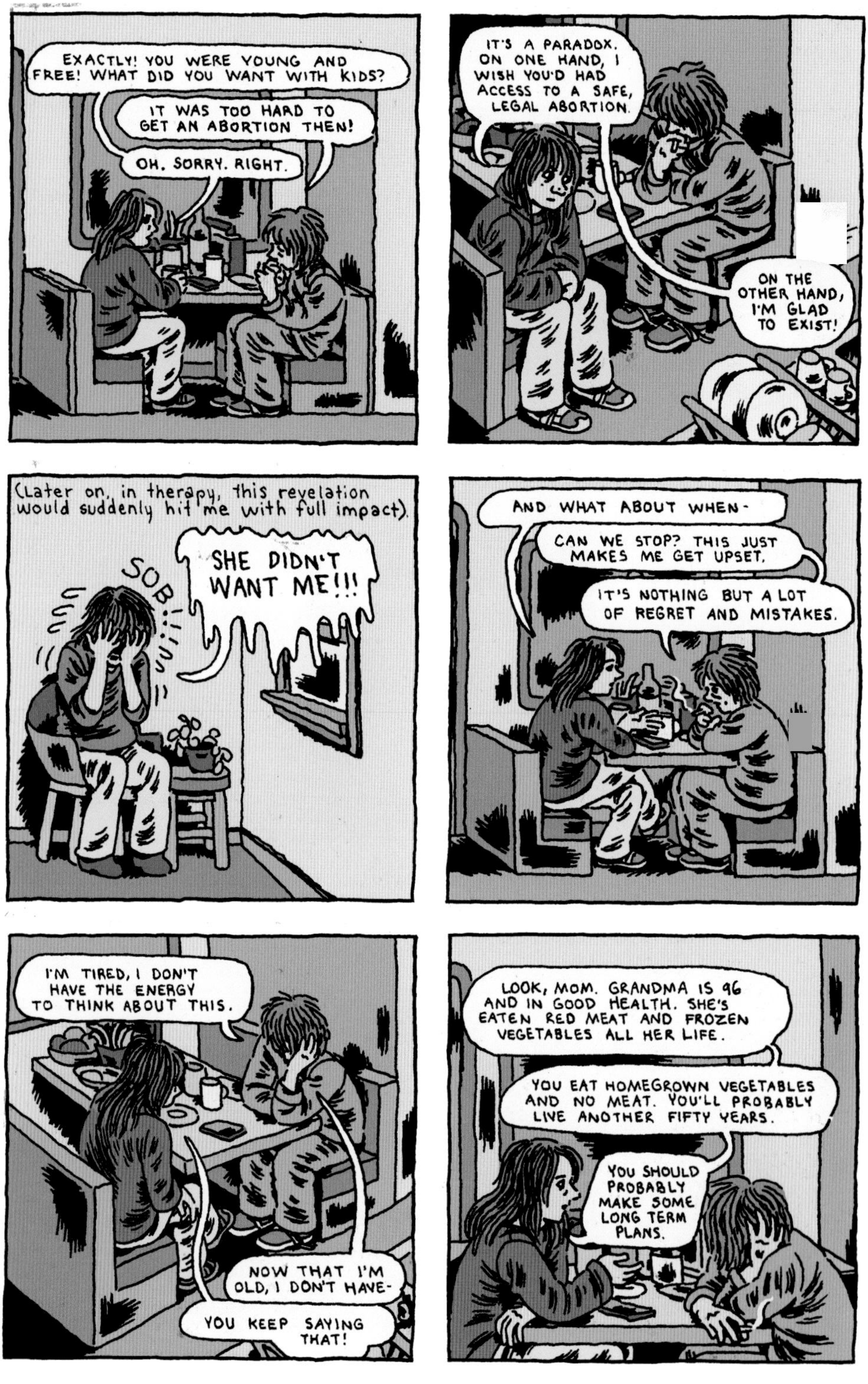
EXACTLY! YOU WERE YOUNG AND FREE! WHAT DID YOU WANT WITH KIDS?
IT WAS TOO HARD TO GET AN ABORTION THEN!
OH. SORRY. RIGHT.
IT'S A PARADOX. ON ONE HAND, I WISH YOU'D HAD ACCESS TO A SAFE, LEGAL ABORTION.
ON THE OTHER HAND, I'M GLAD TO EXIST!
(Later on, in therapy, this revelation would suddenly hit me with full impact).
SOB
SHE DIDN'T WANT ME!!!
AND WHAT ABOUT WHEN-
CAN WE STOP? THIS JUST MAKES ME GET UPSET.
IT'S NOTHING BUT A LOT OF REGRET AND MISTAKES.
I'M TIRED, I DON'T HAVE THE ENERGY TO THINK ABOUT THIS.
NOW THAT I'M OLD, I DON'T HAVE-
YOU KEEP SAYING THAT!
LOOK, MOM. GRANDMA IS 96 AND IN GOOD HEALTH. SHE'S EATEN RED MEAT AND FROZEN VEGETABLES ALL HER LIFE.
YOU EAT HOMEGROWN VEGETABLES AND NO MEAT. YOU'LL PROBABLY LIVE ANOTHER FIFTY YEARS.
YOU SHOULD PROBABLY MAKE SOME LONG TERM PLANS.

Tuna Fish
Mystery, Solved

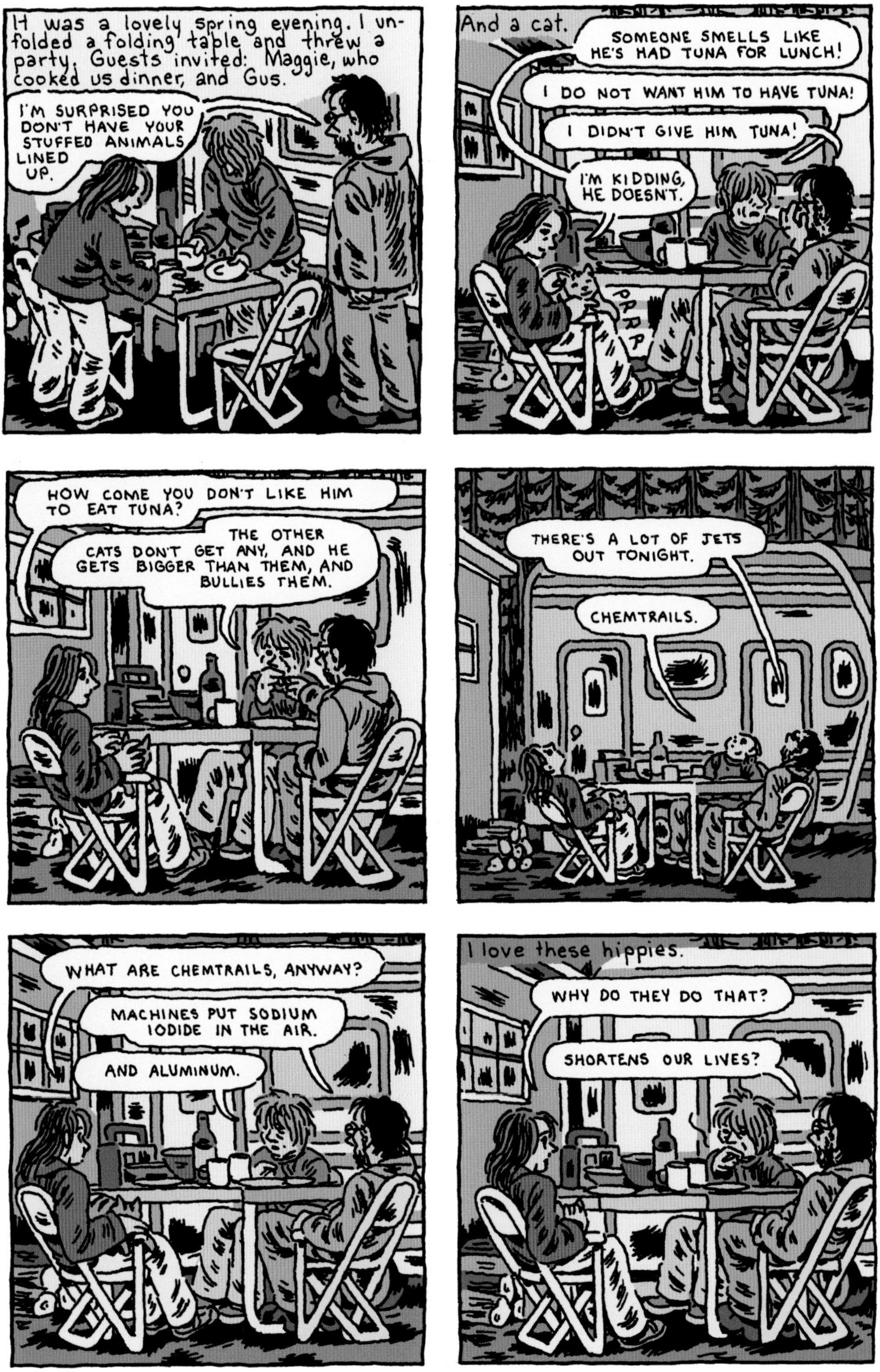
It was a lovely spring evening. I unfolded a folding table and threw a party. Guests invited: Maggie, who cooked us dinner, and Gus.
I'M SURPRISED YOU DON'T HAVE YOUR STUFFED ANIMALS LINED UP.
And a cat.
SOMEONE SMELLS LIKE HE'S HAD TUNA FOR LUNCH!
I DO NOT WANT HIM TO HAVE TUNA!
I DIDN'T GIVE HIM TUNA!
I'M KIDDING, HE DOESN'T.
PRRP
HOW COME YOU DON'T LIKE HIM TO EAT TUNA?
THE OTHER CATS DON'T GET ANY, AND HE GETS BIGGER THAN THEM, AND BULLIES THEM.
THERE'S A LOT OF JETS OUT TONIGHT.
CHEMTRAILS.
WHAT ARE CHEMTRAILS, ANYWAY?
MACHINES PUT SODIUM IODIDE IN THE AIR.
AND ALUMINUM.
I love these hippies.
WHY DO THEY DO THAT?
SHORTENS OUR LIVES?

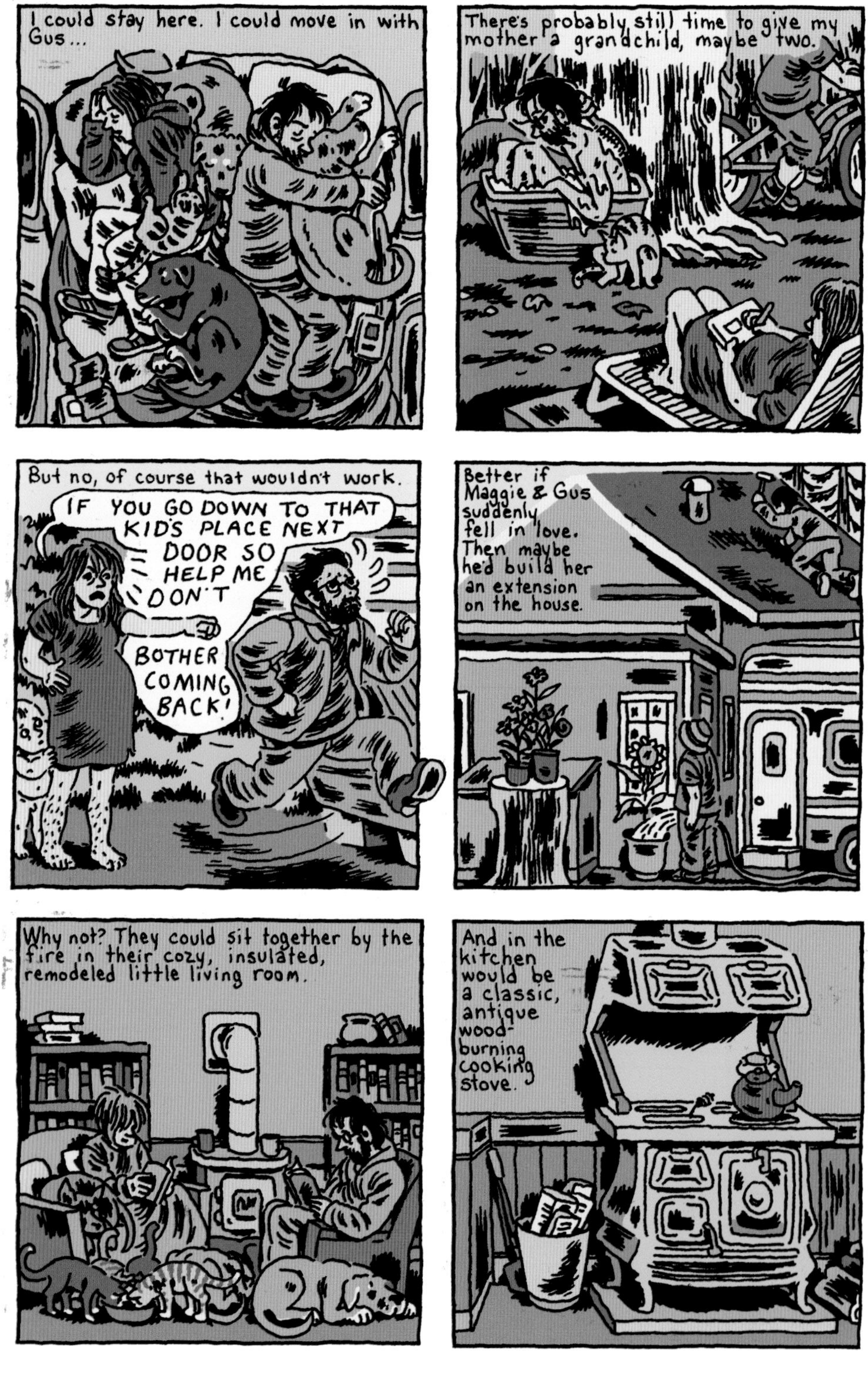
I could stay here. I could move in with Gus...
There's probably still time to give my mother a grandchild, maybe two.
But no, of course that wouldn't work.
IF YOU GO DOWN TO THAT KID'S PLACE NEXT DOOR SO HELP ME DON'T BOTHER COMING BACK!
Better if Maggie & Gus suddenly fell in love. Then maybe he'd build her an extension on the house.
Why not? They could sit together by the fire in their cozy, insulated, remodeled little living room.
And in the kitchen would be a classic, antique wood-burning cooking stove.

Mistakes

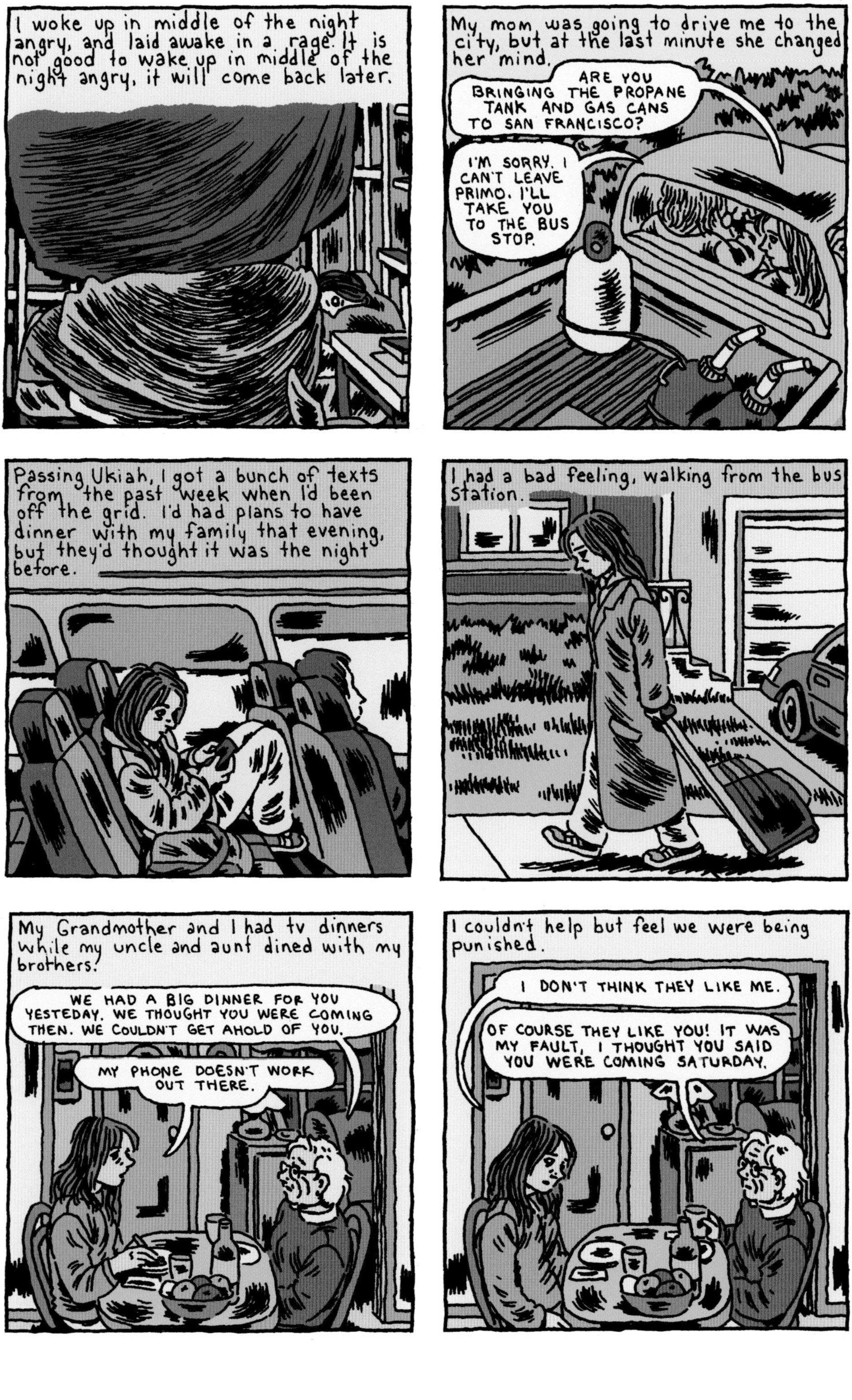
I woke up in middle of the night angry, and laid awake in a rage. It is not good to wake up in middle of the night angry, it will come back later.
My mom was going to drive me to the city, but at the last minute she changed her mind.
ARE YOU BRINGING THE PROPANE TANK AND GAS CANS TO SAN FRANCISCO?
I'M SORRY. I CAN'T LEAVE PRIMO. I'LL TAKE YOU TO THE BUS STOP.
Passing Ukiah, I got a bunch of texts from the past week when I'd been off the grid. I'd had plans to have dinner with my family that evening, but they'd thought it was the night before.
I had a bad feeling, walking from the bus station.
My Grandmother and I had tv dinners while my uncle and aunt dined with my brothers.
WE HAD A BIG DINNER FOR YOU YESTEDAY. WE THOUGHT YOU WERE COMING THEN. WE COULDN'T GET AHOLD OF YOU.
MY PHONE DOESN'T WORK OUT THERE.
I couldn't help but feel we were being punished.
I DON'T THINK THEY LIKE ME.
OF COURSE THEY LIKE YOU! IT WAS MY FAULT, I THOUGHT YOU SAID YOU WERE COMING SATURDAY.

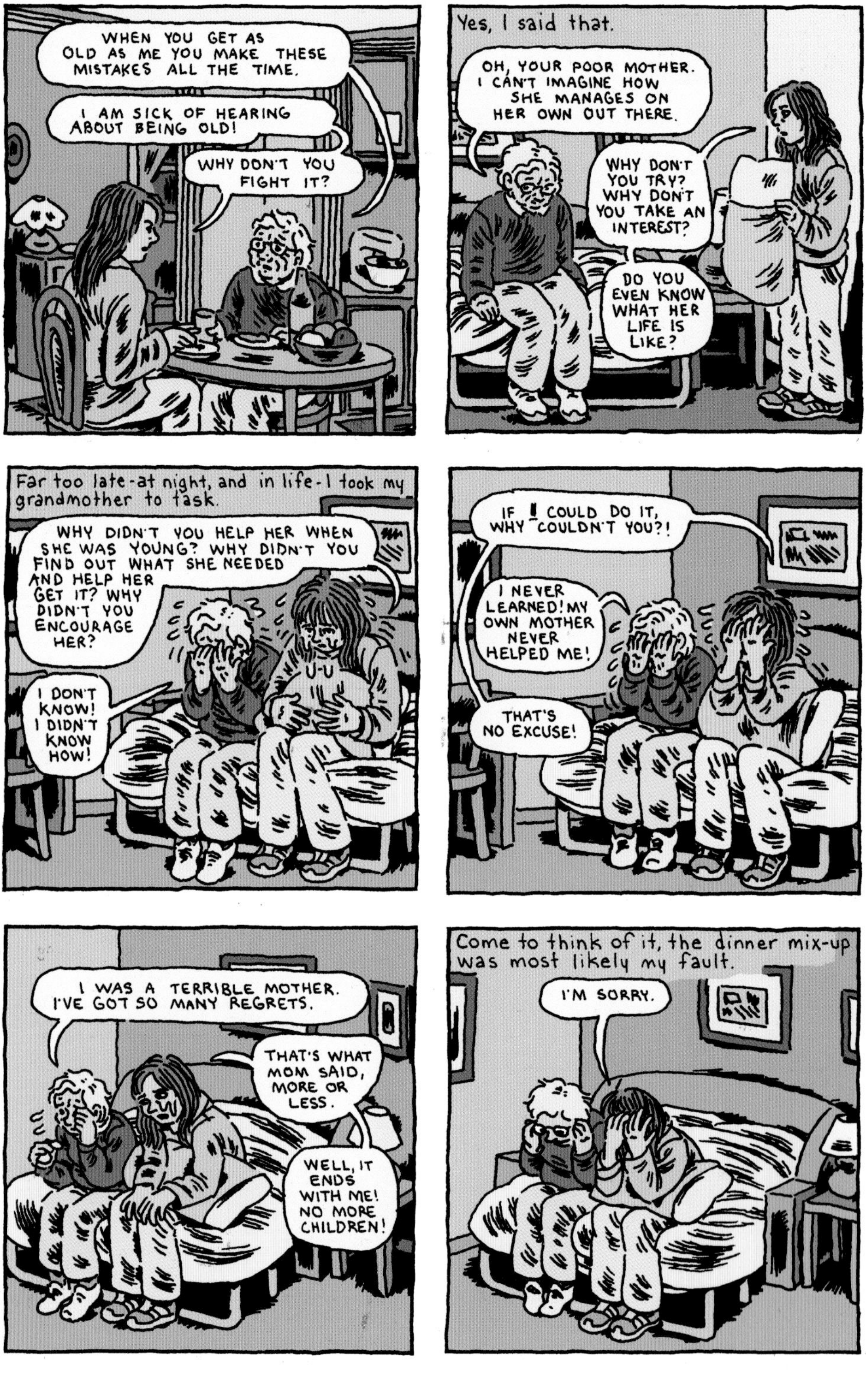
WHEN YOU GET AS OLD AS ME YOU MAKE THESE MISTAKES ALL THE TIME.
I AM SICK OF HEARING ABOUT BEING OLD!
WHY DON'T YOU FIGHT IT?
Yes, I said that.
OH, YOUR POOR MOTHER. I CAN'T IMAGINE HOW SHE MANAGES ON HER OWN OUT THERE.
WHY DON'T YOU TRY? WHY DON'T YOU TAKE AN INTEREST?
DO YOU EVEN KNOW WHAT HER LIFE IS LIKE?
Far too late-at night, and in life-I took my grandmother to task.
WHY DIDN'T YOU HELP HER WHEN SHE WAS YOUNG? WHY DIDN'T YOU FIND OUT WHAT SHE NEEDED AND HELP HER GET IT? WHY DIDN'T YOU ENCOURAGE HER?
I DON'T KNOW! I DIDN'T KNOW HOW!
IF I COULD DO IT, WHY COULDN'T YOU?!
I NEVER LEARNED! MY OWN MOTHER NEVER HELPED ME!
THAT'S NO EXCUSE!
I WAS A TERRIBLE MOTHER. I'VE GOT SO MANY REGRETS.
THAT'S WHAT MOM SAID, MORE OR LESS.
WELL, IT ENDS WITH ME! NO MORE CHILDREN!
Come to think of it, the dinner mix-up was most likely my fault.
I'M SORRY.

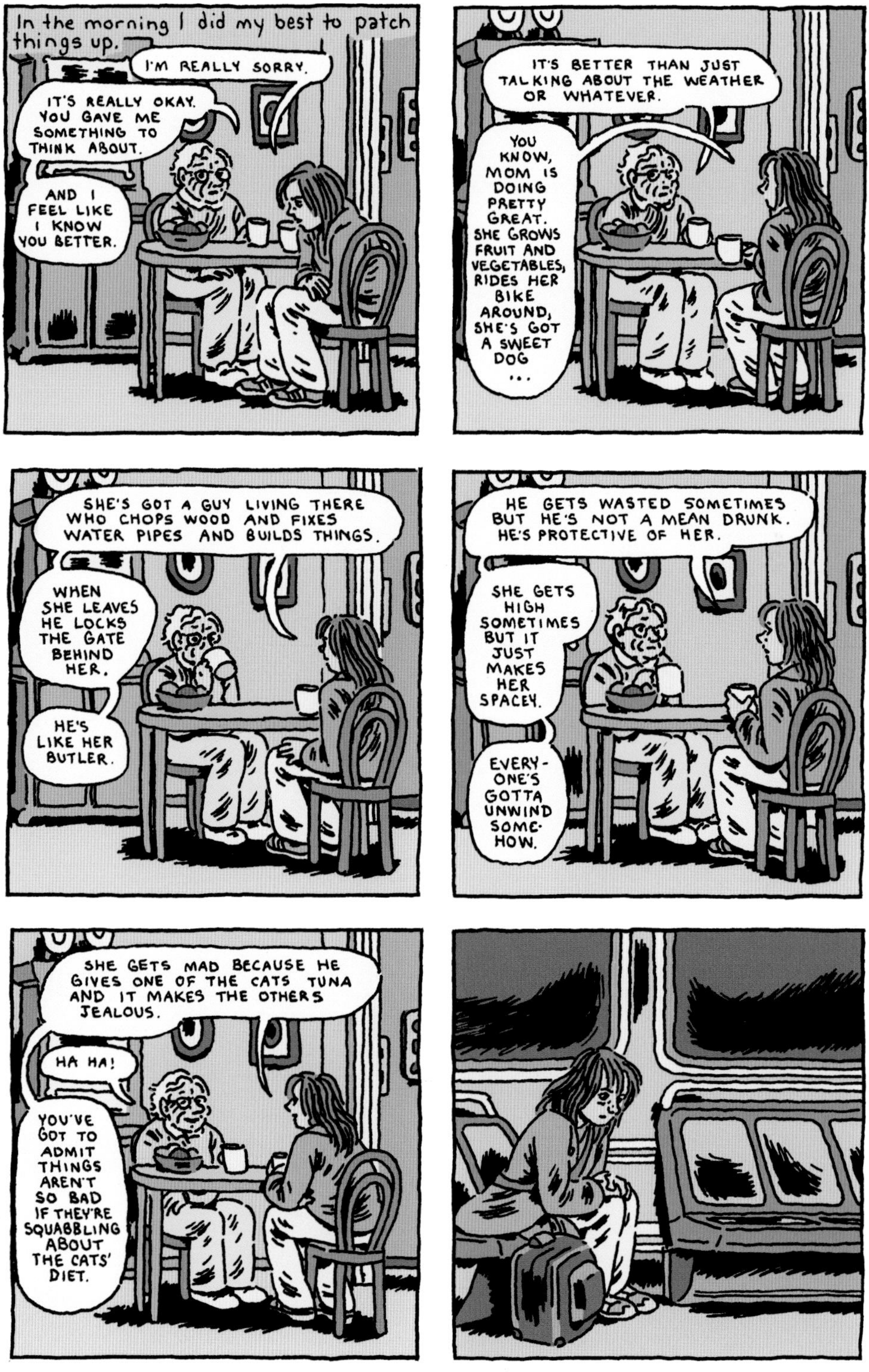
In the morning I did my best to patch things up.
I'M REALLY SORRY.
IT'S REALLY OKAY. YOU GAVE ME SOMETHING TO THINK ABOUT.
AND I FEEL LIKE I KNOW YOU BETTER.
IT'S BETTER THAN JUST TALKING ABOUT THE WEATHER OR WHATEVER.
YOU KNOW, MOM IS DOING PRETTY GREAT. SHE GROWS FRUIT AND VEGETABLES, RIDES HER BIKE AROUND, SHE'S GOT A SWEET DOG ...
SHE'S GOT A GUY LIVING THERE WHO CHOPS WOOD AND FIXES WATER PIPES AND BUILDS THINGS.
WHEN SHE LEAVES HE LOCKS THE GATE BEHIND HER.
HE'S LIKE HER BUTLER.
HE GETS WASTED SOMETIMES BUT HE'S NOT A MEAN DRUNK. HE'S PROTECTIVE OF HER.
SHE GETS HIGH SOMETIMES BUT IT JUST MAKES HER SPACEY.
EVERY-ONE'S GOTTA UNWIND SOME-HOW.
SHE GETS MAD BECAUSE HE GIVES ONE OF THE CATS TUNA AND IT MAKES THE OTHERS JEALOUS.
HA HA!
YOU'VE GOT TO ADMIT THINGS AREN'T SO BAD IF THEY'RE SQUABBLING ABOUT THE CATS' DIET.

Summer
2015

Dog Envy

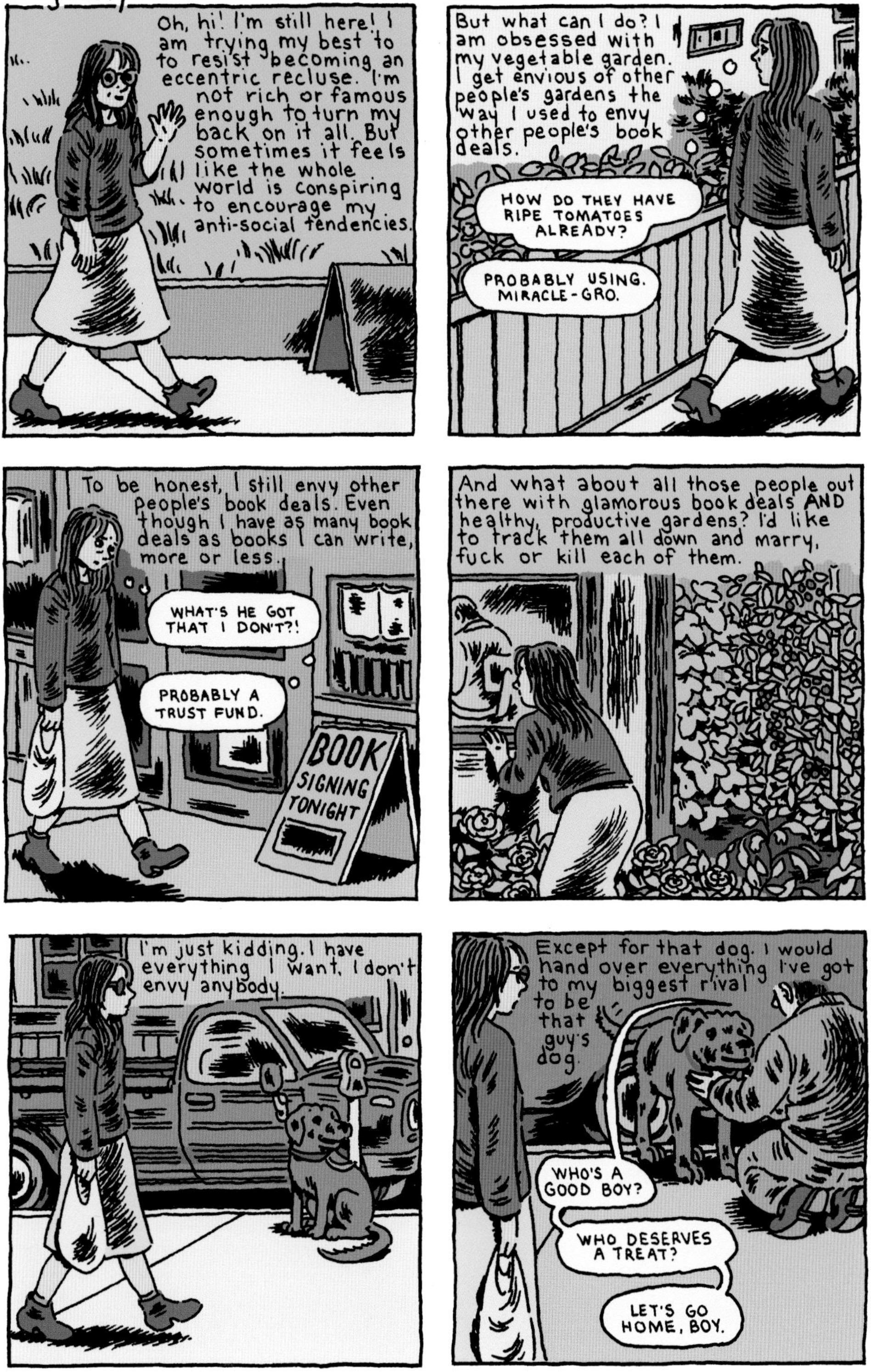
Oh, hi! I'm still here! I am trying my best to to resist becoming an eccentric recluse. I'm not rich or famous enough to turn my back on it all. But sometimes it feels like the whole world is conspiring to encourage my anti-social tendencies.
But what can I do? I am obsessed with my vegetable garden. I get envious of other people's gardens the way I used to envy other people's book deals.
HOW DO THEY HAVE RIPE TOMATOES ALREADY?
PROBABLY USING. MIRACLE-GRO.
To be honest, I still envy other people's book deals. Even though I have as many book deals as books I can write, more or less.
WHAT'S HE GOT THAT I DON'T?!
PROBABLY A TRUST FUND.
BOOK SIGNING TONIGHT
And what about all those people out there with glamorous book deals AND healthy, productive gardens? I'd like to track them all down and marry, fuck or kill each of them.
I'm just kidding. I have everything I want. I don't envy anybody.
Except for that dog. I would hand over everything I've got to my biggest rival to be that guy's dog.
WHO'S A GOOD BOY?
WHO DESERVES A TREAT?
LET'S GO HOME, BOY.

Thought Balloons

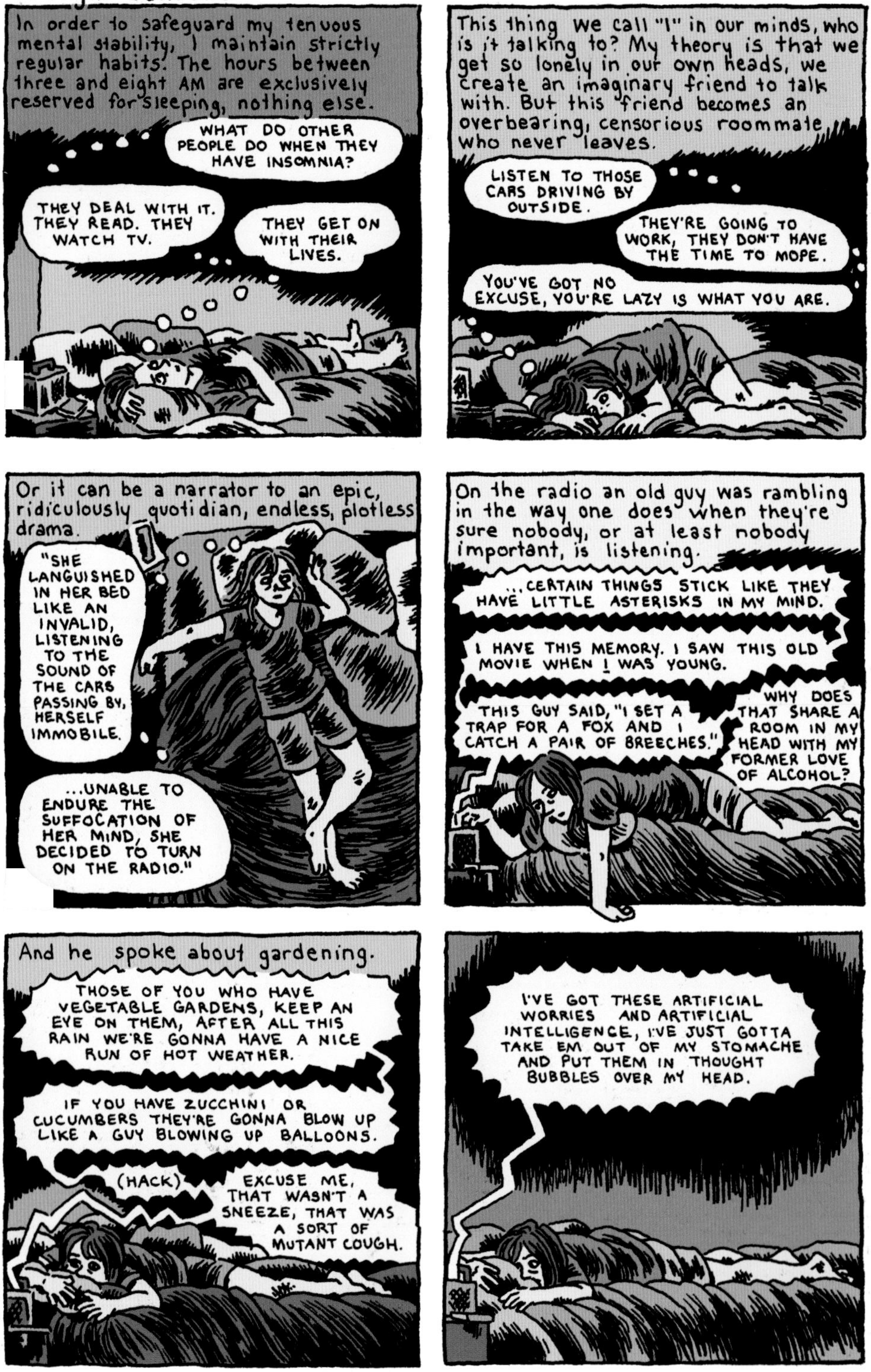
In order to safeguard my tenuous mental stability, I maintain strictly regular habits. The hours between three and eight AM are exclusively reserved for sleeping, nothing else.
WHAT DO OTHER PEOPLE DO WHEN THEY HAVE INSOMNIA?
THEY DEAL WITH IT. THEY READ. THEY WATCH TV.
THEY GET ON WITH THEIR LIVES.
This thing we call "I" in our minds, who is it talking to? My theory is that we get so lonely in our own heads, we create an imaginary friend to talk with. But this friend becomes an overbearing, censorious roommate who never leaves.
LISTEN TO THOSE CARS DRIVING BY OUTSIDE.
THEY'RE GOING TO WORK, THEY DON'T HAVE THE TIME TO MOPE.
YOU'VE GOT NO EXCUSE, YOU'RE LAZY IS WHAT YOU ARE.
Or it can be a narrator to an epic, ridiculously quotidian, endless, plotless drama.
"SHE LANGUISHED IN HER BED LIKE AN INVALID, LISTENING TO THE SOUND OF THE CARS PASSING BY, HERSELF IMMOBILE.
...UNABLE TO ENDURE THE SUFFOCATION OF HER MIND, SHE DECIDED TO TURN ON THE RADIO."
On the radio an old guy was rambling in the way one does when they're sure nobody, or at least nobody important, is listening.
...CERTAIN THINGS STICK LIKE THEY HAVE LITTLE ASTERISKS IN MY MIND.
I HAVE THIS MEMORY. I SAW THIS OLD MOVIE WHEN I WAS YOUNG.
THIS GUY SAID, "I SET A TRAP FOR A FOX AND I CATCH A PAIR OF BREECHES."
WHY DOES THAT SHARE A ROOM IN MY HEAD WITH MY FORMER LOVE OF ALCOHOL?
And he spoke about gardening.
THOSE OF YOU WHO HAVE VEGETABLE GARDENS, KEEP AN EYE ON THEM, AFTER ALL THIS RAIN WE'RE GONNA HAVE A NICE RUN OF HOT WEATHER.
IF YOU HAVE ZUCCHINI OR CUCUMBERS THEY'RE GONNA BLOW UP LIKE A GUY BLOWING UP BALLOONS.
(HACK)
EXCUSE ME, THAT WASN'T A SNEEZE, THAT WAS A SORT OF MUTANT COUGH.
I'VE GOT THESE ARTIFICIAL WORRIES AND ARTIFICIAL INTELLIGENCE, I'VE JUST GOTTA TAKE EM OUT OF MY STOMACHE AND PUT THEM IN THOUGHT BUBBLES OVER MY HEAD.

Invaders

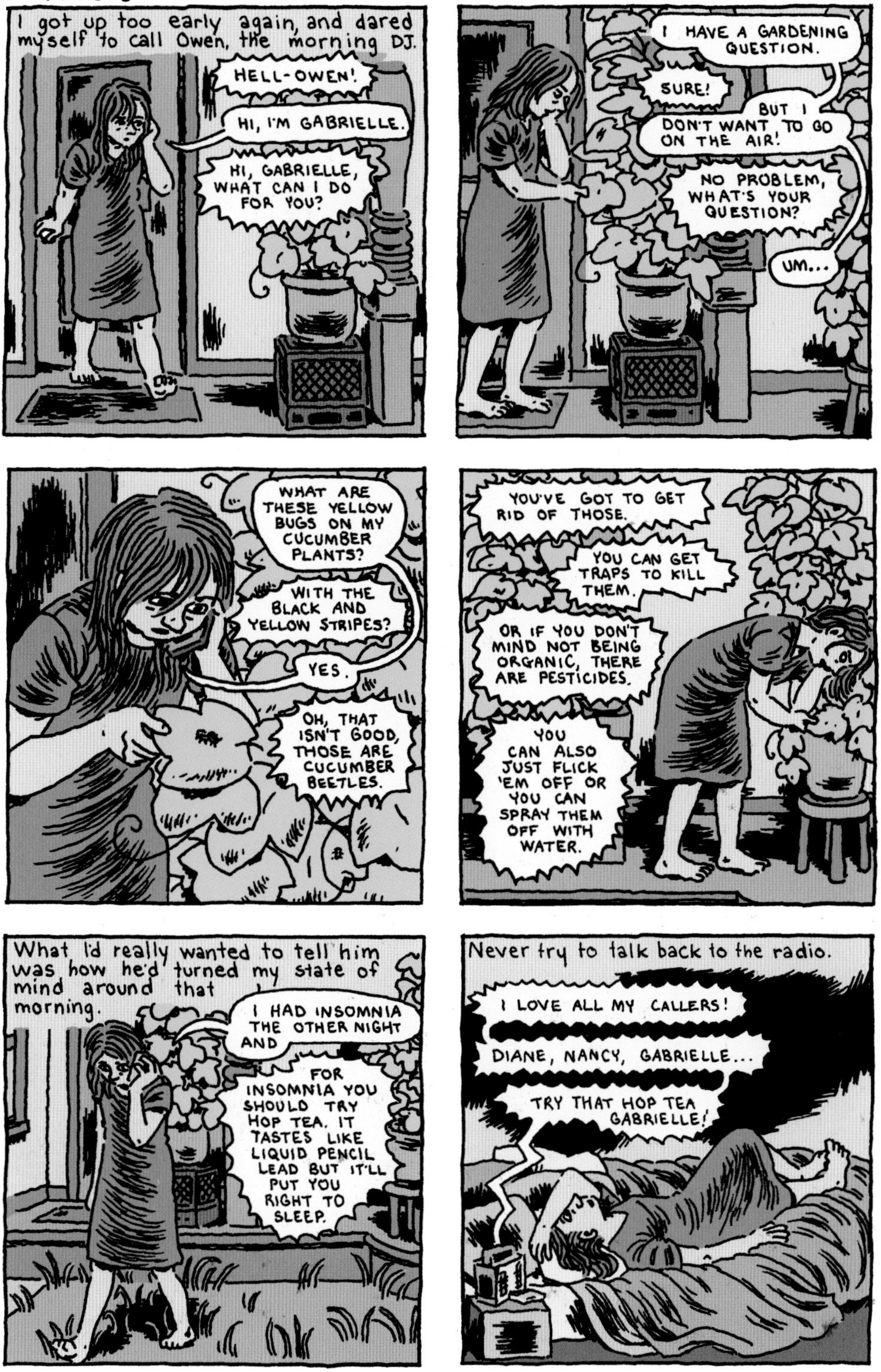

I got up too early again, and dared myself to call Owen, the morning DJ.
HELL-OWEN!
HI, I'M GABRIELLE.
HI, GABRIELLE, WHAT CAN I DO FOR YOU?
I HAVE A GARDENING QUESTION.
SURE!
BUT I DON'T WANT TO GO ON THE AIR!
NO PROBLEM, WHAT'S YOUR QUESTION?
UM...
WHAT ARE THESE YELLOW BUGS ON MY CUCUMBER PLANTS?
WITH THE BLACK AND YELLOW STRIPES?
YES.
OH, THAT ISN'T GOOD, THOSE ARE CUCUMBER BEETLES.
YOU'VE GOT TO GET RID OF THOSE.
YOU CAN GET TRAPS TO KILL THEM.
OR IF YOU DON'T MIND NOT BEING ORGANIC, THERE ARE PESTICIDES.
YOU CAN ALSO JUST FLICK 'EM OFF OR YOU CAN SPRAY THEM OFF WITH WATER.
What I'd really wanted to tell him was how he'd turned my state of mind around that morning.
I HAD INSOMNIA THE OTHER NIGHT AND
FOR INSOMNIA YOU SHOULD TRY HOP TEA. IT TASTES LIKE LIQUID PENCIL LEAD BUT IT'LL PUT YOU RIGHT TO SLEEP.
Never try to talk back to the radio.
I LOVE ALL MY CALLERS!
DIANE, NANCY, GABRIELLE...
TRY THAT HOP TEA GABRIELLE!

Bad News, Revisited.

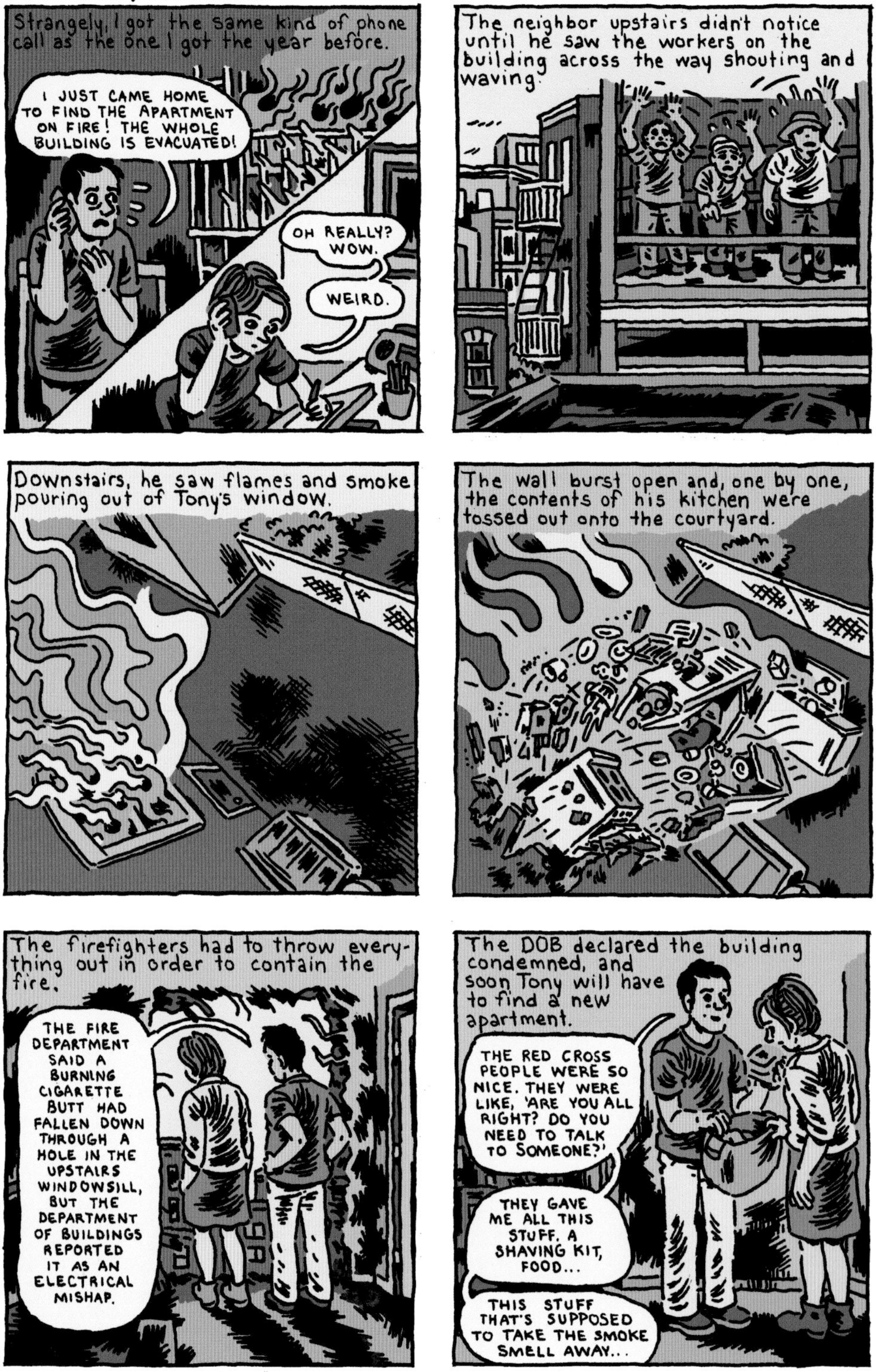
Strangely, I got the same kind of phone call as the one I got the year before.
I JUST CAME HOME TO FIND THE APARTMENT ON FIRE! THE WHOLE BUILDING IS EVACUATED!
OH REALLY? WOW.
WEIRD.
The neighbor upstairs didn't notice until he saw the workers on the building across the way shouting and waving.
Downstairs, he saw flames and smoke pouring out of Tony's window.
The wall burst open and, one by one, the contents of his kitchen were tossed out onto the courtyard.
The firefighters had to throw everything out in order to contain the fire.
THE FIRE DEPARTMENT SAID A BURNING CIGARETTE BUTT HAD FALLEN DOWN THROUGH A HOLE IN THE UPSTAIRS WINDOWSILL, BUT THE DEPARTMENT OF BUILDINGS REPORTED IT AS AN ELECTRICAL MISHAP.
The DOB declared the building condemned, and soon Tony will have to find a new apartment.
THE RED CROSS PEOPLE WERE SO NICE. THEY WERE LIKE, 'ARE YOU ALL RIGHT? DO YOU NEED TO TALK TO SOMEONE?'
THEY GAVE ME ALL THIS STUFF. A SHAVING KIT, FOOD...
THIS STUFF THAT'S SUPPOSED TO TAKE THE SMOKE SMELL AWAY...

Bureaucracy, Revisited

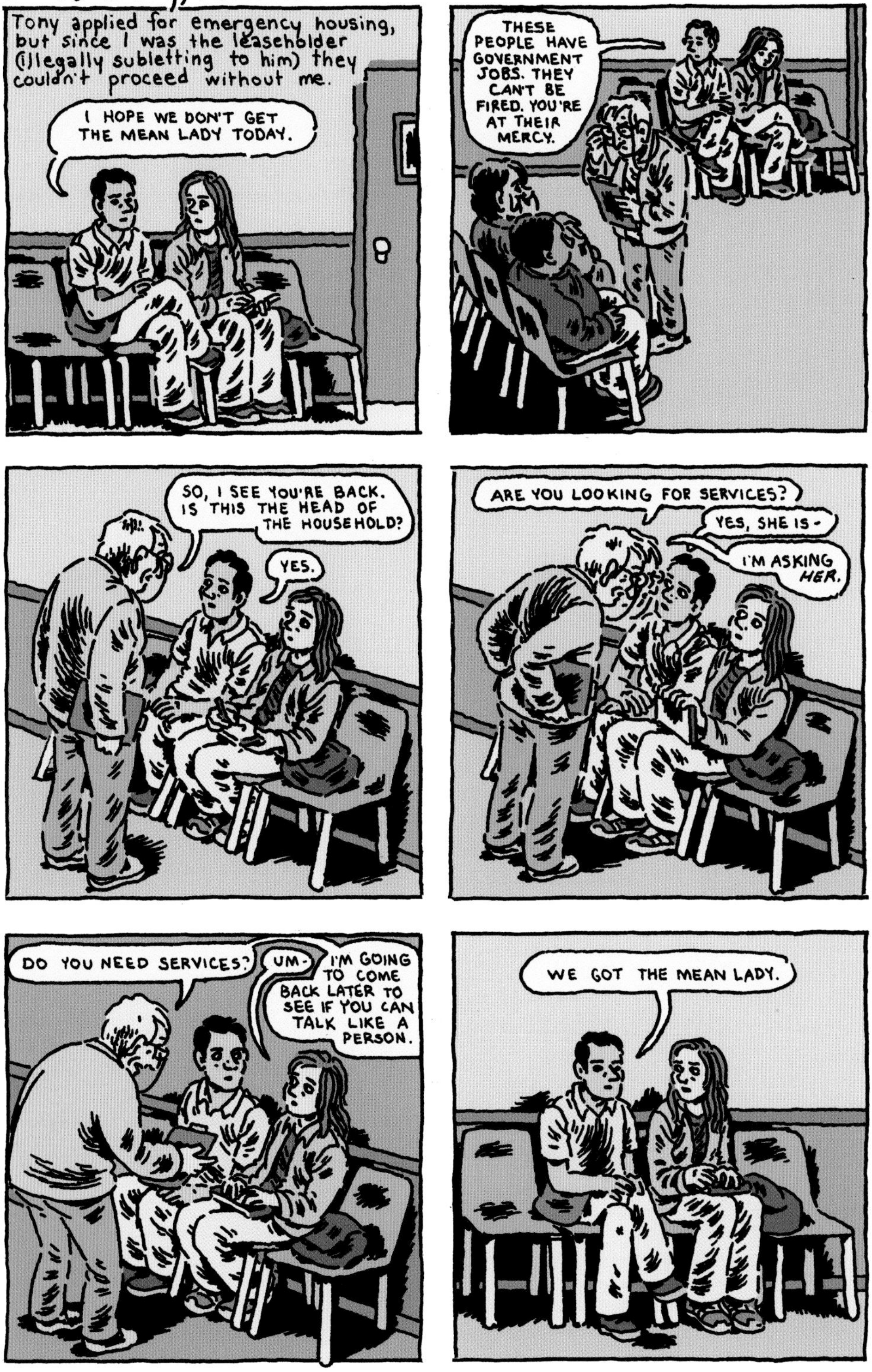

Tony applied for emergency housing, but since I was the leaseholder (illegally subletting to him) they couldn't proceed without me.
I HOPE WE DON'T GET THE MEAN LADY TODAY.
THESE PEOPLE HAVE GOVERNMENT JOBS. THEY CAN'T BE FIRED. YOU'RE AT THEIR MERCY.
SO, I SEE YOU'RE BACK. IS THIS THE HEAD OF THE HOUSEHOLD?
YES.
ARE YOU LOOKING FOR SERVICES?
YES, SHE IS -
I'M ASKING *HER*.
DO YOU NEED SERVICES?
UM-
I'M GOING TO COME BACK LATER TO SEE IF YOU CAN TALK LIKE A PERSON.
WE GOT THE MEAN LADY.

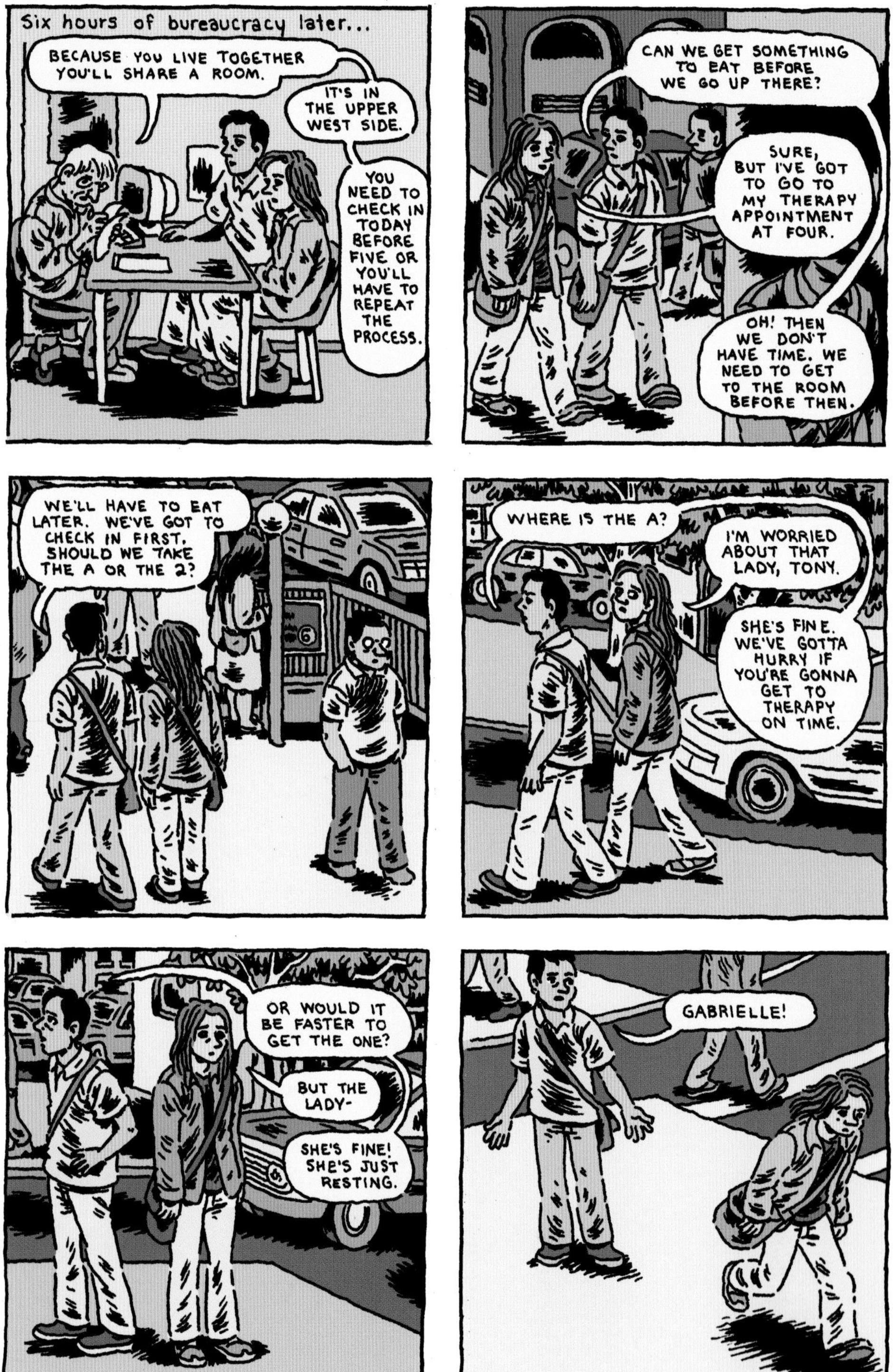
Six hours of bureaucracy later...
BECAUSE YOU LIVE TOGETHER YOU'LL SHARE A ROOM.
IT'S IN THE UPPER WEST SIDE.
YOU NEED TO CHECK IN TODAY BEFORE FIVE OR YOU'LL HAVE TO REPEAT THE PROCESS.
CAN WE GET SOMETHING TO EAT BEFORE WE GO UP THERE?
SURE, BUT I'VE GOT TO GO TO MY THERAPY APPOINTMENT AT FOUR.
OH! THEN WE DON'T HAVE TIME. WE NEED TO GET TO THE ROOM BEFORE THEN.
WE'LL HAVE TO EAT LATER. WE'VE GOT TO CHECK IN FIRST. SHOULD WE TAKE THE A OR THE 2?
WHERE IS THE A?
I'M WORRIED ABOUT THAT LADY, TONY.
SHE'S FINE. WE'VE GOTTA HURRY IF YOU'RE GONNA GET TO THERAPY ON TIME.
OR WOULD IT BE FASTER TO GET THE ONE?
BUT THE LADY-
SHE'S FINE! SHE'S JUST RESTING.
GABRIELLE!

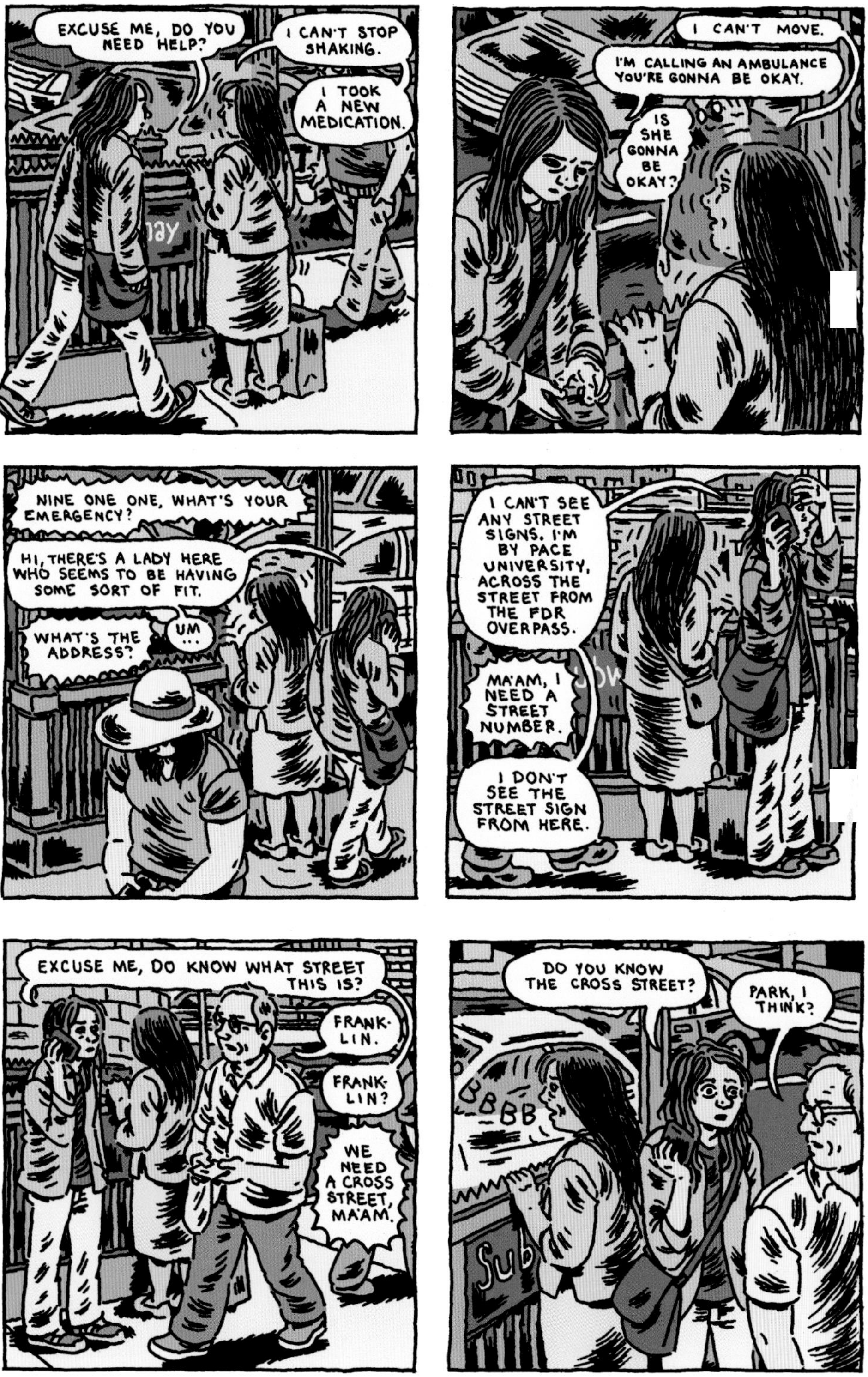
EXCUSE ME, DO YOU NEED HELP?
I CAN'T STOP SHAKING.
I TOOK A NEW MEDICATION.
I CAN'T MOVE.
I'M CALLING AN AMBULANCE YOU'RE GONNA BE OKAY.
IS SHE GONNA BE OKAY?
NINE ONE ONE, WHAT'S YOUR EMERGENCY?
HI, THERE'S A LADY HERE WHO SEEMS TO BE HAVING SOME SORT OF FIT.
WHAT'S THE ADDRESS?
UM ...
I CAN'T SEE ANY STREET SIGNS. I'M BY PACE UNIVERSITY, ACROSS THE STREET FROM THE FDR OVERPASS.
MA'AM, I NEED A STREET NUMBER.
I DON'T SEE THE STREET SIGN FROM HERE.
EXCUSE ME, DO KNOW WHAT STREET THIS IS?
FRANKLIN.
FRANKLIN?
WE NEED A CROSS STREET, MA'AM.
DO YOU KNOW THE CROSS STREET?
PARK, I THINK?
BBBB

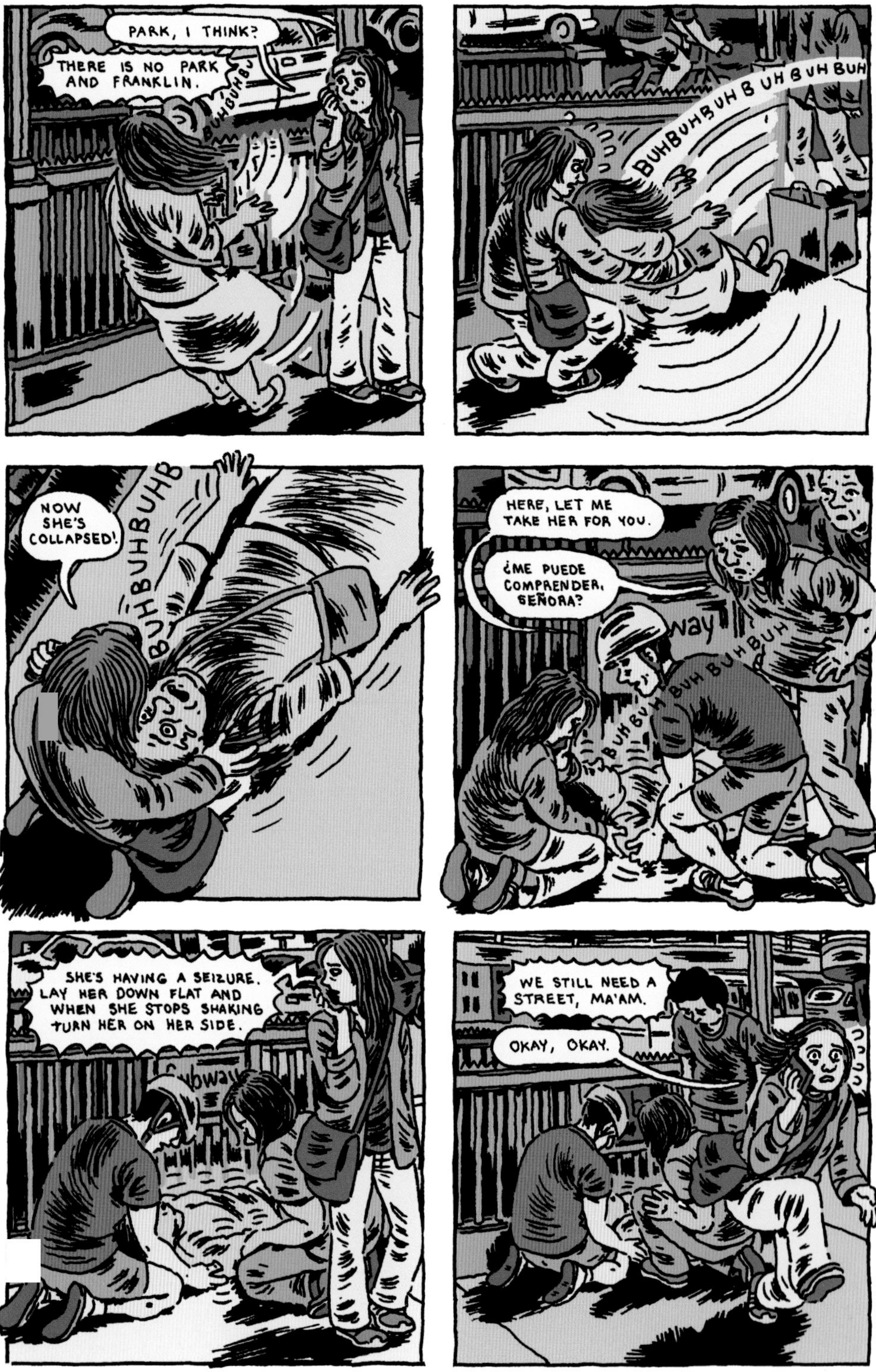
PARK, I THINK?
THERE IS NO PARK AND FRANKLIN.
BUHBUHBU
BUHBUHBUH B UH B UH BUH
NOW SHE'S COLLAPSED!
BUHBUHBUHB
HERE, LET ME TAKE HER FOR YOU.
¿ME PUEDE COMPRENDER, SEÑORA?
BUHBUHBUH BUHBUH
SHE'S HAVING A SEIZURE. LAY HER DOWN FLAT AND WHEN SHE STOPS SHAKING TURN HER ON HER SIDE.
WE STILL NEED A STREET, MA'AM.
OKAY, OKAY.

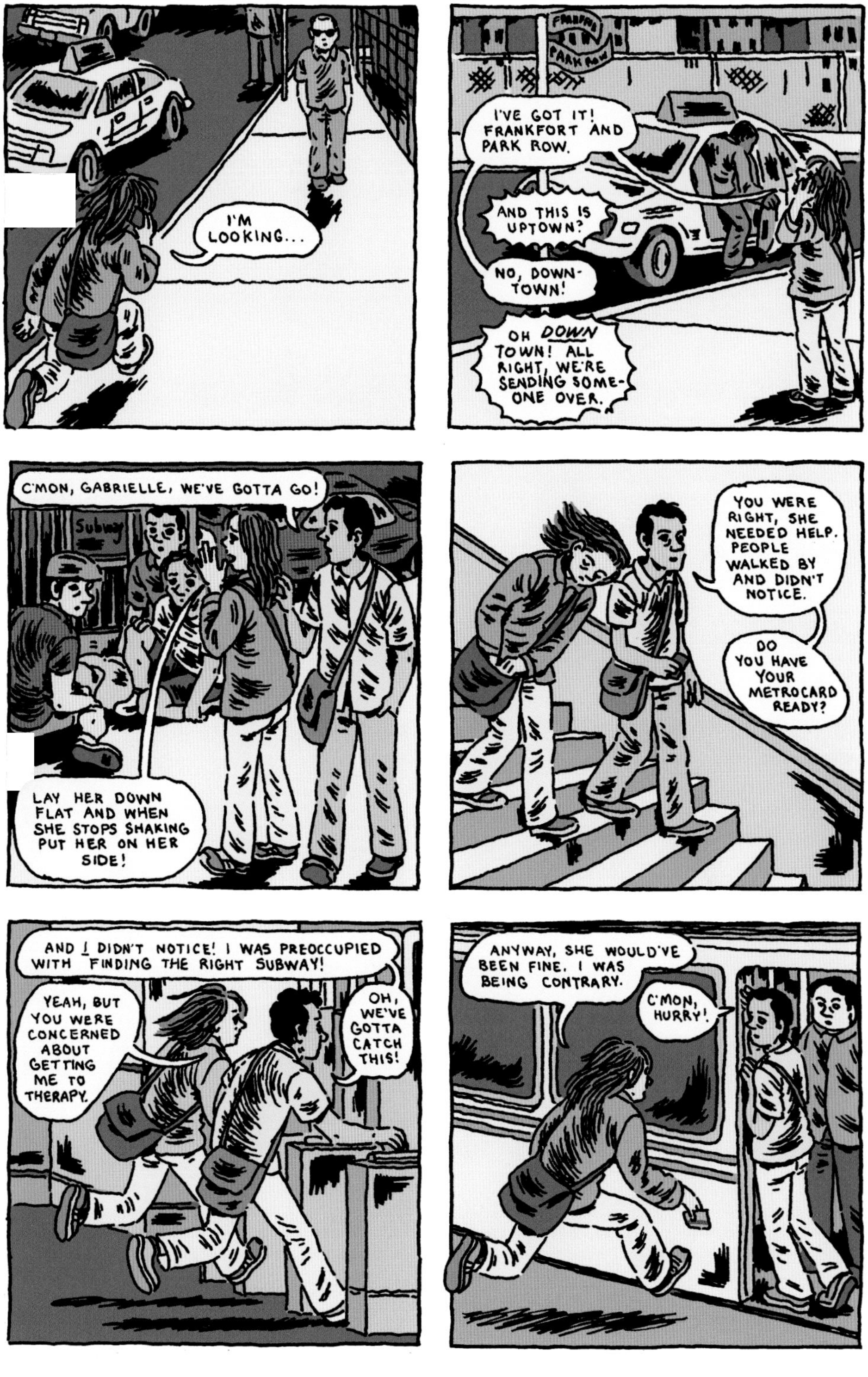
I'M LOOKING...
FRANKFORT
PARK ROW
I'VE GOT IT! FRANKFORT AND PARK ROW.
AND THIS IS UPTOWN?
NO, DOWNTOWN!
OH DOWN TOWN! ALL RIGHT, WE'RE SENDING SOMEONE OVER.
C'MON, GABRIELLE, WE'VE GOTTA GO!
Subway
LAY HER DOWN FLAT AND WHEN SHE STOPS SHAKING PUT HER ON HER SIDE!
YOU WERE RIGHT, SHE NEEDED HELP. PEOPLE WALKED BY AND DIDN'T NOTICE.
DO YOU HAVE YOUR METROCARD READY?
AND I DIDN'T NOTICE! I WAS PREOCCUPIED WITH FINDING THE RIGHT SUBWAY!
YEAH, BUT YOU WERE CONCERNED ABOUT GETTING ME TO THERAPY.
OH, WE'VE GOTTA CATCH THIS!
ANYWAY, SHE WOULD'VE BEEN FINE. I WAS BEING CONTRARY.
C'MON, HURRY!

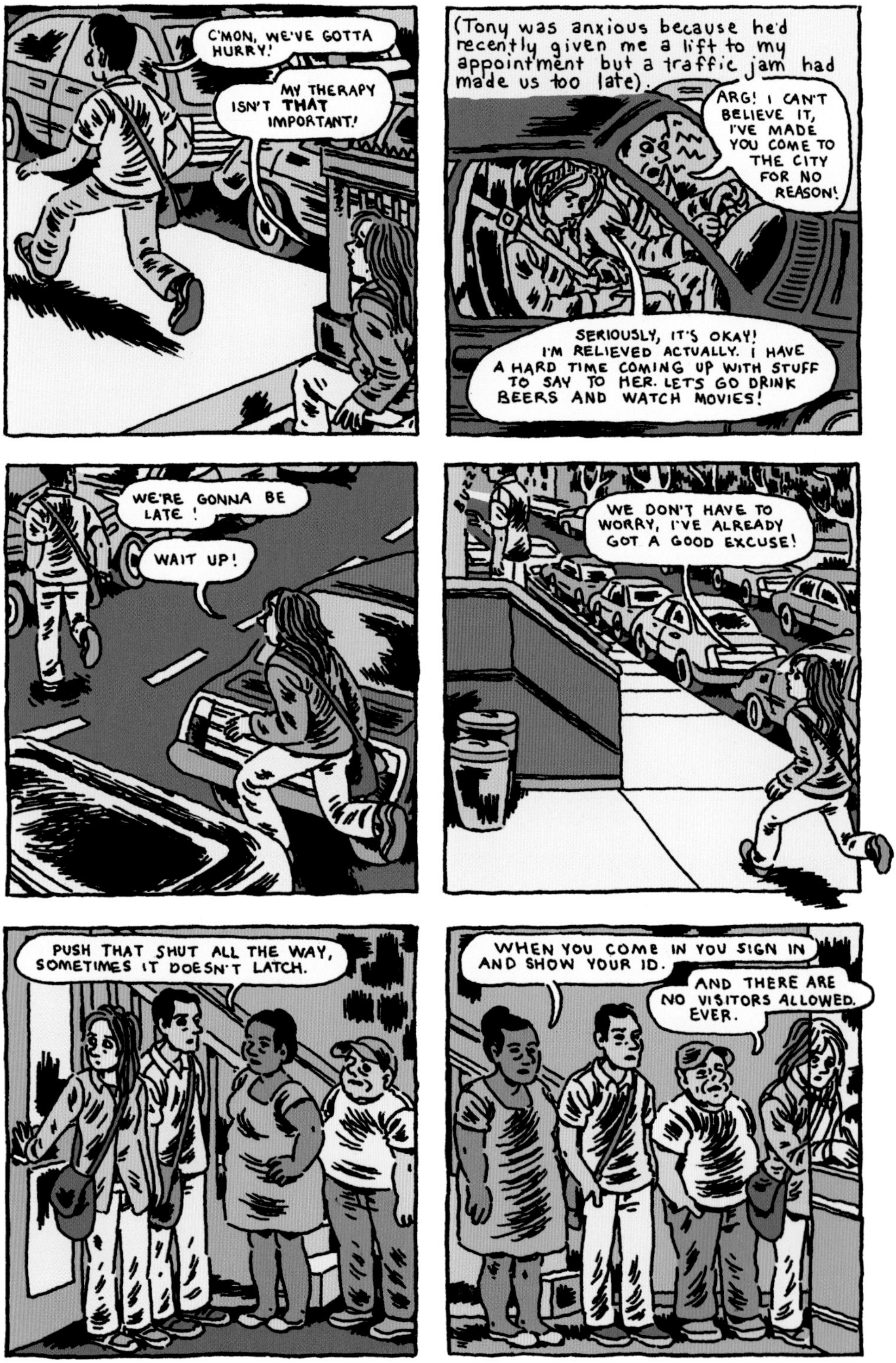
C'MON, WE'VE GOTTA HURRY!
MY THERAPY ISN'T THAT IMPORTANT!
(Tony was anxious because he'd recently given me a lift to my appointment but a traffic jam had made us too late).
ARG! I CAN'T BELIEVE IT, I'VE MADE YOU COME TO THE CITY FOR NO REASON!
SERIOUSLY, IT'S OKAY! I'M RELIEVED ACTUALLY. I HAVE A HARD TIME COMING UP WITH STUFF TO SAY TO HER. LET'S GO DRINK BEERS AND WATCH MOVIES!
WE'RE GONNA BE LATE !
WAIT UP!
WE DON'T HAVE TO WORRY, I'VE ALREADY GOT A GOOD EXCUSE!
PUSH THAT SHUT ALL THE WAY, SOMETIMES IT DOESN'T LATCH.
WHEN YOU COME IN YOU SIGN IN AND SHOW YOUR ID.
AND THERE ARE NO VISITORS ALLOWED. EVER.

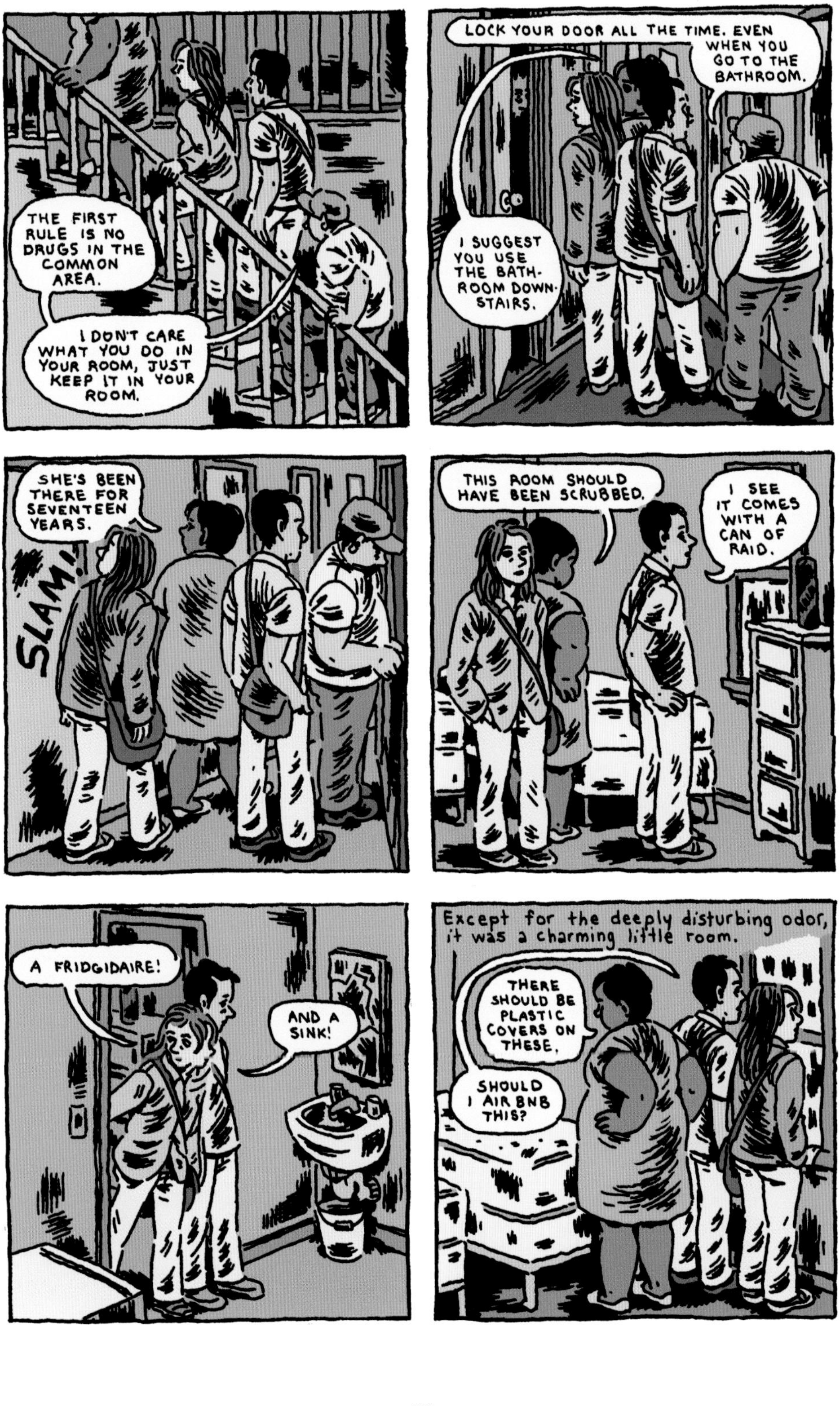
THE FIRST RULE IS NO DRUGS IN THE COMMON AREA.
I DON'T CARE WHAT YOU DO IN YOUR ROOM, JUST KEEP IT IN YOUR ROOM.
LOCK YOUR DOOR ALL THE TIME. EVEN WHEN YOU GO TO THE BATHROOM.
I SUGGEST YOU USE THE BATH-ROOM DOWN-STAIRS.
SHE'S BEEN THERE FOR SEVENTEEN YEARS.
SLAM!
THIS ROOM SHOULD HAVE BEEN SCRUBBED.
I SEE IT COMES WITH A CAN OF RAID.
A FRIDGIDAIRE!
AND A SINK!
Except for the deeply disturbing odor, it was a charming little room.
THERE SHOULD BE PLASTIC COVERS ON THESE.
SHOULD I AIR BNB THIS?

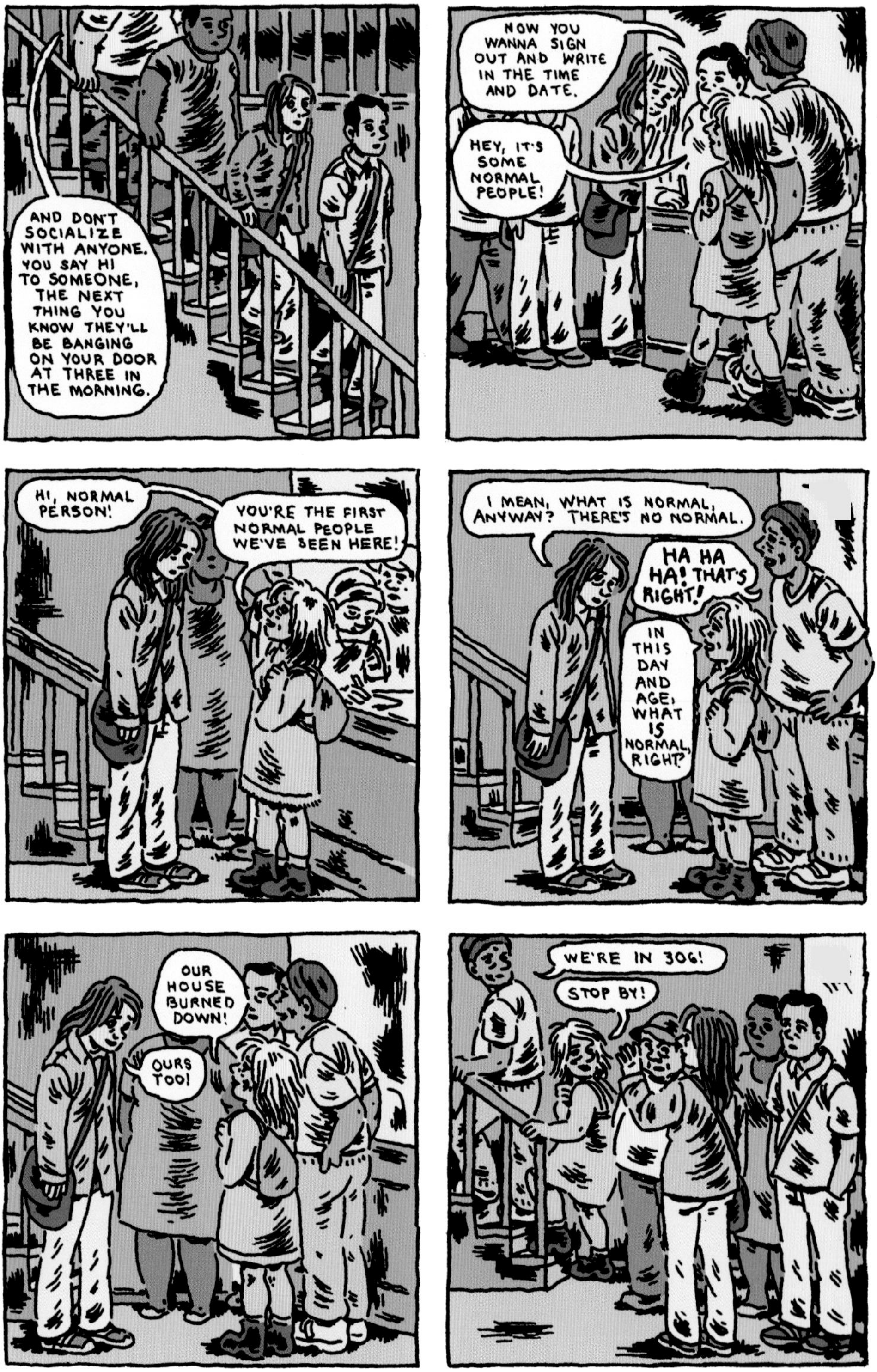
AND DON'T SOCIALIZE WITH ANYONE. YOU SAY HI TO SOMEONE, THE NEXT THING YOU KNOW THEY'LL BE BANGING ON YOUR DOOR AT THREE IN THE MORNING.
NOW YOU WANNA SIGN OUT AND WRITE IN THE TIME AND DATE.
HEY, IT'S SOME NORMAL PEOPLE!
HI, NORMAL PERSON!
YOU'RE THE FIRST NORMAL PEOPLE WE'VE SEEN HERE!
I MEAN, WHAT IS NORMAL, ANYWAY? THERE'S NO NORMAL.
HA HA HA! THAT'S RIGHT!
IN THIS DAY AND AGE, WHAT IS NORMAL, RIGHT?
OUR HOUSE BURNED DOWN!
OURS TOO!
WE'RE IN 306!
STOP BY!

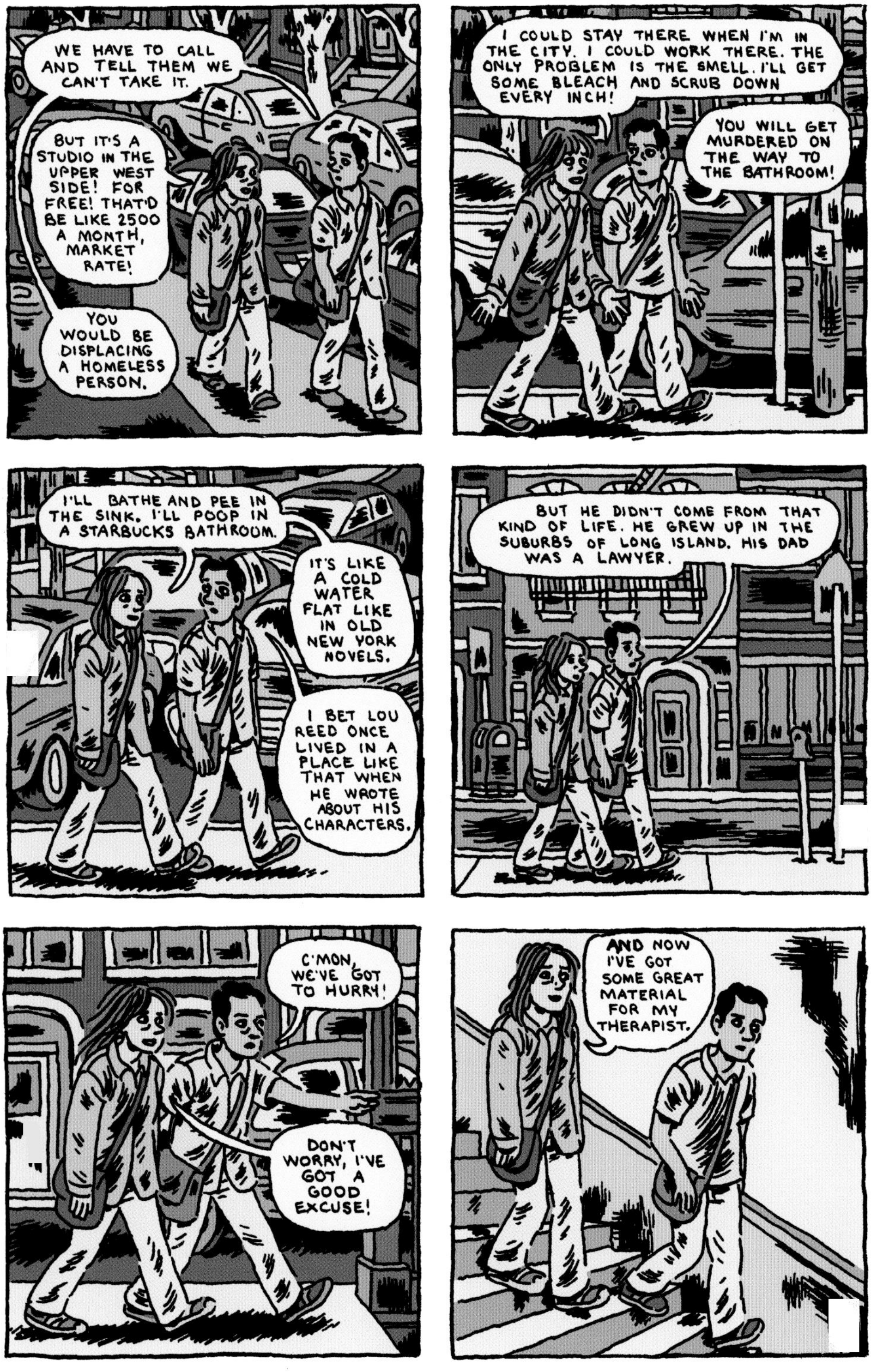
WE HAVE TO CALL AND TELL THEM WE CAN'T TAKE IT.
BUT IT'S A STUDIO IN THE UPPER WEST SIDE! FOR FREE! THAT'D BE LIKE 2500 A MONTH, MARKET RATE!
YOU WOULD BE DISPLACING A HOMELESS PERSON.
I COULD STAY THERE WHEN I'M IN THE CITY. I COULD WORK THERE. THE ONLY PROBLEM IS THE SMELL. I'LL GET SOME BLEACH AND SCRUB DOWN EVERY INCH!
YOU WILL GET MURDERED ON THE WAY TO THE BATHROOM!
I'LL BATHE AND PEE IN THE SINK. I'LL POOP IN A STARBUCKS BATHROOM.
IT'S LIKE A COLD WATER FLAT LIKE IN OLD NEW YORK NOVELS.
I BET LOU REED ONCE LIVED IN A PLACE LIKE THAT WHEN HE WROTE ABOUT HIS CHARACTERS.
BUT HE DIDN'T COME FROM THAT KIND OF LIFE. HE GREW UP IN THE SUBURBS OF LONG ISLAND. HIS DAD WAS A LAWYER.
C'MON, WE'VE GOT TO HURRY!
DON'T WORRY, I'VE GOT A GOOD EXCUSE!
AND NOW I'VE GOT SOME GREAT MATERIAL FOR MY THERAPIST.

That Insidious Smell

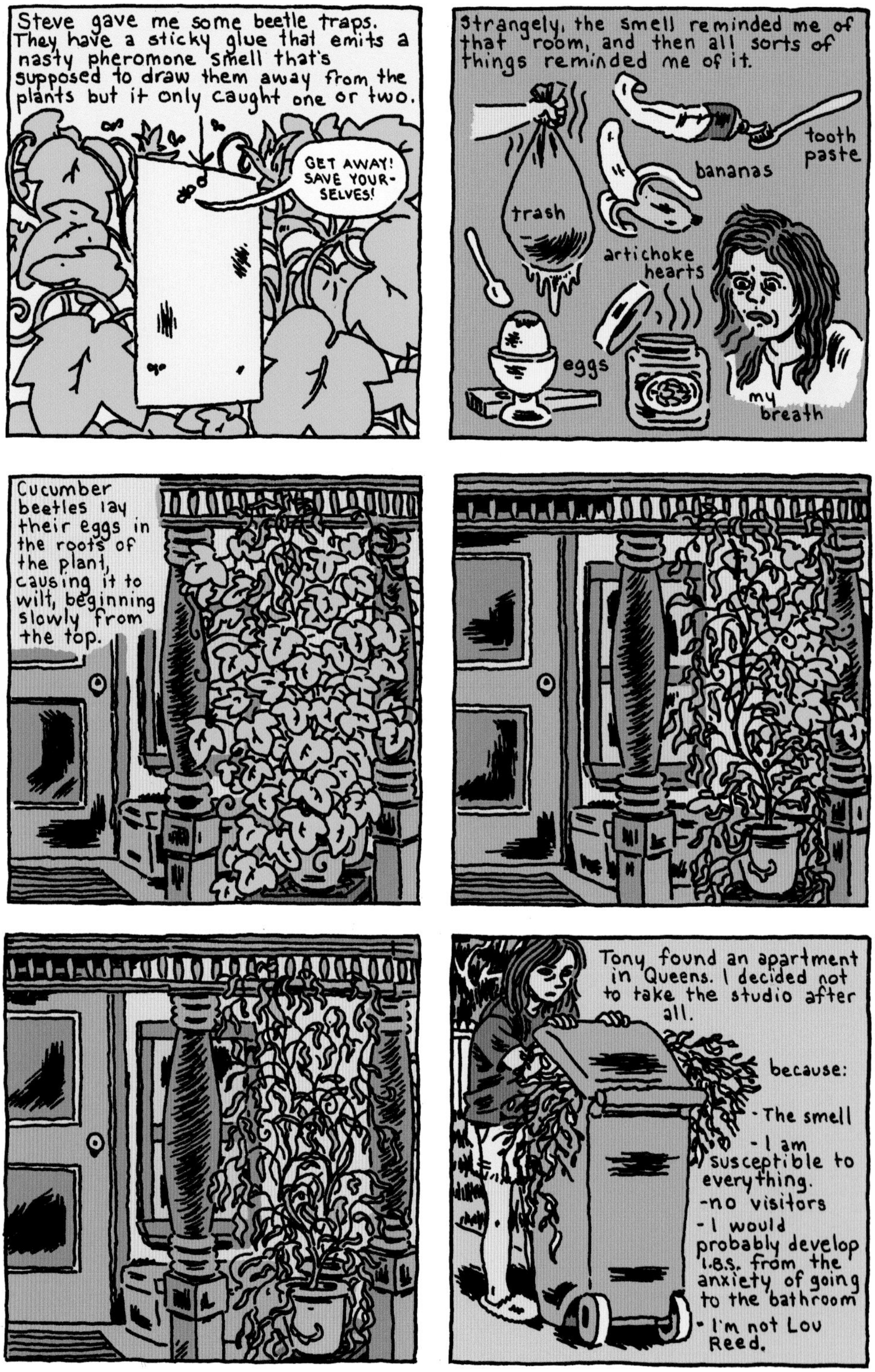
Steve gave me some beetle traps. They have a sticky glue that emits a nasty pheromone smell that's supposed to draw them away from the plants but it only caught one or two.
GET AWAY! SAVE YOUR-SELVES!
Strangely, the smell reminded me of that room, and then all sorts of things reminded me of it.
trash
bananas
tooth paste
artichoke hearts
eggs
my breath
Cucumber beetles lay their eggs in the roots of the plant, causing it to wilt, beginning slowly from the top.
Tony found an apartment in Queens. I decided not to take the studio after all.
because:
- The smell
- I am susceptible to everything.
-no visitors
- I would probably develop I.B.S. from the anxiety of going to the bathroom
- I'm not Lou Reed.

One More Trip
Out West

Hands Across America

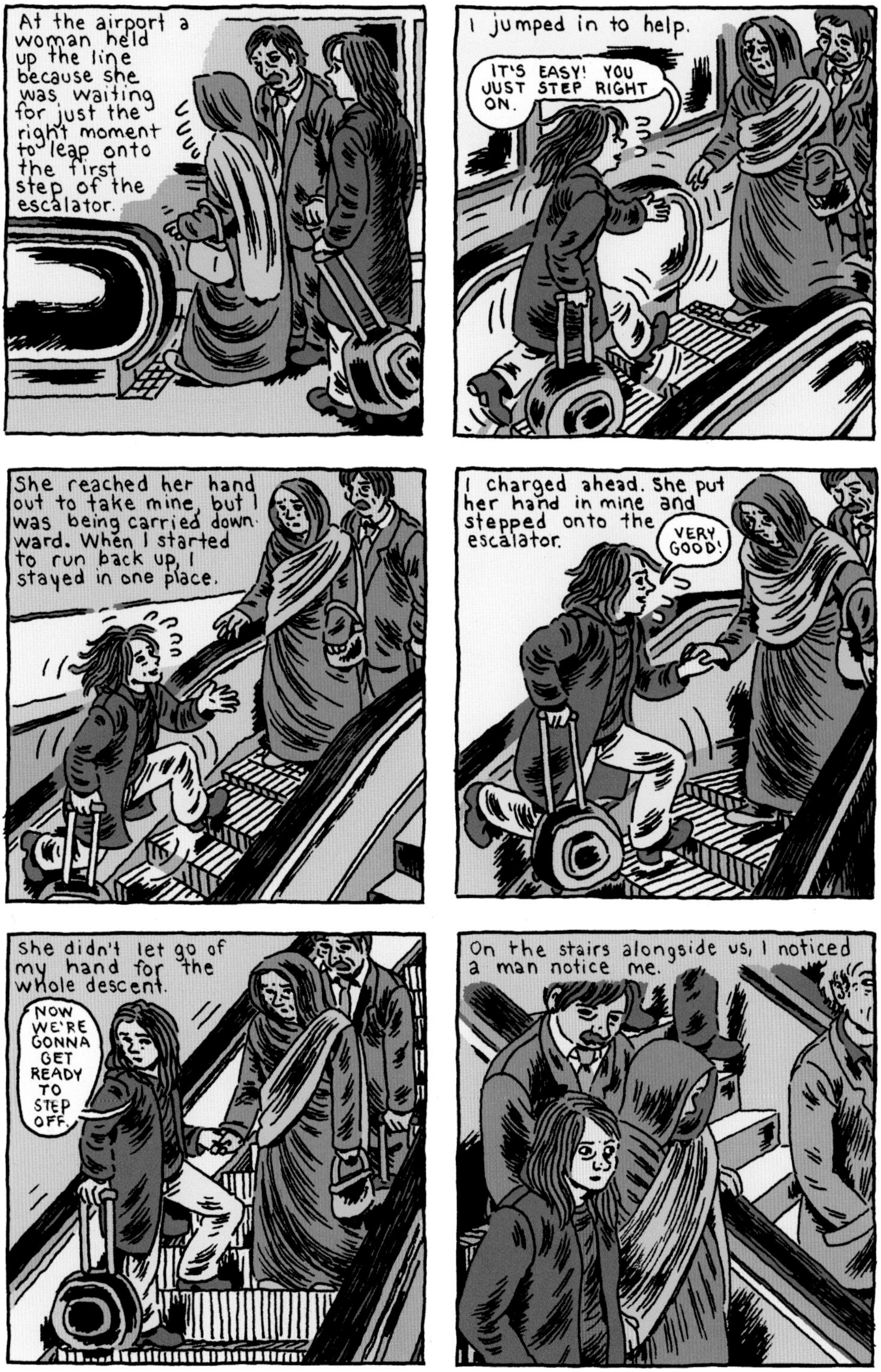
At the airport a woman held up the line because she was waiting for just the right moment to leap onto the first step of the escalator.
I jumped in to help.
IT'S EASY! YOU JUST STEP RIGHT ON.
She reached her hand out to take mine, but I was being carried downward. When I started to run back up, I stayed in one place.
I charged ahead. She put her hand in mine and stepped onto the escalator.
VERY GOOD!
She didn't let go of my hand for the whole descent.
NOW WE'RE GONNA GET READY TO STEP OFF.
On the stairs alongside us, I noticed a man notice me.

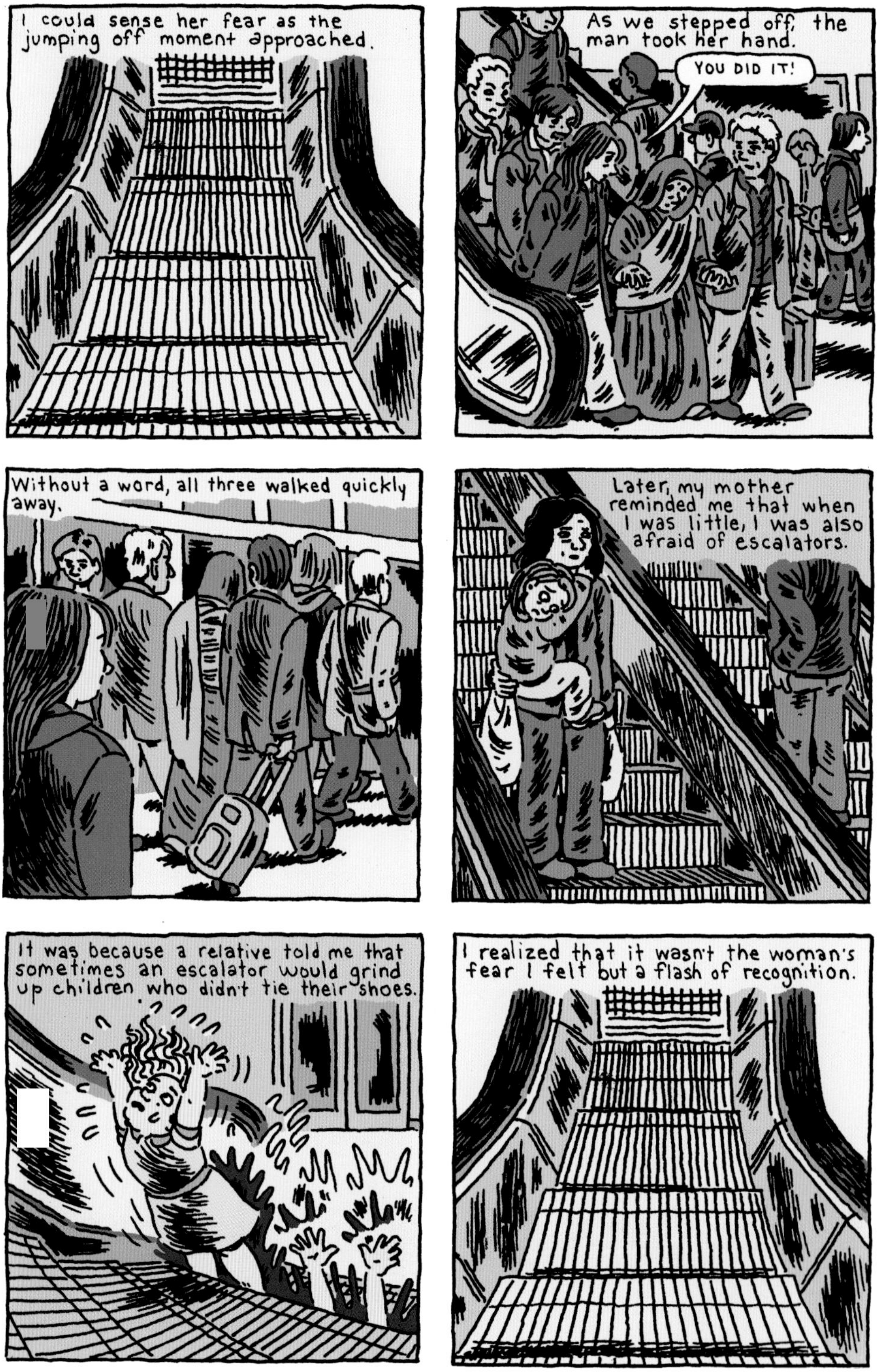
I could sense her fear as the jumping off moment approached.
As we stepped off, the man took her hand.
YOU DID IT!
Without a word, all three walked quickly away.
Later, my mother reminded me that when I was little, I was also afraid of escalators.
It was because a relative told me that sometimes an escalator would grind up children who didn't tie their shoes.
I realized that it wasn't the woman's fear I felt but a flash of recognition.

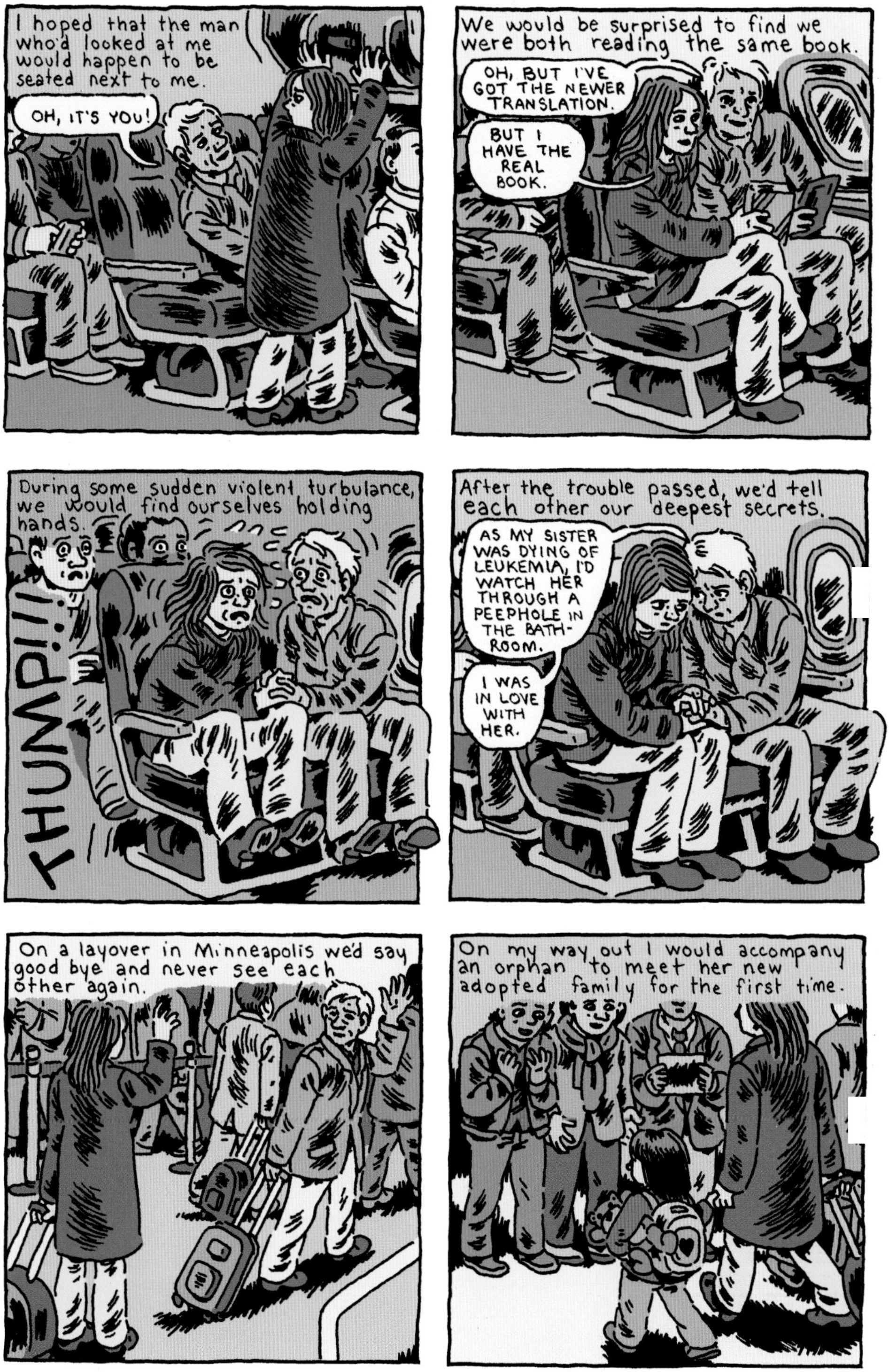
I hoped that the man who'd looked at me would happen to be seated next to me.
OH, IT'S YOU!
We would be surprised to find we were both reading the same book.
OH, BUT I'VE GOT THE NEWER TRANSLATION.
BUT I HAVE THE REAL BOOK.
During some sudden violent turbulance, we would find ourselves holding hands.
THUMP!!!
After the trouble passed, we'd tell each other our deepest secrets.
AS MY SISTER WAS DYING OF LEUKEMIA, I'D WATCH HER THROUGH A PEEPHOLE IN THE BATHROOM.
I WAS IN LOVE WITH HER.
On a layover in Minneapolis we'd say good bye and never see each other again.
On my way out I would accompany an orphan to meet her new adopted family for the first time.

Doggy

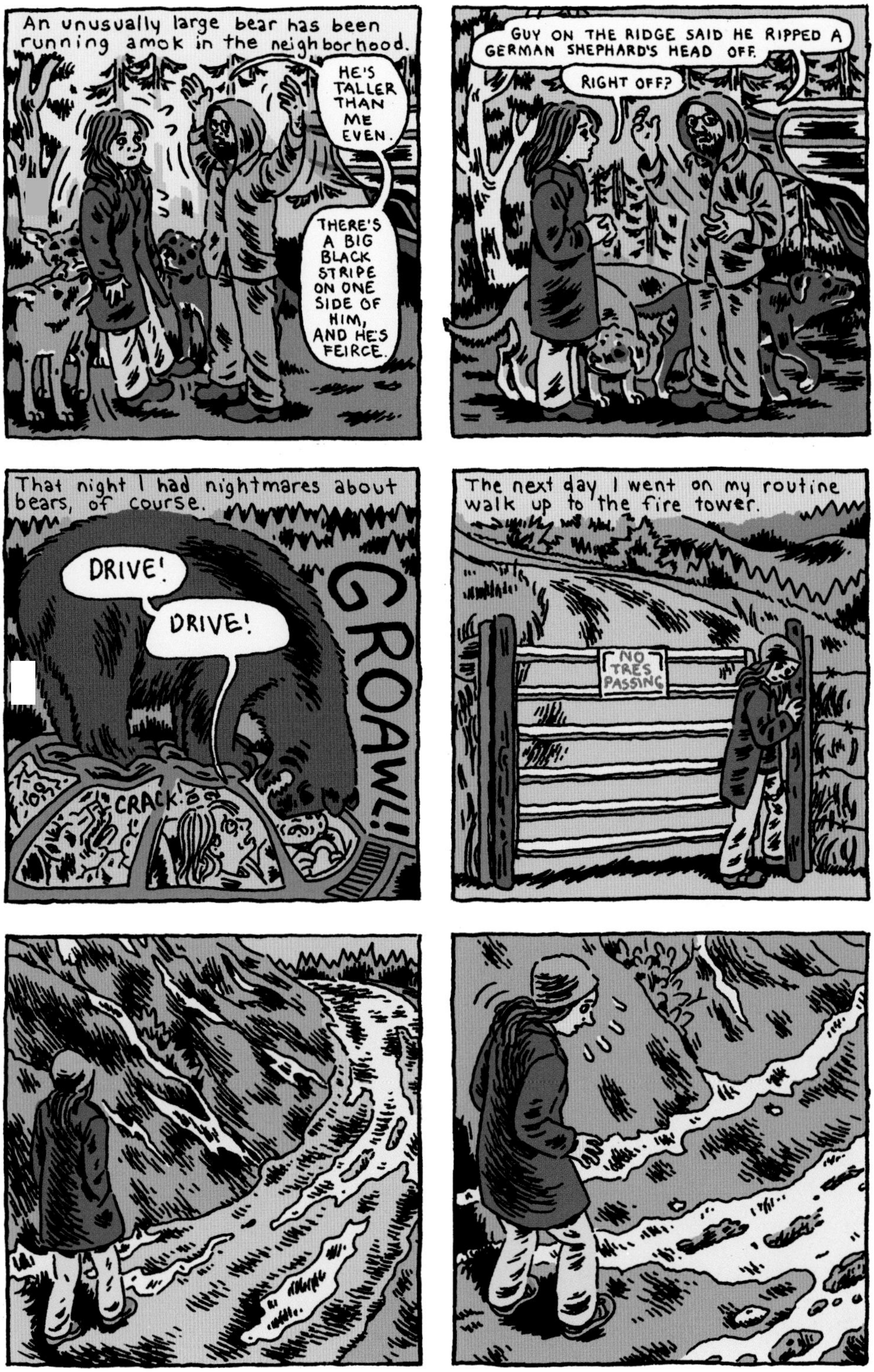
An unusually large bear has been running amok in the neighborhood.
HE'S TALLER THAN ME EVEN.
THERE'S A BIG BLACK STRIPE ON ONE SIDE OF HIM, AND HE'S FEIRCE.
GUY ON THE RIDGE SAID HE RIPPED A GERMAN SHEPHARD'S HEAD OFF.
RIGHT OFF?
That night I had nightmares about bears, of course.
DRIVE!
DRIVE!
GROAWL!
CRACK
The next day I went on my routine walk up to the fire tower.
NO TRES PASSING

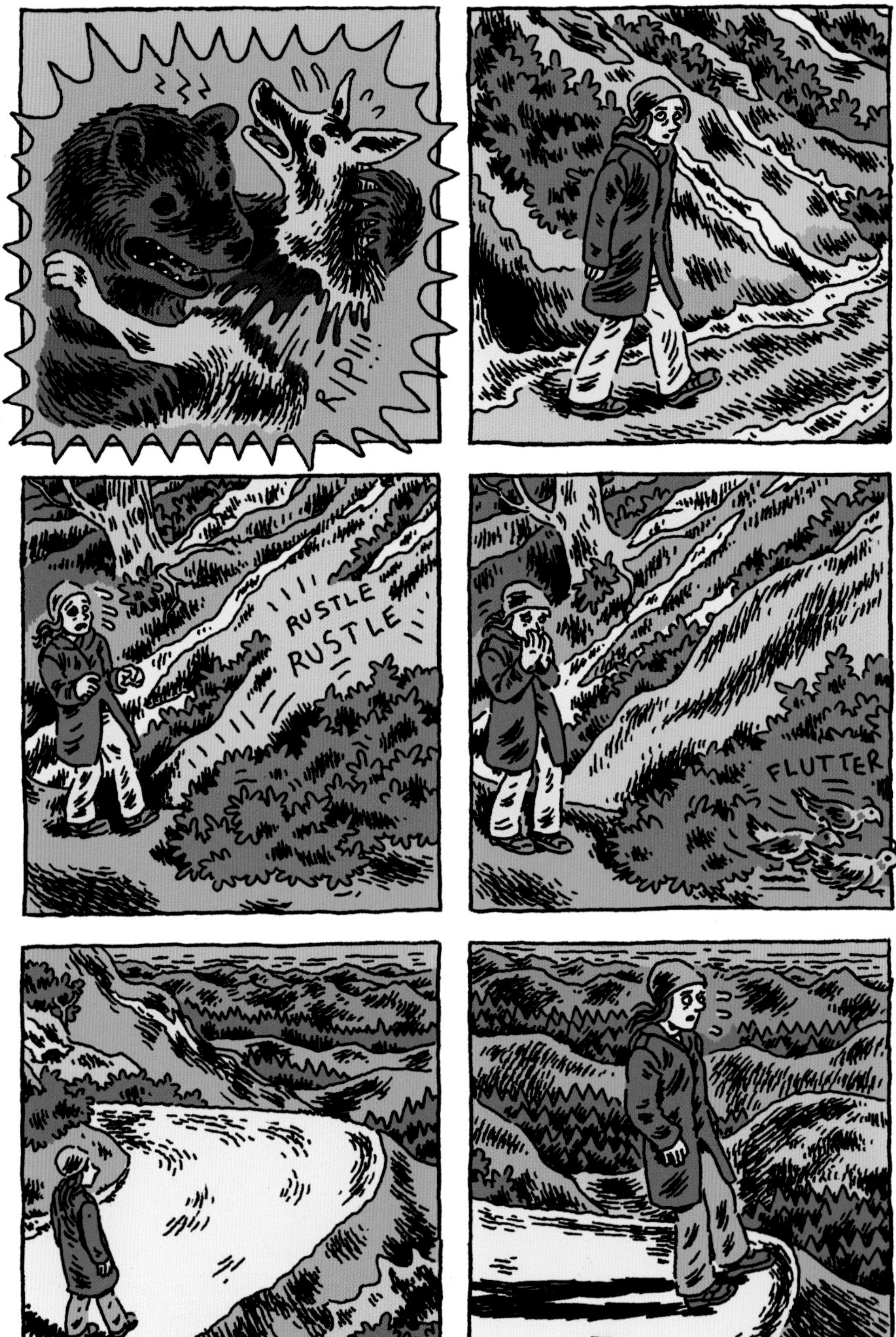
RIP!!!
RUSTLE
RUSTLE
FLUTTER

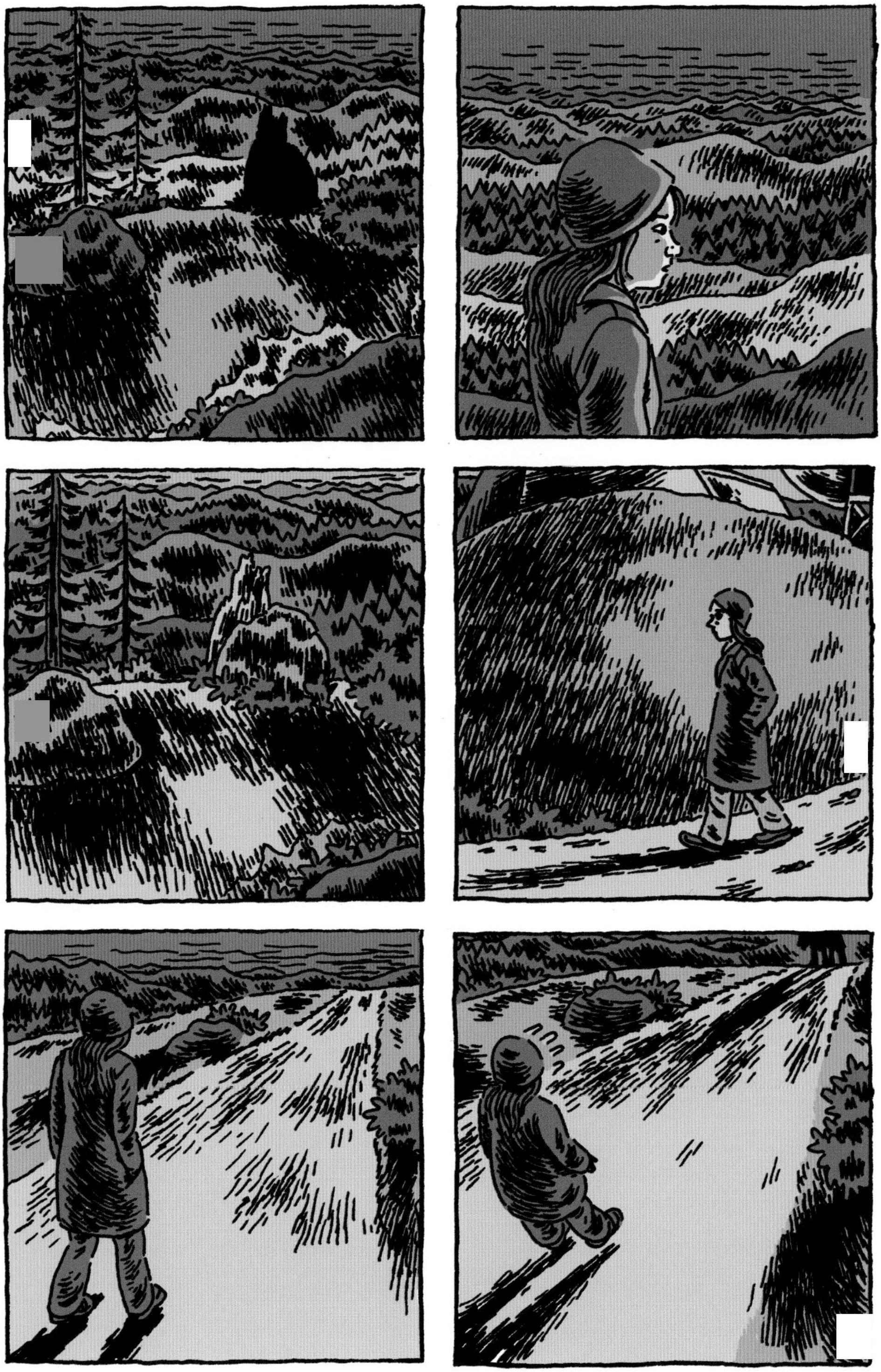

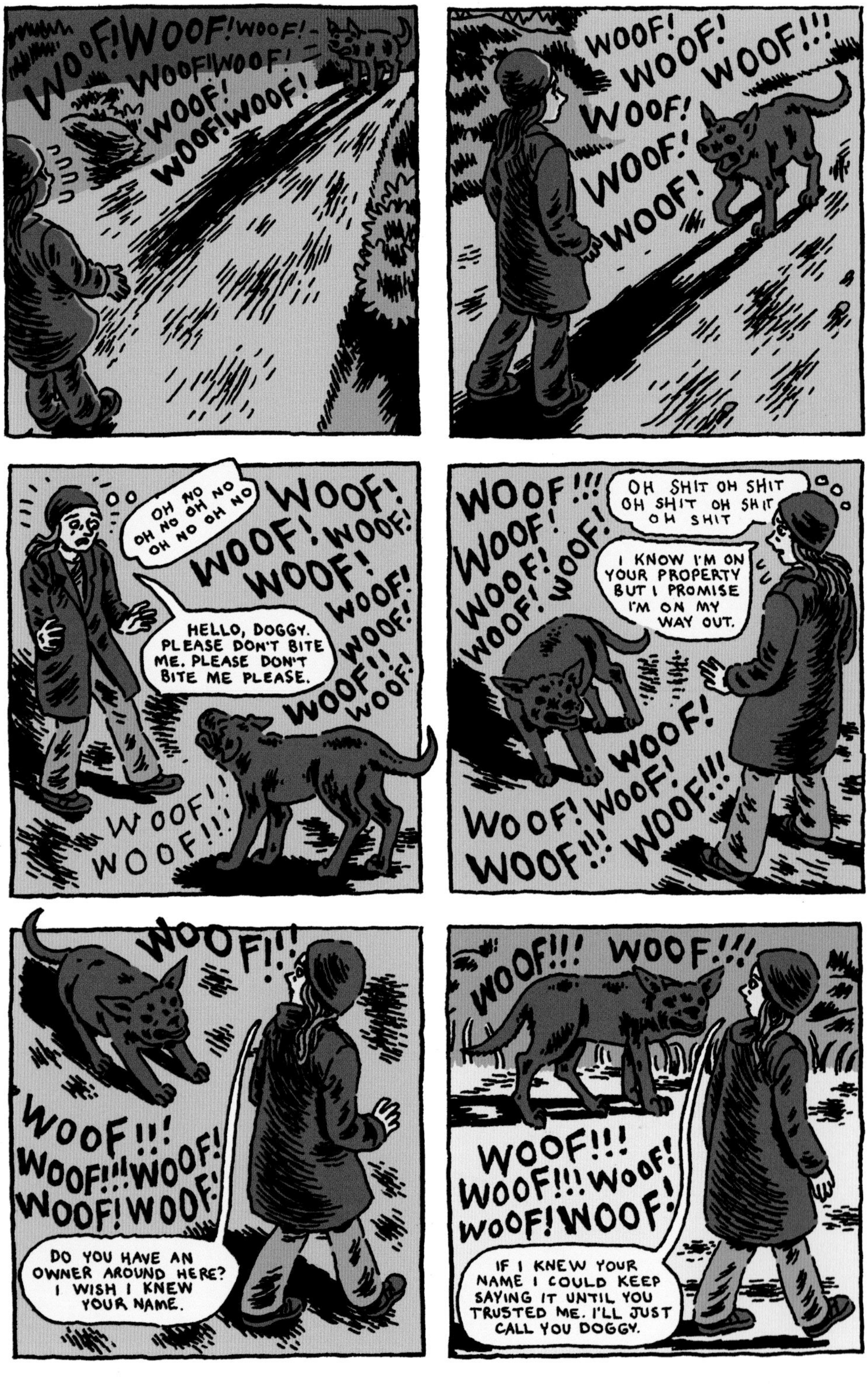
WOOF! WOOF! WOOF!
WOOF! WOOF!
WOOF!
WOOF! WOOF!
WOOF! WOOF! WOOF!!!
WOOF!
WOOF!
WOOF!
OH NO OH NO OH NO OH NO OH NO
HELLO, DOGGY. PLEASE DON'T BITE ME. PLEASE DON'T BITE ME PLEASE.
WOOF! WOOF! WOOF! WOOF! WOOF! WOOF! WOOF!!! WOOF!
WOOF!! WOOF!!!
WOOF!!! WOOF! WOOF! WOOF! WOOF!
OH SHIT OH SHIT OH SHIT OH SHIT OH SHIT
I KNOW I'M ON YOUR PROPERTY BUT I PROMISE I'M ON MY WAY OUT.
WOOF! WOOF! WOOF! WOOF!!! WOOF!!!
WOOF!!!
WOOF!!! WOOF!!! WOOF! WOOF! WOOF!
DO YOU HAVE AN OWNER AROUND HERE? I WISH I KNEW YOUR NAME.
WOOF!!! WOOF.!!!
WOOF!!! WOOF!!! WOOF! WOOF! WOOF!
IF I KNEW YOUR NAME I COULD KEEP SAYING IT UNTIL YOU TRUSTED ME. I'LL JUST CALL YOU DOGGY.

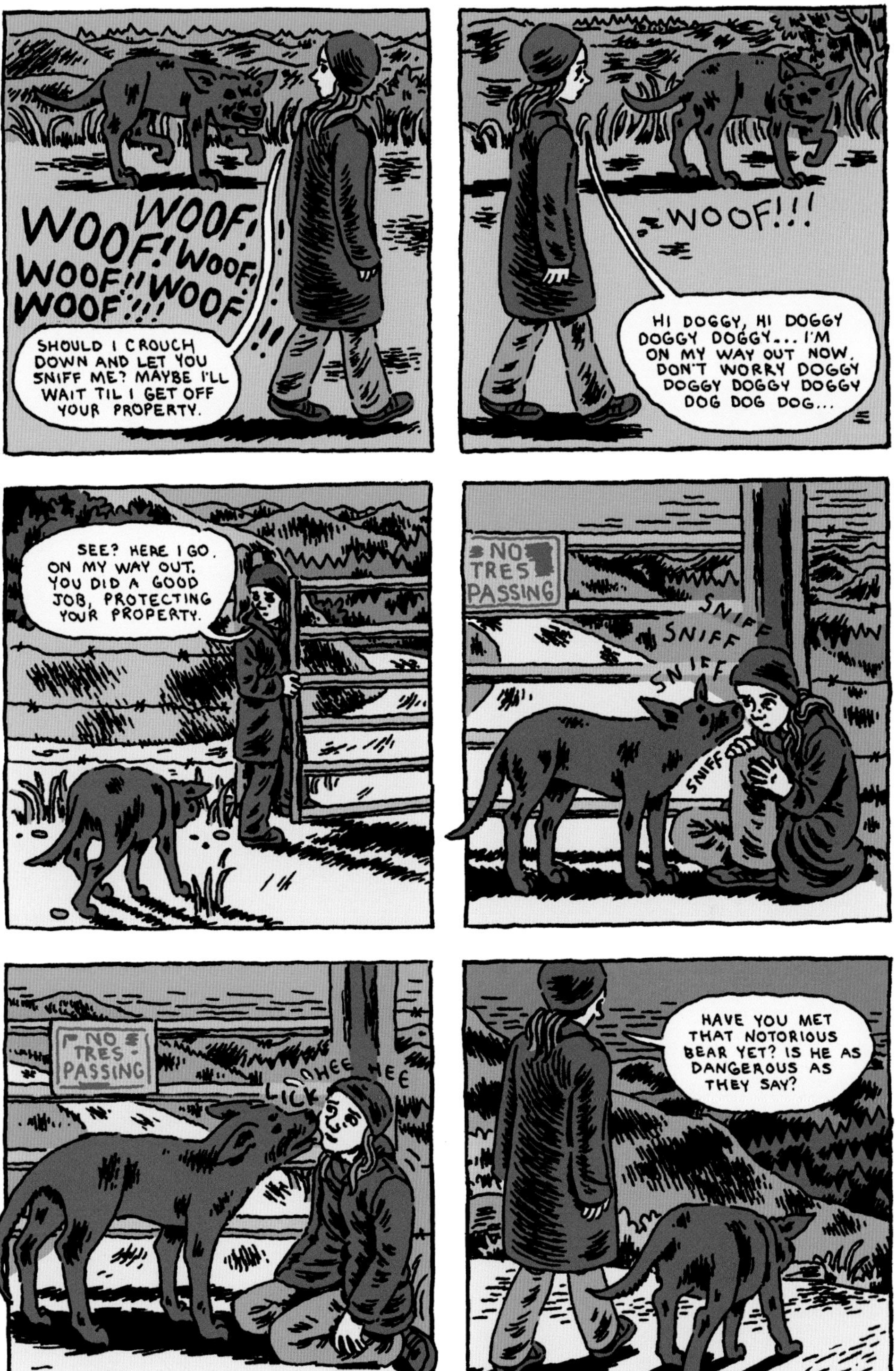
WOOF! WOOF! WOOF! WOOF!! WOOF WOOF!!!
SHOULD I CROUCH DOWN AND LET YOU SNIFF ME? MAYBE I'LL WAIT TIL I GET OFF YOUR PROPERTY.
WOOF!!!
HI DOGGY, HI DOGGY DOGGY DOGGY... I'M ON MY WAY OUT NOW. DON'T WORRY DOGGY DOGGY DOGGY DOGGY DOG DOG DOG...
SEE? HERE I GO. ON MY WAY OUT. YOU DID A GOOD JOB, PROTECTING YOUR PROPERTY.
NO TRES PASSING
SNIFF SNIFF SNIFF SNIFF
NO TRES PASSING
LICK
HEE HEE
HAVE YOU MET THAT NOTORIOUS BEAR YET? IS HE AS DANGEROUS AS THEY SAY?

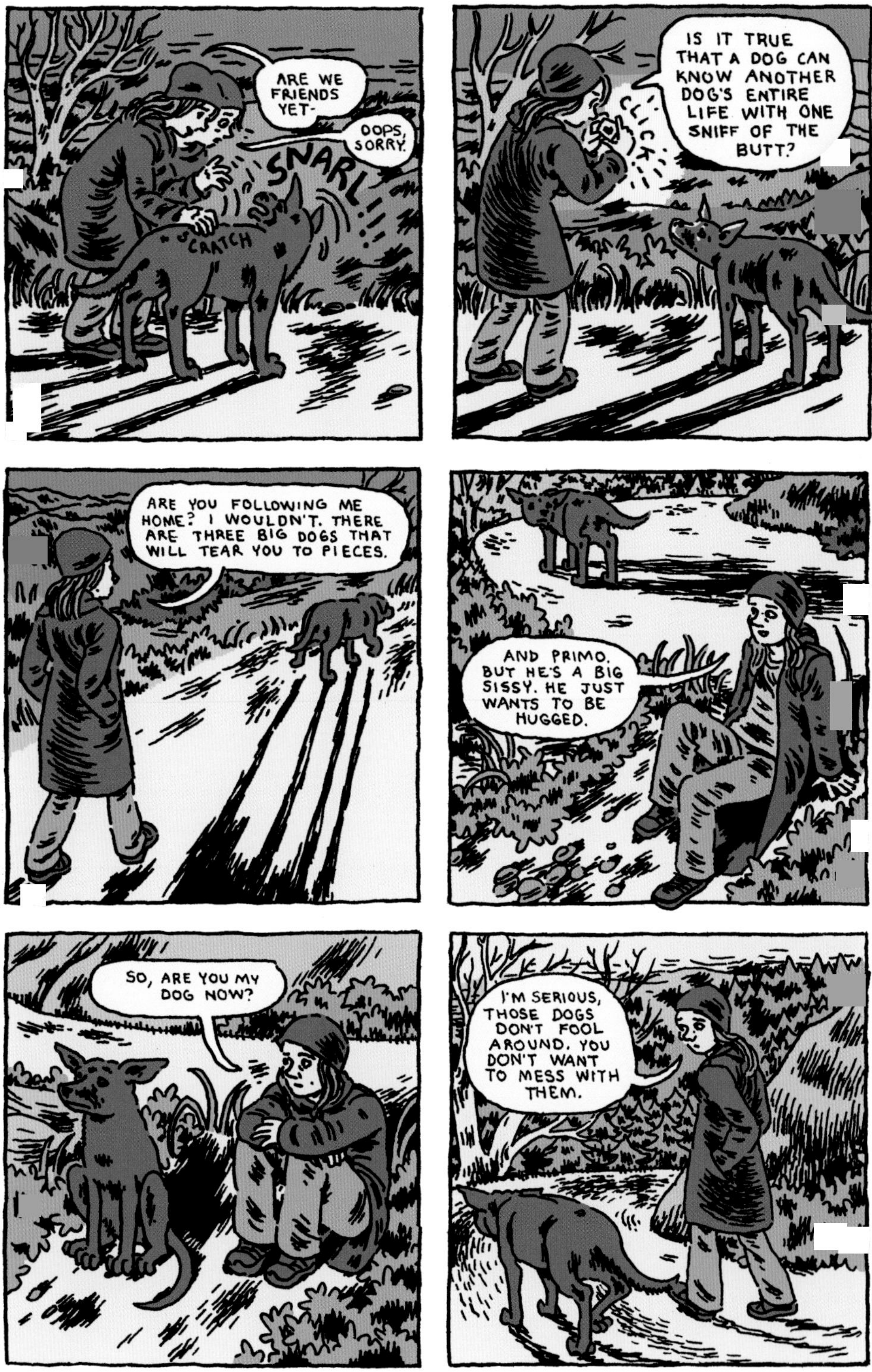
ARE WE FRIENDS YET-
OOPS, SORRY.
SNARL
SCRATCH
IS IT TRUE THAT A DOG CAN KNOW ANOTHER DOG'S ENTIRE LIFE WITH ONE SNIFF OF THE BUTT?
CLICK
ARE YOU FOLLOWING ME HOME? I WOULDN'T. THERE ARE THREE BIG DOGS THAT WILL TEAR YOU TO PIECES.
AND PRIMO. BUT HE'S A BIG SISSY. HE JUST WANTS TO BE HUGGED.
SO, ARE YOU MY DOG NOW?
I'M SERIOUS, THOSE DOGS DON'T FOOL AROUND. YOU DON'T WANT TO MESS WITH THEM.

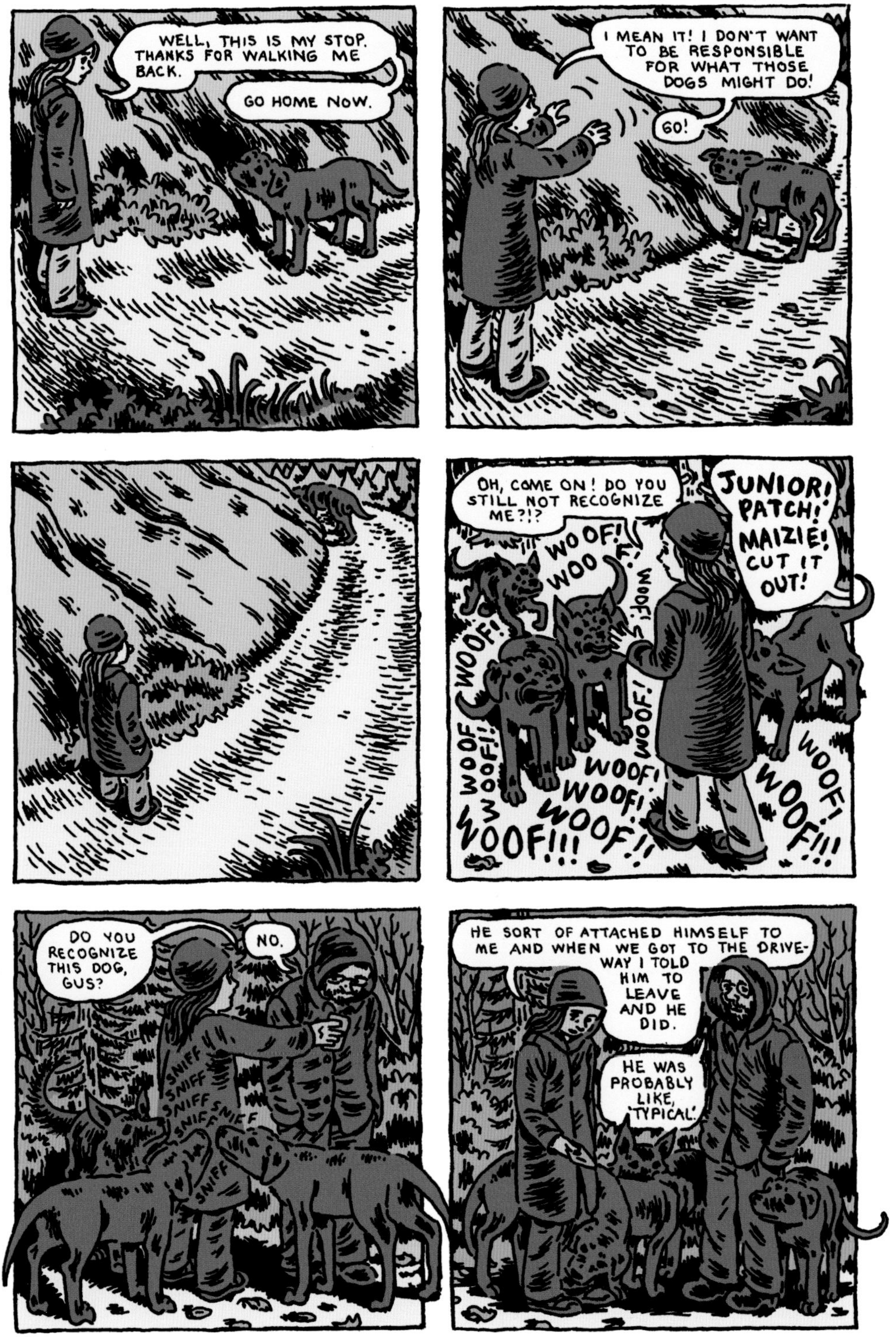
WELL, THIS IS MY STOP. THANKS FOR WALKING ME BACK.
GO HOME NOW.
I MEAN IT! I DON'T WANT TO BE RESPONSIBLE FOR WHAT THOSE DOGS MIGHT DO!
GO!
OH, COME ON! DO YOU STILL NOT RECOGNIZE ME?!?
JUNIOR! PATCH! MAIZIE! CUT IT OUT!
WOOF! WOOF!
WOOF!
WOOF! WOOF!
WOOF!
WOOF! WOOF! WOOF!!
WOOF!!!
WOOF! WOOF!!!
DO YOU RECOGNIZE THIS DOG, GUS?
NO.
SNIFF SNIFF SNIFF SNIFF SNIFF SNIFF
HE SORT OF ATTACHED HIMSELF TO ME AND WHEN WE GOT TO THE DRIVE-WAY I TOLD HIM TO LEAVE AND HE DID.
HE WAS PROBABLY LIKE, 'TYPICAL.'

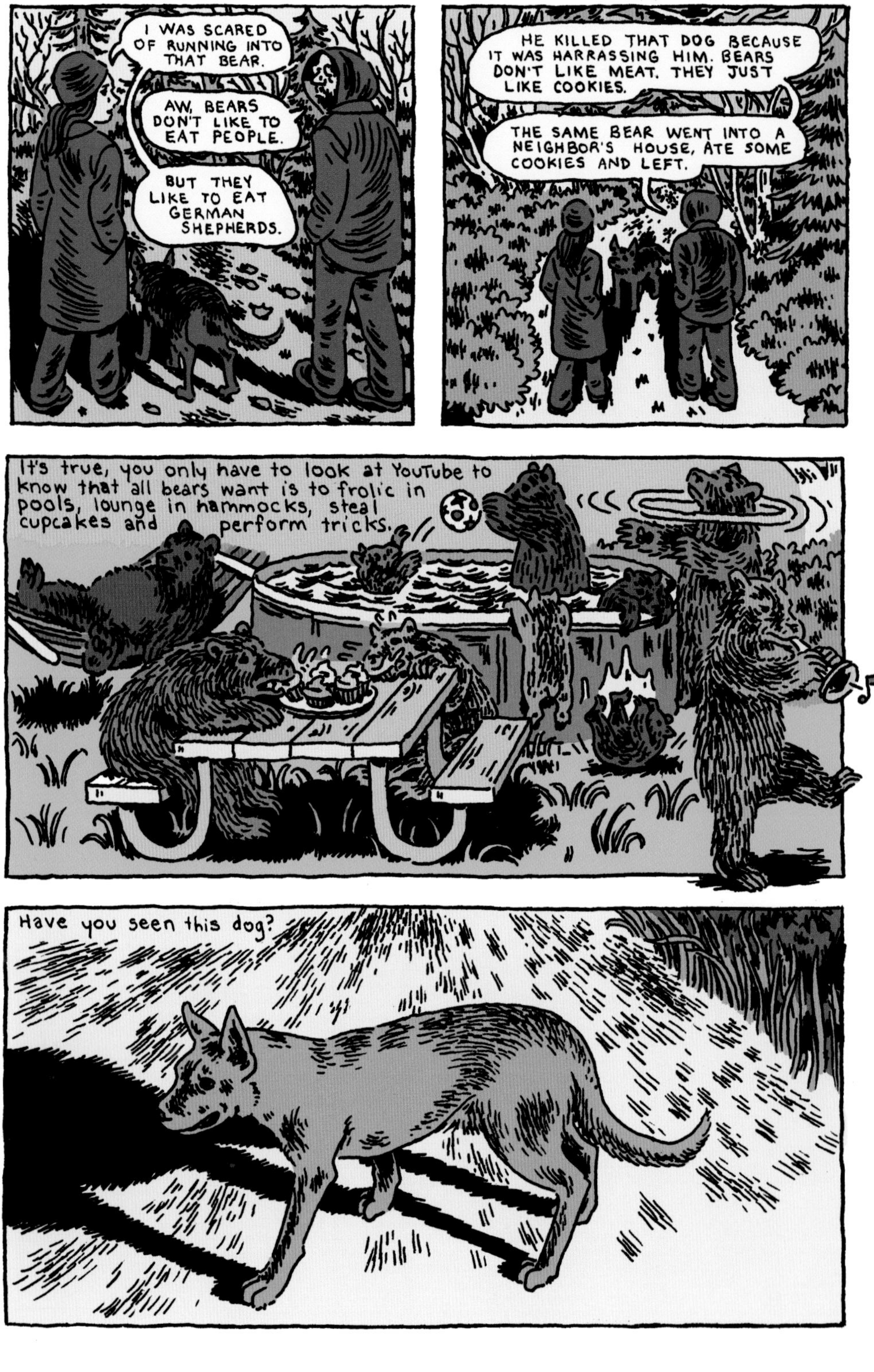
I WAS SCARED OF RUNNING INTO THAT BEAR.
AW, BEARS DON'T LIKE TO EAT PEOPLE.
BUT THEY LIKE TO EAT GERMAN SHEPHERDS.
HE KILLED THAT DOG BECAUSE IT WAS HARRASSING HIM. BEARS DON'T LIKE MEAT. THEY JUST LIKE COOKIES.
THE SAME BEAR WENT INTO A NEIGHBOR'S HOUSE, ATE SOME COOKIES AND LEFT.
It's true, you only have to look at YouTube to know that all bears want is to frolic in pools, lounge in hammocks, steal cupcakes and perform tricks.
Have you seen this dog?

The Extension

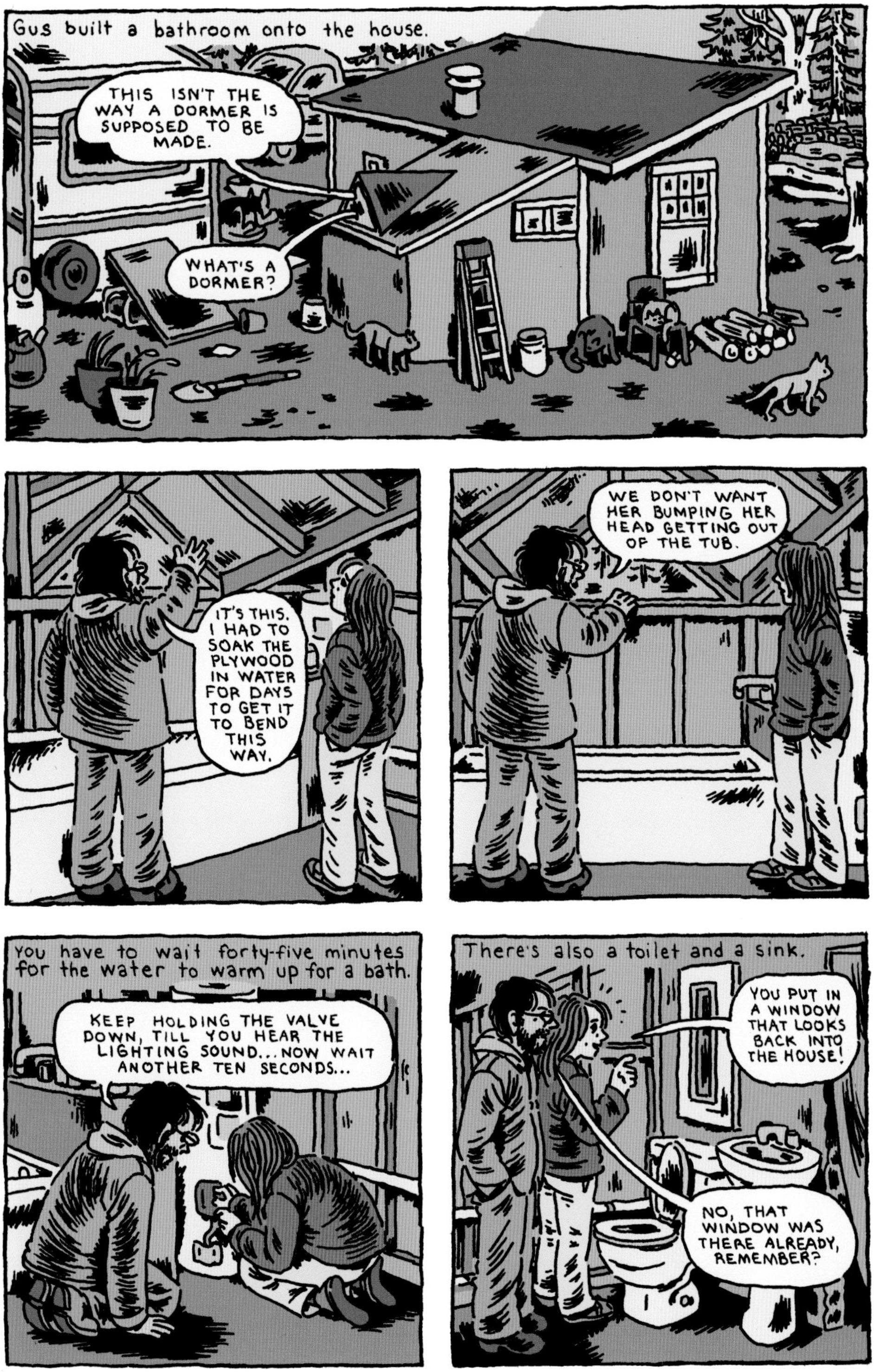
Gus built a bathroom onto the house.
THIS ISN'T THE WAY A DORMER IS SUPPOSED TO BE MADE.
WHAT'S A DORMER?
IT'S THIS. I HAD TO SOAK THE PLYWOOD IN WATER FOR DAYS TO GET IT TO BEND THIS WAY.
WE DON'T WANT HER BUMPING HER HEAD GETTING OUT OF THE TUB.
You have to wait forty-five minutes for the water to warm up for a bath.
KEEP HOLDING THE VALVE DOWN, TILL YOU HEAR THE LIGHTING SOUND... NOW WAIT ANOTHER TEN SECONDS...
There's also a toilet and a sink.
YOU PUT IN A WINDOW THAT LOOKS BACK INTO THE HOUSE!
NO, THAT WINDOW WAS THERE ALREADY, REMEMBER?

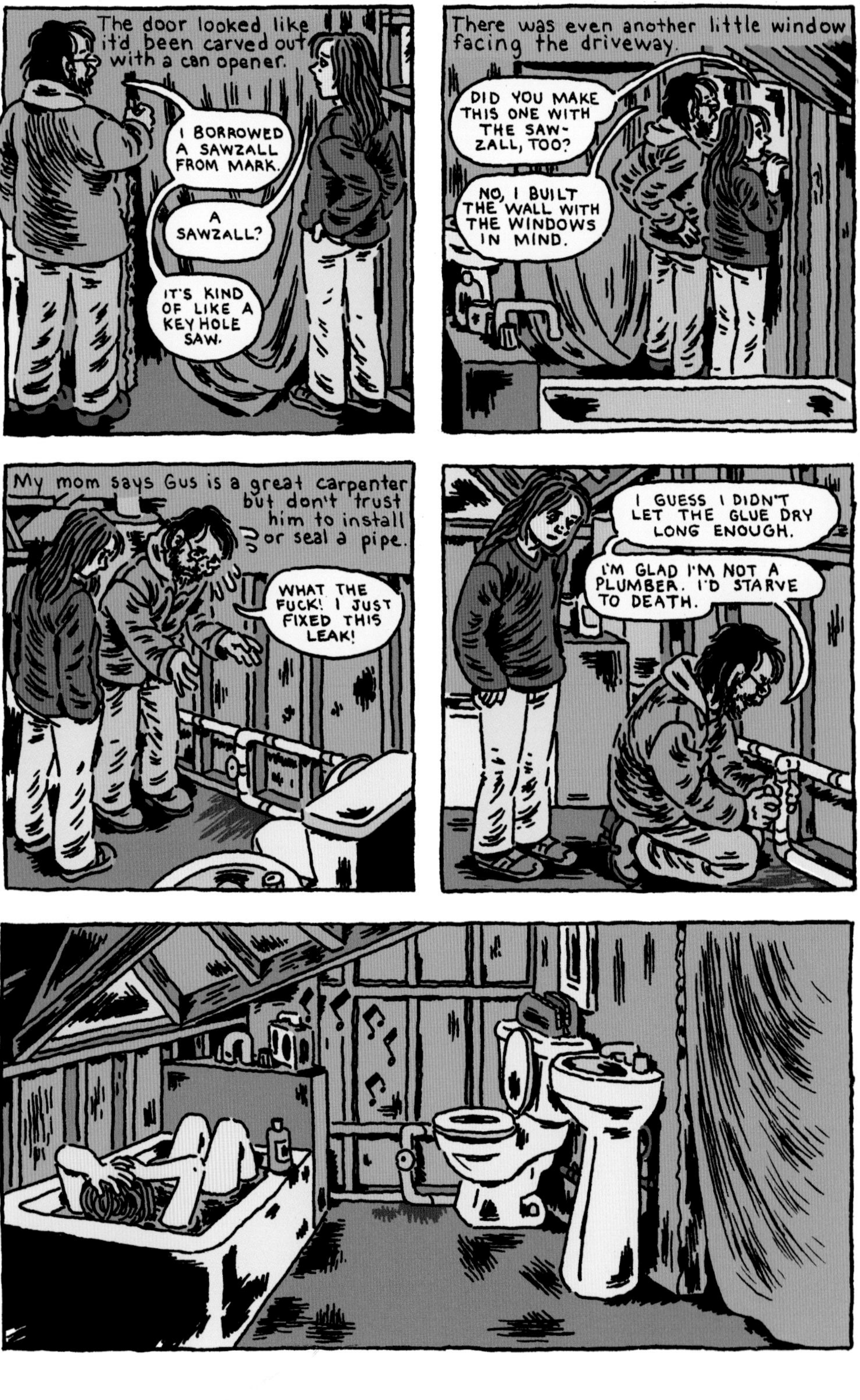
The door looked like it'd been carved out with a can opener.
I BORROWED A SAWZALL FROM MARK.
A SAWZALL?
IT'S KIND OF LIKE A KEY HOLE SAW.
There was even another little window facing the driveway.
DID YOU MAKE THIS ONE WITH THE SAW-ZALL, TOO?
NO, I BUILT THE WALL WITH THE WINDOWS IN MIND.
My mom says Gus is a great carpenter but don't trust him to install or seal a pipe.
WHAT THE FUCK! I JUST FIXED THIS LEAK!
I GUESS I DIDN'T LET THE GLUE DRY LONG ENOUGH.
I'M GLAD I'M NOT A PLUMBER. I'D STARVE TO DEATH.

Photo by Joseph Radoccia

THANK YOU

Margaret Hayes, Charles Schulz, Lois Hayes, Larry Livermore, Tom Kaczynski, Alyson Sinclair, Jordan Shiveley, Steven Thornton, Tony Groutsis, Clara Lucie Jetsmark, Lilly Richard, Roz Chast, Patton Oswalt, Tom Hart, Richard Mcguire, Sadie Hales, Ariel Schrag, Tania Schrag, Karen Sneider, Lauren Weinstein, Julia Gfrörer, Julia Wertz, Liana Finck, Tahneer Oksman, Jon Lewis, Jordann Davis, George Mansfield, Phil Nerestan, Joe Radoccia, Jon Reichert, Erica Hauser, Jerry & Jane Duncan, Jed Collins, Emma Gregoline & Stephen Nye